African Society and Culture

孙丽华　韩红　穆育枫　蒋春生　编著

非洲社会与文化（一）

知识产权出版社
全国百佳图书出版单位
—北京—

图书在版编目（CIP）数据

非洲社会与文化. 一 / 孙丽华等编著. —北京：知识产权出版社, 2019.10
ISBN 978-7-5130-6502-3

Ⅰ.①非… Ⅱ.①孙… Ⅲ.①非洲—概况 Ⅳ.①K94

中国版本图书馆 CIP 数据核字（2019）第 214282 号

责任编辑：国晓健　　　　　　　　　　责任校对：谷　洋
封面设计：臧　磊　　　　　　　　　　责任印制：孙婷婷

非洲社会与文化（一）

孙丽华　韩红　穆育枫　蒋春生　编著

出版发行：	知识产权出版社有限责任公司	网　址：	http://www.ipph.cn
社　址：	北京市海淀区气象路 50 号院	邮　编：	100081
责编电话：	010-82000860 转 8385	责编邮箱：	anxuchuban@126.com
发行电话：	010-82000860 转 8101/8102	发行传真：	010-82000893/82005070/82000270
印　刷：	北京九州迅驰传媒文化有限公司	经　销：	各大网上书店、新华书店及相关专业书店
开　本：	720mm×1000mm　1/16	印　张：	13.75
版　次：	2019 年 10 月第 1 版	印　次：	2019 年 10 月第 1 次印刷
字　数：	244 千字	定　价：	68.00 元

ISBN 978-7-5130-6502-3

出版权专有　侵权必究
如有印装质量问题，本社负责调换。

前　言

多年来，北京物资学院非洲研究团队的老师们深入非洲不同国家和地区进行田野调研，广泛探访非洲社会各阶层民众，积累了大量第一手文字和图片资料，于2012年率先在国内高校开设"非洲社会与文化"素质拓展课。

"非洲社会与文化"丛书共分三册，以社会透视和文化鉴赏为主线，旨在展示一个全面真实而又精彩纷呈的非洲。非洲有54个国家[1]、近13亿人口，是世界上国家最多、人口第二的大陆。

非洲不同国家甚至同一国家不同地区间在宗教、语言、传统习俗和地理环境等方面都存在很大的差异。因篇幅有限，本套丛书只能选取部分有代表性的国家和地区的部分情况加以介绍，难免挂一漏万。此外，由于作者水平有限，不足之处在所难免，敬请读者指正。

韩红　孙丽华
2019年6月18日于北京

---

[1] 关于非洲国家的具体数目存在不同说法。非洲联盟（African Union）承认的非洲国家一共有55个，包括阿拉伯撒哈拉民主共和国(the Sahrawi Arab Democratic Republic)，但是联合国和世界上大多数国家（包括中国）并不承认。

Contents

前　言 1
Unit I　An Introduction to Africa 1
Unit II　Ancient Civilizations in Africa 26
Unit III　Ethnic Groups in Africa 60
Unit IV　Colonization of Africa 86
Unit V　African Religions 116
Unit VI　Festivals and Values in Africa 144
Key to questions 167
Reference 180
Vocabulary List 188

Unit I   An Introduction to Africa

这是一片广袤神秘的土地，这里有原始深邃的森林、一望无垠的大草原、辽阔无比的沙漠、星罗棋布的湖区以及世界第一长河；这里是种类繁多的野生动植物的家园；这里有多样的语言、文化和族群；这里被认为是"人类的摇篮"。

Sunset in Africa
(Photographer: Jiang Chunsheng)

"Since man walked out of Africa, man must find its way back to The Source."
—Wole Soyinka, Nigerian playwright and novelist, 1986 Nobel Laureate in Literature

> ◎ **Think and Talk**
> ☆ What do you know about Africa?
> ☆ What is your impression of Africa?
> ☆ Can you name some African countries?

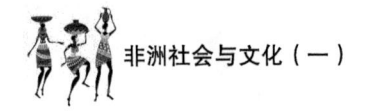

I. OVERVIEW

Africa is the second largest continent on earth, including some **adjacent** islands. Its landmass is more than three times that of the United States of America. Broad to the north, Africa **straddles** the equator and stretches 8,050 km from **Cape Blanc** (Tunisia) in the north to **Cape Agulhas** (South Africa) in the south. It is connected with Asia by the **Sinai Peninsula**, from which it is separated by **the Suez Canal**, and is **bounded** on the north by **the Mediterranean Sea**, on the west and south by the Atlantic Ocean, and on the east and south by the Indian Ocean. The largest offshore island is **Madagascar**.

Of Africa's 54 countries,[1] Sudan used to be the largest before the peaceful separation of Sudan and South Sudan. As they are now separate countries, the title of the largest country in Africa now falls to Algeria. **Seychelles** is the smallest, covering only 45,600 **hectares**. In terms of population density, **Mauritius** was in 2001 the most densely populated with 583 people per 100 hectare, compared to Namibia, the least densely populated at 2 people per 100 hectare.

Africa was the birthplace of the human species between 8 million and 5 million years ago. Today, the vast majority of its inhabitants are of **indigenous** origin. People across the continent are remarkably diverse by just about any measure. They speak a vast number of different languages, practice hundreds of distinct religions, live in a variety of types of **dwellings**, and engage in a wide range of economic activities. The vast continent of Africa is so rich and diverse in its culture that there are not only many different cultures from one country to another, within an individual country many different cultures can be found. Currently Algeria is the largest African country in terms of territory, with 2,381,740 km^2, followed by **the Democratic Republic of the Congo** at 2,344,858 km^2.

II. GEOGRAPHY AND ECOSYSTEM

Most of Africa is a series of stable and ancient **plateau** surfaces, low in the north and west and higher in the south and east. The **escarpment** of the plateau is often in close **proximity** to the coast, thus leaving the continent with a generally narrow coastal plain; in addition, the escarpment forms barriers of falls and **rapids** in the lower courses of rivers that **impede** their use as transportation routes into the **interior**. Northern Africa is **underlain** by folded **sedimentary** rock and is, geologically, more closely related to Europe than to the rest of the continent of Africa. The entire African continent is surrounded by a narrow **continental shelf**. The continent's largest river is **the Nile** (the world's longest river), and the largest lake is **Lake Victoria**, which is also the world's second largest **freshwater** lake. The lakes and major rivers, most of which are **navigable** in stretches above the escarpment of the plateau, form an important inland transportation system.

The African landscape is a rich and dynamic **mosaic** of resources, which includes five main kinds of ecosystems: forests and woodlands, **savanna** grasslands, deserts and semi-deserts, mountain environments, and coastal environments. Each ecosystem has its typical environment and climate, and the people who live there have adapted to its conditions and learned to use its resources.

1. Forests and Woodlands

A forest is a continuous group of trees whose **crowns interlock** and cast enough shade to prevent grasses from growing. Africa's various forest ecosystems include tropical rainforests; thick, high-branched forests that wind through savanna woodlands along rivers; and small groups of tiny **dwarf** trees that grow high on **mist-wrapped** peaks.

About 16.8 percent of global forest cover is found in Africa, with **the Congo Basin** home to the second largest **contiguous** block of tropical rainforest in the world. Tropical and humid forests occupy about 7 percent of the continent's total land areas. Five thousand years ago, before human activities such as burning and clearing land began on a large scale, forests covered three times as much ground. Today, the major forest areas are along the eastern and southern coasts, the central mountains, and in the Congo Basin that is in west **equatorial** Africa.

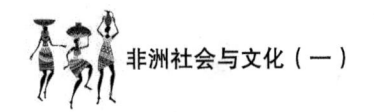

The forests' boundaries are mainly established by water and human activity. Rainfall is the most important factor in determining what type of forest will develop and how far it will extend—although groundwater from rivers or **swamps** can also support forest. The influence of humans has also been enormous. Forests provide many useful products, including **timber**, skins, meat and medicines.

2. Savannas

Savannas occupy more than half of Africa's land surface. A savanna is a tropical plain with both trees and grass. The typical image consists of a broad grassland dotted with large trees and herds of **grazing** animals such as zebra and **antelope**. However, in some savanna ecosystems, trees cover more than half of the areas.

Africa has two main types of savannas, **fine-leaved** and **broad-leaved**. Fine-leaved savannas occur in dry areas with fertile soil. Trees, typically the short and thorny **acacia**, cover less than 30 percent of the land. Grasses grow evenly and are rich sources of food. In these savannas, animals consume a substantial amount of the plant growth.

Broad-leaved savannas are found in moist areas with relatively poor soil. Trees, mostly thornless, cover more than 30 percent of the land. The grass, which is low in food value, tends to grow in tall bunches. People who live on this type of savanna often set fires to the vegetation to improve the soil for crops. But generally the major plant-eaters on the savannas are not human. **Caterpillars** may suddenly appear and devastate the broad-leaved savannas, while swarms of **grasshoppers** and **locusts** may **descend** on the fine-leaved savannas.

3. Deserts and Semi-deserts

Africa has two large areas of little rainfall and scarce vegetation—the Sahara Desert across the northern part of the continent and the combined **Namib Desert** and **Kalahari Desert** in the southwest. Each region consists of both true desert and semi-desert, which is somewhat moister.

The Sahara Desert in northern Africa is the largest desert in the world, which is home to about 2 million people, excluding those in the Nile valley. In some places in the Sahara, there is water coming up through a **crack** in the rocks. This water is called a "spring" and wherever one is found, trees and grass will grow. Such a place is called an "**oasis**". In the big oases, there are villages and towns. But the sun is so hot that before the water from the spring has flowed very far, it is dried up, and beyond that nothing will grow. It is a journey of many months to cross the Sahara, and day after day there is nothing to see but sand—sand, not flat, but in **ridges** of hills like great waves of the sea. When people are travelling across this desert, they get very tired of looking at nothing but sand all day. Then, at last, as the sun sets, they reach an oasis where there is water and bananas and **date-trees**, and perhaps houses and people. Sometimes great winds blow in the desert and bring a sandstorm. Then the sand beats hard against everything. If travelers meet a sandstorm, they have to throw themselves face downwards on the ground to keep the sand out of their eyes and mouth. Very often people who live in the desert have bad eyes, and many are blind because of the sandstorms.

4. Mountains

Some of the physically smallest countries in Africa also have the highest percentage of mountainous areas. These include **Lesotho, Rwanda** and **Swaziland**. The three countries are in the top twenty countries in the world with the highest percentage of mountainous areas. African mountain ranges are the **headwaters** of most of the large African rivers such as the Nile and **Tana River**.

Samien Mountains in northern Ethiopia
(Photographer: Han Hong)

In terms of economic activity, mountains support forestry and tourism, as they support bird watching, hiking and climbing, among other **recreational** activities. They are, therefore, key in both local and national economies. Mountain water generates **hydroelectricity**, facilitates industrial processes, and is critical in irrigated agriculture.

Mountains in Africa have been described as "islands of high **productivity**" in a continent where dryness and **aridity** are increasing at an alarming rate. People also settle in mountain areas as the lowlands are difficult to manage due to poor soils and **erratic** rainfall patterns, and are usually home to **pests** such as mosquitoes and **tsetse flies**.

Mountains are also important **biodiversity** areas. Stretching across Tanzania and into Kenya, **the Eastern Arc Mountains** and coastal forests are recognized as one of 32 globally important "hotspots" for biodiversity.

5. Coastal Ecosystems

Africa has 3 coastlines—along the Mediterranean Sea in the north, the Atlantic Ocean in the west, and the Indian Ocean in the east. These shores consist of stretches of sand, soil, or rock. In general, plants and animals on Africa's western coast are less varied and numerous than on the eastern coast. The coastal environments of Africa include **coral reef**, **lagoon**, **mangrove**, **salt marsh**, and seagrass ecosystems.

Coral reefs are made of the **skeletons** and shells of millions of tiny sea creatures. Long chains of coral just off the eastern coastline of Africa have created sheltered warm-water environments in which many species of marine life can flourish. Fewer reefs are found on the west coast, where unprotected cliffs are subjected to cold water and heavy waves.

Fishing boats along the Indian Ocean in east Africa
(Photographer: Sun Lihua)

All African coasts have lagoons (shallow bodies of water separated from the sea by a strip of land) and river **deltas**—fan-shaped areas at the mouth of a river formed by deposits of mud and sand. Because lagoons and deltas harbor large populations of fish, shrimp, and shellfish, they are among the most economically important coastal ecosystems. However, some of them have been harmed by pollution and construction projects, notably in western Africa's **Gulf of Guinea**. A floating weed called **water hyacinth** has also caused damage to lagoons and deltas.

Mangroves are trees that grow along warm muddy coastlines. In Africa, mangrove ecosystems occur most commonly in sheltered deltas and lagoons along the continent's tropical and subtropical coasts. In the vast swamps of **the Niger River and Delta**, mangrove trees reach heights of 5.2 meters, though elsewhere they are shorter. The tree's roots rise out of the water, providing **habitats** for snails, **barnacles, oysters**, and **algae.** Mangroves also protect shorelines from storm damage and **erosion** and serve as a local source of wood. Throughout Africa, however, mangrove ecosystems are threatened by **oil spills** and by the clearing of coastal lands for industrial, agricultural, or construction purposes.

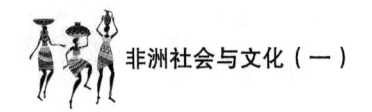

Water hyacinth on Lake Naivasha, Kenya
(Photographer: Han Hong)

Salt marsh ecosystems, found at the mouths of rivers in southern Africa, are dominated by low-growing grasses and plants that tolerate high levels of salt in the water. Seagrass ecosystems occur in shallow, protected areas of offshore sand or mud. They consist of underwater plant meadows that nurture a variety of creatures. Seagrass meadows are more widespread and diverse off the eastern coast, but they are also found off the coast of Angola in the west.

III. CLIMATE

Africa's climatic zones are largely controlled by the continent's location **astride** the equator and its almost **symmetrical** extensions into the northern and southern **hemispheres**. Thus, except where **altitude** exerts a **moderating** influence on temperature or **precipitation**, Africa may be divided into six general climatic regions.[2] Areas near the equator and on the **windward** shores of southeast Madagascar have a tropical rain forest climate, with heavy rain and high temperature throughout the year. North and south of the rain forest are belts of tropical savanna climate, with high temperature all year around and a seasonal distribution of rain during the summer season. The savanna grades **poleward** in both hemispheres into a region of **semiarid steppe** and then into the arid conditions of the extensive Sahara and the Kalahari.[3] Belts of semiarid steppe with limited winter rain occur on the poleward sides of the desert regions. At the northern and southern **extremities** of the continent are narrow belts of Mediterranean-type climate with subtropical temperature and a concentration of rainfall mostly in the autumn and winter months.

Two main factors influencing temperature patterns in Africa are **solar radiation** and **elevation**. Since the annual variation of radiation is very small, the range of monthly average temperature variations is also small, i.e. between 3°C and 6°C. The daily range of temperature is somewhat greater, however, ranging from less than 10°C in many coastal areas to over 15°C in southwest Libya. Even so, temperature variations are generally less **pronounced** in Africa than in **temperate latitudes**.

IV. THE PEOPLES

Africans, who account for over 12% of the world's population, is a term which encompasses all the indigenous **ethnicities** of the African continent. Therefore an African is **exclusively** a person from the indigenous ethnic groups found on the continent of Africa and people who trace their **ancestry** to these groups in the African **diaspora**.

Africa is diverse and rich with at least 3,000 distinct ethnic groups, 2,000 languages, and also is home to the most genetically diverse people on the earth. So diverse that two Africans are more genetically different from each other than a Chinese and a European are from each other.[4]

Africa is an amazing continent. It has such a huge number of countries residing in its expanse that it is just amazing to even **ponder** the amount of cultural diversity found in the **labyrinths** of the African lands. The diversity is so huge between the countries that it'll take ages just to sort them out by their various tribes. Even more so, the cultural difference inside the countries is greater.[5] You will find the cultures of **Zulu** tribes and other peoples all residing within an area and still they have a drastic diversity in languages and customs. Most of the diversity is found in customs and ethnic groups if we **disregard** the minor differences. Each ethnic group diversifies in the matter of religion, the custom they follow and the tongues they speak. Different African countries have different national languages. The most commonly spoken are Arabic, **Swahili** and **Hausa**. Many people also speak English, French, and Spanish as well.

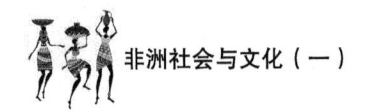

Everything is very different regarding each tribe or ethnic groups. **Islam** and **Christianity** are the two most followed upon religions in the African continent. Though there are various numbers of other religions residing and prospering as well. But the religions have the most power. A minority of people in the African cities are after the western culture and doing their customs and norms. Disregarding the identity crisis, the majority of African cities now follow their own cultural values and customs with **awe** and dedication. That is on such a large extent that people are inspired by them each and every day. The people are very **steadfast** in their lives and for making their life's decisions. They always stay by who they really are.

Local people in a market in Bamako, Mali
(Photographer: Chen Yong)

Most of the people in Africa earn their bread with **crafts** of different types, or live on livestock, farming, fishing or trade between cities and villages. Christianity is the most common religion practised in Africa, but Muslim **practitioners** are increasing day by day. Many other religions are also practiced freely. Art, craft, music and festivals are **customary** to different areas of Africa. But these are the most important traditions. Each and every city, village, and town celebrates one or another type of festival. These festivals are colorful and attract scores of visitors from around the world.

Soups are an important part of dining tables in most African homes. Most traditional dishes are soups of different variety. African food is a **fusion** of vegetables, fruits, milk and meat. Hot species and peppers are used in African cuisine frequently. Coastal areas use dried fish mixed with meat. Rice and bread are also consumed. **Yams** and **cassava** are popular among Africans.

Art and craft is an important tool. Wood craft, **weaving**, **pottery** making, hand-made **embroidery** items and hand printed clothes are famous crafts of Africa. Painting and **sculptures** are important features of African arts, especially sculpture. Sculptures in wood, **brass** and other metals have unique African styles. The common themes seen in painting and sculptures are couples, women holding a child, weapons, animals and outsiders. These entire themes represent true African culture.

V. THE CULTURE

The culture of Africa is varied and **manifold**, consisting of a mixture of tribes that each have their own unique characteristics. It is a product of the diverse populations that today **inhabit** the continent of Africa and the African diaspora. African culture is expressed in its arts and crafts, **folklore** and religion, clothing, **cuisine**, music and languages. Africa is so full of culture, with it not only changing from one country to another, but within a single country, many cultures can be discovered. Even though African cultures are widely diverse, they are also, when closely studied, seen to have many similarities. For example, the **morals** they uphold, their love and respect for their culture as well as the strong respect they hold for the aged and the important, i.e. kings and **chiefs**.

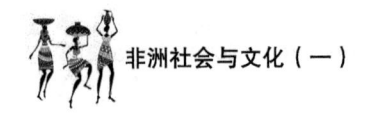

Africa has influenced and been influenced by other continents. This can be portrayed in the willingness to adapt to the ever changing modern world rather than staying rooted to their static culture. The westernized few, persuaded by European culture and Christianity, first denied African traditional culture, but with the increase of African **nationalism**, a cultural **revival** occurred. The governments of most African nations encourage national dance and music groups, museums, and to a lower degree, artists and writers.

Africa is divided into a great number of ethnic cultures. The continent's cultural **regeneration** has also been an **integral** aspect of post-independence nation-building on the continent, with a recognition of the need to **harness** the cultural resources of Africa to enrich the process of education, requiring the creation of an enabling environment in a number of ways. In recent times, the call for much greater emphasis on the cultural dimension in all aspects of development has become increasingly **vocal**. During the Roman colonization of North Africa[6] (parts of Algeria, Libya, Egypt and the whole of Tunisia), provinces such as **Tripolitania** became major producers of food for the republic and the empire, and generated much wealth during their 400 years of occupation. During colonialism in Africa, Europeans possessed attitudes of **superiority** and a sense of mission. The French were able to accept an African as French if that person gave up their African culture and adopted French ways. Knowledge of the Portuguese language and culture and abandonment of traditional African ways defined one as civilized. Kenyan social **commentator** Mwiti Mugambi argues that the future of Africa can only be forged from accepting and mending the sociocultural present. For Mugambi, colonial cultural **hangovers**, **pervasive** Western cultural **inundation**, and **arm-twisting** aid-giving **donors** are, he argues, here to stay and no amount of looking into Africa's past will make them go away.[7]

VI. HISTORY

1. Ancient Africa

Africa has the longest human history of any continent. African **hominids** date from at least 4 million years ago; agriculture, brought from Asia, appears to date from the 6th or 5th **millennium** B.C..

For most of their long history, Africans, similar to other humans everywhere, survived and thrived by constantly adapting to different and rapidly changing natural and human environments. They also used their collective imagination to invent **communal** ways to better their living conditions and, in general, to make life more interesting. But fundamental choices once made were never questioned again. With the passage of centuries and even millennia, African communities have thus adapted ever more efficiently to particular surroundings, and cultures gradually **diverged** more and more from each other. Yet at the same time, different communities found that it was needed to learn from others' experiences and to exchange both **know-how** and the products of their different environments with each other. Over time, repeated borrowing of this sort then made the societies and cultures involved more **convergent**, that is, more similar to each other, thus **counterbalancing** the trend toward divergence.

Olduvai Handaxe, made 1.2-1.4 million years ago, in Olduvai Gorge, Tanzania
(Photographer: Han Hong)

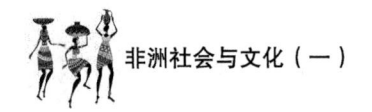

There is enough **archaeological** and historical evidence in the early 21st century to follow these dynamics of divergence and convergence over the centuries and even millennia almost everywhere in Africa.[8] And as people nearly always chose to add additional refinements to further **elaborate** on choices once made, rather than to abandon them, they built up their societies and cultures to increasingly intricate levels. In doing so, convergence eventually gained the upper hand over **divergence** in their **seesaw** dynamic.[9] The result was the emergence of regional cultural traditions. The most famous of these grew even larger in the area along the shores of the Mediterranean, to eventually **culminate** in the Roman Empire and then the **realm** of Christianity. Some six centuries later, Islam was born within this area and rapidly spread over nearly all of western Asia and the northern half of Africa. Meanwhile, convergence had created a few other cultural traditions elsewhere in the continent, especially during the first millennium and the first half of the second. As a result, by about 1200-1500, there were a small but recognizable number of thriving, still growing, and internally fairly complex regional traditions that were linked by webs of trade and communication covering most of the continent and extending well into the two adjacent continents from Spain.

Such integrated development did take place, however, and rather suddenly, too, because it occurred within somewhat less than three generations between the mid-15th century and 1525. It was part of the rise of new era in Africa.

First, Portuguese ships encircled Africa and then Europeans planted scattered **mercantile** settlements along the coasts of the Atlantic and Indian Oceans to **complement** others that already existed along the Mediterranean, This train of events is especially significant in African history because it was the first time that Africans from all parts of the continent shared a single common experience. Soon thereafter, Europeans began to export slaves from the coasts of the southern Atlantic to the Americas, thus completing a ring of slave trading around the continent, as slaves had already been carried for almost a millennium to the shores of the Mediterranean from points south of the Sahara and from eastern Africa to the Middle East and India. By the 18th century, however, the ever-increasing numbers of persons exported by Europeans to the Americas **dwarfed** all earlier exports. From the early 1600s onward, this traffic in humans lowered **demographic** growth rates in many regions of the continent, and bred insecurity, moral **callousness**, violence, and war.[10] In addition, it **bolstered** class formation as well as more **autocratic** leadership in many of the affected societies. But perhaps the most durable and most **nefarious** effect of the slave trade has been to foster worldwide racism against Africans as an **outgrowth** of the contempt attached to the Atlantic slave status, a contempt later transferred to that of colonial subject.[11] Meanwhile the Atlantic slave trade also sped up the existing older trends toward sociocultural convergence within the continent. It did so as this trade, **abetted** by a **parallel** commerce in other products, increased in spatial reach, volume, and frequency, affected an ever-widening circle of societies and cultures and created **diasporic** cultures in the Americas.[12] The trend accelerated even further during the industrial age as the continent came to be flooded with **hitherto** undreamed of quantities of all sorts of old and new commodities.

2. The Colonial Era

After the encirclement of the continent, the next turn in African history that affected its inhabitants in all parts of the continent almost simultaneously was its military colonization by European powers during the 19th and 20th centuries.[13]

The Berlin Conference established national borders in Africa based upon the competing claims of the European powers. Africans themselves did not take part in any discussion about the fate of their continent. The **legitimacy** of many European territorial claims was supposedly based on treaties with local rulers, but the rulers had no say in the future of their lands. At another meeting in **Brussels** in 1890, European leaders prohibited the sale of weapons to Africans. With Africans thus denied access to modern weapons, European mastery of the continent was assured.

The drawing of colonial borders at the Berlin Conference had profound consequence for the future of Africa. These boundaries were created without regard to ethnic and **linguistic** divisions within the continent. In many cases, the borders placed members of rival groups to share the same land. It increased the likelihood that they would come into conflict with settled communities over access to land and resources.

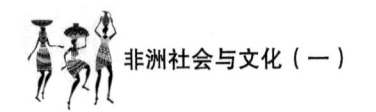

The European nations that colonized Africa hoped to exploit the continent's natural resources for their own benefit. From the start, however, their efforts were **hampered** by lack of familiarity with Africa and by inadequate funding.[14]

At first, most colonial powers granted European companies a **monopoly** over the production of resources such as rubber or timber. In return, the companies agreed to build much of the infrastructure needed to **extract** the resources and bring them to Europe. This included building towns for workers, roads and railroads to ship the goods to ports, and harbor facilities to **service** the ships carrying goods between Africa and Europe.

The agreements between colonial rulers and European companies caused major disruptions in Africans' access to the land's resources. In many cases, Africans were forced to work for the companies for little or no pay, often under brutal conditions. Hundreds of thousands of Africans died working in mines, fields, and factories, and while building roads and railroads through Africa's difficult **terrain**. Despite efforts to control expenses, most of these undertakings were very costly. The large coffee and **cocoa plantations** set up by European companies, for example, were far less efficient than the many small African farms that produced the same crops.

Despite many years under European rule, most African countries were still very underdeveloped when they achieved independence in the 1950s—1960s. Few roads or railroads had been built, and most of these served limited areas. Because the European powers saw Africa as a market for their manufactured goods, they established very little industry in their colonies. Instead, African raw materials were sent to Europe, where they were used to produce finished goods that were then shipped back to Africa. African dependence on foreign manufactured goods would contribute heavily to economic problems after independence.[15]

Colonial efforts to cut costs were not confined to economic activities. The administrations that were set up to govern African colonies were often **understaffed** and overworked. European leaders did not want to invest more resources in their colonies in Africa than they could get out of them. As a result, the amount spent on governments was limited to whatever **revenue** the colonial authorities could raise from taxes and fees charged on imports and exports.[16]

With only small staffs to govern their colonies, the European powers developed other ways to maintain control. Britain and France, the most important colonial powers, adopted different strategies. The British kept many traditional sources of authority in place. They relied on existing African leaders to maintain order at the local level and **incorporated** them into the general structure of colonial government. The French, on the other hand, eliminated local governing institutions and replaced them with councils and other organizations based on French models. In all colonies, the rights and needs of the colonial powers and white settlers came before those of Africans.

The most drastic form of white domination arose in South Africa, where a highly segregated state began to emerge during the early 1900s.[17] Although white and black populations lived separately in all parts of **Sub-Saharan Africa**, in South Africa's policy of **segregation**, non-white residents lost virtually all their civil rights, including the right to move freely within the country. Blacks were forced into separated schools, driven out of "white" areas in towns and cities, and made into a permanent **underclass** with no chance of improving their lives.

3. Movement Toward Independence

The Union of South Africa was formed and became virtually self-governing in 1910, Egypt achieved a measure of **sovereignty** in 1922, and in 1925 **Tangier**, previously attached to Morocco, was made an international zone. At the end of World War II, a rise in international trade spurred renewed exploitation of Africa's resources. France and Britain began campaigns to improve conditions in their African **holdings**, including access to education and investment in infrastructure. Africans were also able to pressure France and Britain into a degree of self-administration. Belgium and Portugal did little in the way of colonial development and sought greater control over their colonies during this period.

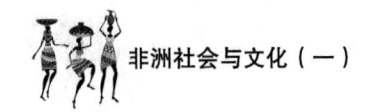

Imperial rule by Europeans would continue until after the conclusion of World War II, when almost all remaining colonial territories gradually obtained formal independence. Independence Movements in Africa gained **momentum** following World War II, which left the major European powers weakened. In 1951, Libya, a former Italian colony, gained independence. In 1956, Tunisia won its independence from France. The year 1956 also witnessed the end of French and Spanish colonial administration in Morocco. Ghana followed suit the next year (March, 1957), becoming the first of the Sub-Saharan colonies to be granted independence. Most of the rest of the continent became independent over the next decade.

Portugal's overseas presence in Sub-Saharan Africa (most notably in Angola, **Cape Verde**, Mozambique, **Guinea-Bissau** and **São Tomé and Príncipe**) lasted from the 16th century to 1975, after the Estado Novo regime[18] was overthrown in a military **coup** in **Lisbon**. **Southern Rhodesia unilaterally** declared independence from the United Kingdom in 1965, under the white minority government of **Ian Smith**, but was not internationally recognized as an independent state (as Zimbabwe) until 1980, when black **nationalists** gained power after a bitter **guerrilla** war. Although South Africa was one of the first African countries to gain independence, the state remained under the control of the country's white minority through a system of racial segregation known as **apartheid** until 1994.

4. Africa since Independence

Worldwide economic and political crises, World War I, **the Great Depression** and World War II caused European nations to reduce their investment in African colonies. During this time, the first African **labor unions** and political parties arose to challenge white privileges and white rule.[19] After World War II, the European powers moved to grant more rights and freedoms to Africans. Most colonies achieved some form of self-rule, although final authority remained in Europe. Despite such changes, calls for greater freedom intensified, and during the 1960s, most African countries gained independence.

Following independence, most African nations faced serious political problems. Traditional forms of authority had been destroyed during the colonial era, leaving most countries with a system of government inherited from their European rulers. The system, run by a small group of educated Africans, excluded the majority of the population from political power.

The most pressing issue for most African leaders was to build strong central governments in countries with deep racial and ethnic divisions. The boundaries created during the colonial period remained after independence, producing nations composed of rival groups, often long-standing enemies. Struggles among competing ethnic groups and violence marked politics in countries such as Nigeria, Sudan, Rwanda, and Burundi. Military leaders emerged as rulers in nations where the army was the only effective way of gaining and maintaining power. In some countries, public order broke down completely, and civil war has raged in many African nations since independence.

African nations have also experienced economic problems in the years since independence. Because of colonial neglect, few countries had the infrastructure needed to support a modern economy. In addition, African economies have been dependent on exports of raw materials such as minerals and agricultural products, items with unstable prices that cannot produce steady income. African nations also have had to import most of the expensive manufactured goods they need from Europe and other parts of the world. The imbalance of trade revenues forced African nations to borrow heavily to finance improvements such as roads, railroads, seaports, **power plants**, and schools, leaving many countries in debt.

In the 1980s, Africa faced a continent-wide financial crisis, and most nations were unable to pay back the money they had borrowed. Lenders agreed to forgive or refinance debts if borrowers reduced the size of the governments and cut back on spending. Doing so, however, left even less money to spend on development and social services. In fact, many of those social services—such as education and transportation—rapidly decline once spending is cut. Most African nations had targeted such services for growth after the end of colonialism, but rising populations combined with spending cuts led to **underfunded** schools and **crumbling** roadways and railroads. The inability of African leaders to meet the needs of their citizens resulted in political unrest, leading some nations to use severe measures to control the people. The most brutal **regimes** often were very corrupt, with leaders stealing government funds and gaining advantages through **bribery** and threats.

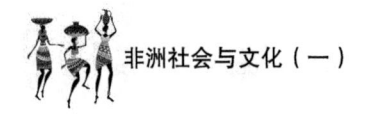

5.African's Dilemma

At the beginning of the 21st century, Africa stands at a crossroads. While many developing countries in Latin America and Asia have advanced both politically and economically, most of Africa **lags** far behind. A number of African nations still face the threat of internal conflicts and some, such as Somalia and Liberia, are so torn by civil **strife** that their governments have completely collapsed.[20]

Many of Africa's problems can be traced back to the slave trade and colonial policies that disrupted or destroyed the continent's traditional social, economic, and political institutions. Modern African leaders now face the challenge of building stable nations on weak economic foundations and governmental structures that are not generally accepted as **legitimate** by the people.

To solve Africa's problems and help the continent move forward, its leaders must take steps to repair the damage done by slavery and colonialism. This will almost certainly require the cooperation of the nations that profited from the exploitation of Africa for so many years. Until that occurs, most Africans will continue to be denied the benefits of the independence they won nearly 50 years ago.

Explanations

[1] **Africa's 54 countries:** 非洲目前一共有54个国家和1个地区（西撒哈拉地区 Western Sahara）。南苏丹于2011年7月9日正式独立，是迄今为止最年轻的非洲国家。

[2] **Thus, except where altitude exerts a moderating influence on temperature or precipitation, Africa may be divided into six general climatic regions:** 因此，如果不考虑海拔对温度或降水量的影响因素，非洲大体上可以划分为六个气候带。

[3] **The savanna grades poleward in both hemispheres into a region of semiarid steppe and then into the arid conditions of the extensive Sahara and the Kalahari:** 从赤道向南北两极方向降水逐渐减少，依次分布着热带稀树草原、半干旱草原以及一望无际的撒哈拉沙漠和卡拉哈里沙漠。

[4] **So diverse that two Africans are more genetically different from each other than a Chinese and a European are from each other:** 与一个中国人和一个欧洲人的基因差异相比，两个非洲人的遗传基因差别更加显著。

[5] **The diversity is so huge between the countries that it'll take ages just to sort them out by their various tribes. Even more so, the cultural difference inside the countries is greater:** 非洲国家之间存在明显的差异，仅仅以部族为依据将国家分类的工作就旷日持久，更何况国家内部的文化差异更加显著。

[6] **the Roman colonization of North Africa:** 公元534年，东罗马帝国皇帝查士丁尼一世（Justinian I, 527—565A.D.）派将军贝利萨留（Belisarius）消灭了汪达尔王国（Vandal Kingdom），兼并北非，建立了罗马帝国的阿非利加行省（African Prefecture），中心设在迦太基（Carthage）。此后15年中，由于和摩尔人之间的战争以及部队叛乱的缘故，阿非利加行省一直处在摇摇欲坠的边缘。公元548年安定以后，经济才获得发展。

[7] **For Mugambi, colonial cultural hangovers, pervasive Western cultural inundation, and arm-twisting aid-giving donors are, he argues, here to

stay and no amount of looking into Africa's past will make them go away: 在穆刚毕看来，无论怎样反思非洲历史，都无法消除殖民时期遗留下来的、无处不在的西方文化的影响，也无法摆脱财大气粗的捐赠国的掌控。

[8] **There is enough archaeological and historical evidence in the early 21st century to follow these dynamics of divergence and convergence over the centuries and even millennia almost everywhere in Africa:** 21世纪初期的大量考古成果足以证明：在数百年乃至数千年的时间里，融合和偏离的趋势在非洲几乎所有地区交替上演。

[9] **In doing so, convergence eventually gained the upper hand over divergence in their seesaw dynamic:** 在融合和偏离这两种趋势此消彼长的过程中，前者最终占据了上风。

[10] **From the early 1600s onward, this traffic in humans lowered demographic growth rates in many regions of the continent, and bred insecurity, moral callousness, violence, and war:** 从17世纪初开始，奴隶贸易使得非洲很多地区人口锐减，人口买卖的罪恶行径使得人人自危，道德沦丧，甚至导致暴力冲突、引发战争。

[11] **But perhaps the most durable and most nefarious effect of the slave trade has been to foster worldwide racism against Africans as an outgrowth of the contempt attached to the Atlantic slave status, a contempt later transferred to that of colonial subject:** 奴隶贸易最持久、最为人不齿的影响可能就是：世人对地位卑微的奴隶、遭受殖民统治的人民的鄙视后来发展成为全世界范围内针对黑人的种族歧视。

[12] **It did so as this trade, abetted by a parallel commerce in other products, increased in spatial reach, volume, and frequency, affected an ever-widening circle of societies and cultures and created diasporic cultures in the Americas:** 奴隶贸易和非洲其他商品贸易的范围、规模以及频率不断增长，对越来越多的社会和文化产生影响，还创造出南北美洲的非洲离散文化，这一切加速了非洲社会文化融合的进程。

[13] **After the encirclement of the continent, the next turn in African history that**

Unit 1　An Introduction to Africa

affected its inhabitants in all parts of the continent almost simultaneously was its military colonization by European powers during the 19th and 20th centuries: 在包围非洲大陆以后，欧洲殖民主义者在19和20世纪用武力手段对非洲各国进行残酷统治，严重影响了当地居民，非洲历史就此进入下一个转折点。

[14] **From the start, however, their efforts were hampered by lack of familiarity with Africa and by inadequate funding:** 尽管如此，因为不了解非洲，而且经费不足，欧洲殖民者一开始就举步维艰。

[15] **African dependence on foreign manufactured goods would contribute heavily to economic problems after independence:** 由于严重依赖外国工业品，所以在取得民族独立以后，非洲各国的经济发展都遭遇了重重危机。

[16] **As a result, the amount spent on governments was limited to whatever revenue the colonial authorities could raise from taxes and fees charged on imports and exports:** 因此，宗主国征收的税款以及进出口关税的总和决定了殖民政府的运营费用。

[17] **The most drastic form of white domination arose in South Africa, where a highly segregated state began to emerge during the early 1900s:** 最严苛的白人统治出现在南非：从20世纪初开始，全体南非人民被严格依照种族区分开来。

[18] **Estado Novo regime:** "新国家政权"是1933年由葡萄牙右翼军事独裁者安东尼奥·德·奥利维拉·萨拉查（António de Oliveira Salazar, 1889—1970）建立的带有法西斯性质的新国家体制。该政权对内实行独裁统治，对外无情地压榨葡属非洲殖民地。1974年4月25日，发生在葡萄牙首都里斯本的左派军事政变——康乃馨革命（The Carnation Revolution）推翻了新国家政权。

[19] **During this time, the first African labor unions and political parties arose to challenge white privileges and white rule:** 在此期间，为了反抗白人特权及其统治，非洲大陆的第一批工会和政党应运而生。

[20] **A number of African nations still face the threat of internal conflicts and**

23

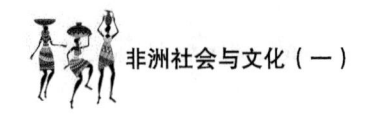

some, such as Somalia and Liberia, are so torn by civil strife that their governments have completely collapsed: 非洲很多国家目前依然可能爆发国内冲突。内战使得一些国家，例如索马里和利比里亚满目疮痍，政府已经彻底垮台。

Exercises

I. Read the following statements and decide whether they are true (T) or false (F).

_____ 1. South Africa is the largest country in Africa.

_____ 2. Africans speak very few different languages.

_____ 3. Africa has 5 main kinds of ecosystems: forests and woodlands, savanna grasslands, deserts and semi-deserts, mountain environments, and coastal environments.

_____ 4. A savanna is a tropical oasis with both water and grass.

_____ 5. Africa may be divided into six general climatic regions.

_____ 6. Madagascar has a tropical rain forest climate, with heavy rain and high temperature throughout the year.

_____ 7. Though the diversity is huge between the countries, the cultural difference inside the countries is quite tiny.

_____ 8. The most widely spoken languages in Africa are Arabic, Swahili and Hausa.

_____ 9. The European nations that colonized Africa hoped to exploit the continent's natural resources for their own benefit.

_____ 10. Because of colonial neglect, many countries had the infrastructure needed to support a modern economy.

II. Fill in the following blanks with words that best complete the sentences.

1. Africa was _____ of the human species between 8 million and 5 million years ago.

Unit I   An Introduction to Africa

2. The forests' boundaries are mainly established by water and _____.

3. Africa has two main types of savannas, _____ and _____.

4. _____ in Northern Africa is the largest desert in the world.

5. African mountain ranges are the headwaters of most of the large African rivers such as _____ and _____.

6. _____ and _____ are the most followed upon religions on the African continent.

7. Africa has the longest _____ of any continent.

8. After World War II, the European powers moved to grant more _____ and _____ to Africans.

9. At the end of World War II, a rise in _____ spurred renewed exploitation of Africa's resources.

10. The most pressing issue for most African leaders was to build _____ in countries with deep racial and ethnic divisions.

Review and Reflect

- What is the biggest benefit of sustainable development of the ecosystem in Africa?
- What have you learned from the history of Africa?
- What are the most possible reasons for the largest desert in Africa?

Unit II Ancient Civilizations in Africa

分布在非洲撒哈拉沙漠以南地区的各黑人民族在历史上创造的物质文明和精神文明的总和构成了非洲黑人文明。这些黑人民族不仅有自己的语言文字（麦罗埃文、斯瓦希里语、豪萨语等）、文学、史学、宗教和其他著作留存，而且还有大量精湛的艺术、音乐、舞蹈、建筑、医学以及科学技术遗存。对世界上任何一种文明的研究，都没有像非洲黑人文明一样遭遇重重质疑。但是毋庸置疑的是，丰富多彩的非洲黑人文明在人类历史上占有重要的一席之地。

The Great Mosque in Djenné, Mali

(Photographer: Chen Yong)

"Timbuktu had no equal among the cities of the blacks... And was known for its solid institutions, political liberties, purity of morals, security of its people and their goods, compassion towards the poor and strangers, as well as courtesy and generosity towards students and scholars."

—The 17th century chronicle Tarikh al-fattash, completed in 1665

Unit II   Ancient Civilizations in Africa

> ◎ **Think and Talk**
>
> ☆ Have you heard of any ancient city in Africa?
>
> ☆ Have you heard of any ancient kingdom in Africa?
>
> ☆ What a role has African civilization played in the world history?

I. HUMAN ORIGINS IN AFRICA

Scientific evidence, which began with the study of **fossils**, shows that Africa was the **cradle** of human beings. Fossils, found in various parts of Africa, dated more than four million years ago. The early human species spread throughout the world and built a culture upon which modern humans have developed.

The role of **archaeology** cannot be overlooked in the prehistory of Africa. Archaeology and its **interpretations** present the scientific part of the history of Africa. Where **oral traditions** fail to provide some needed information for the reconstruction of African past, archaeology fills the gap. The recovery and interpretation of **artifacts** produce vital information on the early history and culture of the peoples of Africa. In his *The Descent of Man, and Selection in Relationship to Sex* (1871), Charles Darwin suggested that Africa was the cradle of humankind and subsequent scientific researches and **archaeological** discoveries proved him right. The shift in focus of the cradle of humans moved from Asia to Africa. Africans themselves had only oral traditions and culture to show, but not scientific evidence to prove their long existence. **Paleoanthropologists**, archaeologists, and **anthropologists** then began to carry out researches into the origins of human beings. **Excavations** have been carried out in Africa with new findings, producing new information and new interpretations. The discovery of **fossilized** bones places Africa as the cradle of modern humankind. Although human fossils are rare because it takes a long time and certain conditions for humans to form into fossilized bones, some have been found in Kenya, Tanzania, Ethiopia, and South Africa.

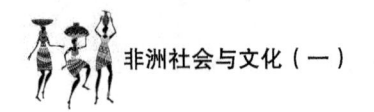

An international group led by **Donald Johanson** made a scientifically informative discovery at the Afar Triangle[1] in Ethiopia in 1974. The fossil was identified as **Australopithecus afarensis** and nicknamed "Lucy". Dated between 3 and 4 million years ago, Lucy was **bipedal** with the **morphology** of its bones functionally **identical** to that of more recent humans. Aside from Lucy, Johanson found a group of **hominid** bones, which has been called the "first family".

II. PREHISTORY IN AFRICA

1. The Stone Age in Africa

Prehistoric archaeologists divide the past into different periods based on the kinds of tools people made. Several of these periods are grouped under the name the Stone Age.

Broadly speaking, the **Early Stone Age** in Africa began about 2.6 million years ago, when the **ancestors** of humans shaped the first large, handheld cutting tools of stone to carve the **carcasses** of animals. Scientists believe that these early beings hunted **small game** and looked for carcasses that had been killed by large animals. This way of life continued until around 200,000 years ago.

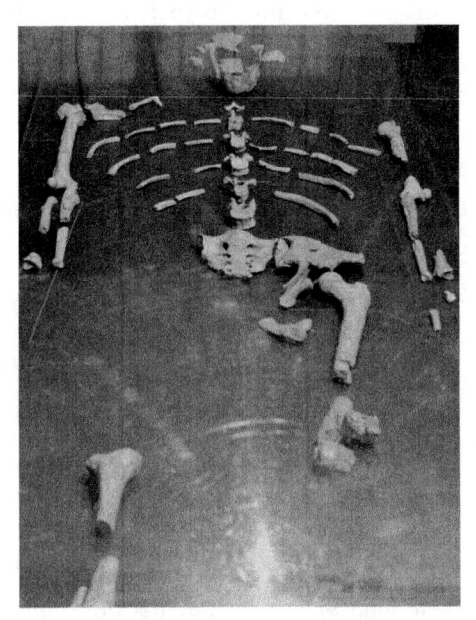

Fossilized remains of Lucy in the National Museum of Ethiopia
(Photographer: Sun Lihua)

During the **Middle Stone Age**, from about 200,000 to 45,000 years ago, large stone tools were replaced by smaller tools made of sharp **flakes** struck from specially prepared rocks. As in the Early Stone Age, people lived on game killed by animals and gathering wild foods. Hunting probably played an increasing role during the

Middle Stone Age. However, archaeologists differ as to whether people hunted large game animals, and if so, how and when they learned to do so.

Africa's climate became cooler and drier during the Middle Stone Age, producing environmental changes that challenged people to adapt to new conditions. Archaeologists who study the Middle Stone Age are trying to determine what the environment was like and how it affected human life.

The **Late Stone Age**, which began about 45,000 years ago, marked the appearance of very small stone **blades** and tools that people attached to **handles** of wood or bone. In the Late Stone Age, people hunted and gathered a wide variety of plants and animals to eat, including seafood. They made **beads**, painted pictures on rock walls, and formally buried their dead. They also produced many artifacts of **perishable** organic materials such as wood, bone, leather, and shell, which have survived at a few sites. Among the oldest such artifacts are 10,000-year-old tools of wood, **bark**, and grass, found at Gwisho **hot springs** in Zambia.

By 7000 B.C., people living in what is now **the Sahara** had **domesticated** cattle. Between 6500 and 4000 B.C., climate changes caused these cattle-**herding** societies to move southward, introducing domestic animals into **Sub-Saharan Africa.** The development of economies based on **livestock** herding and farming marked the end of the Late Stone Age. At around the same time, ironworking technologies appeared in some regions, and new cultures began to develop.

Some of these new cultures were settled; others were **nomadic**. Some were based on agriculture, others on **pastoralist** activities. In a few desert areas and within deep forests, small bands of hunter-gatherers continued to live much as their ancestors had done. Elsewhere, however, African societies grew more complex and began interacting with each other. Around the edges of the continent, they began to encounter people of other races and cultures. Each region of Africa followed its own route to the present, a route that can be retraced through archaeology.

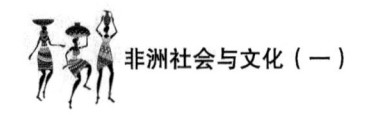

2. Western Africa

Western Africa includes Mauritania, Mali, Niger, Nigeria, Chad, Cameroon, Benin, Burkina Faso, Togo, Ghana, Côte d'Ivoire, Liberia, Sierra Leone, Guinea, Guinea-Bissau, Gambia, and Senegal.[2] The region stretches into the Sahara desert in the north, but its coastal area consists primarily of tropical rain forests. Archaeologists believe that changes in climate—especially shifts between wetter and drier periods—play a key role in shaping the past societies of the region.

Prehistory

Although archaeologists think that parts of western Africa were **inhabited** more than 2 million years ago, they do not yet have a clear picture of the earliest settlements. In 1995, scientists found a fossil **jaw** and seven teeth at Koro Toro, Chad. The fossils came from an **australopithecine**, an early kind of human ancestor previously known only from sites in eastern and southern Africa. Stone tools from both the Early Stone Age and the Middle Stone Age occur widely in western Africa, especially in the Sahara and northern Nigeria. At Asokrochona in Ghana and other sites in the southern part of the region, archaeologists have found tools from the Middle Stone Age that may have been used in woodworking.

Relics of the Late Stone Age show how climate affected human life in the region. During a very dry period between 20,000 and 12,000 years ago, the Sahara desert extended farther than it does today, and no traces of human life from that time have been found in the northern part of the region. During the wetter years that followed, the Sahara was reoccupied, probably from the north. Rock paintings of elephants and wild **buffalo** in areas that are now extremely dry may date from this period.

Work at a number of Saharan sites has revealed **harpoons** and the **remains** of fish, crocodiles, and **hippopotamuses**, suggesting that people of this period had access to lakes and rivers. In 1998, archaeologists discovered a boat more than 25

Unit II Ancient Civilizations in Africa

feet (7.6 meters) long near the Yobe River in northeastern Nigeria. Known as the Dufuna **canoe**, it dates from around 6500 B.C. and is thought to be Africa's oldest boat.

Archaeological sites throughout western Africa **highlight milestones** in the region's prehistory. At a place called Iwo Eleru in the forested area of southwestern Nigeria, scientists have **uncovered** a rock shelter that was inhabited as early as 10,000 years ago. The shelter contained many small stone blades that may have been used as **arrowheads** or, attached to handles, as cutting tools. **Pottery** found in the Sahara dates from the same period. Cattle **skeletons excavated** at a site called Adrar Bous in Niger show that people were herding domestic cattle, sheep, and goats about 4,000 years ago. Other archaeological discoveries in Mali and Mauritania suggest that agriculture—specifically, the farming of **millet**, a cereal grain—began in the region between 4,000 and 3,000 years ago.

Beginning around 2000 B.C., agricultural production increased and settled communities developed in the forest and savanna regions in the southern part of western Africa. More than two dozen sites in Ghana and Côte d'Ivoire have revealed houses in large settlements, complete with a variety of stone tools, remains of sheep and goats, and pottery **vessels** and **figurines**.

Around the same time, people in the area began to work metal. They may have learned techniques from cultures in Sudan and North Africa or developed them on their own. Discoveries in Niger show that people there worked **copper** as early as 2000 B.C. The earliest evidence of iron-working, also in Niger, dates from about 1000 B.C., although iron tools did not completely replace stone tools. A few centuries later, Nigeria, Mali, Ghana, Chad, and Senegal were also producing iron.

Historians used to think that western Africa developed large urban centers and complex social structures as a result of contact with Arabs from North Africa after the 600s A.D.. Growing archaeological evidence, however, reveals large, complex societies in western Africa long before that time. Some of the earliest such evidence comes from the Saharan borderlands, where archaeologists excavated the city of **Djenné-Djenno** in Mali. Established by 250 B.C., the town entered a period of rapid growth some 500 years later.

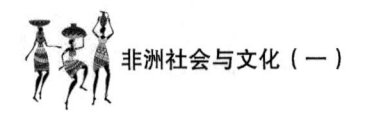

Elsewhere in western Africa, large **earthen mounds** have been found. These contain **burial chambers**, **human sacrifices**, and various objects buried with the dead. Some archaeologists believe that such sites, together with evidence of expanding trade across the region, suggest the development of larger states and kingdoms. The trend toward **centralization** of power would eventually produce a number of great empires in Western Africa.

The historic period

Oral tradition and a few written records including accounts by Arab travelers, provide archaeologists with additional insights into western African states after 1000. Ancient Ghana, the subject of many of these reports, extended over much of present-day Mauritania, Mali, and Senegal. Arabic sources refer to Ghana as a flourishing kingdom. One description of a king's burial has shed light on the **ritual** purpose of burial mounds in the area. At Koumbi Saleh, a site in Mauritania thought to have been Ghana's capital, researchers have **unearthed multistory** stone buildings and **graveyards**.

As Ghana's influence faded, the kingdom of Mali became powerful in the region, reaching its peak in the 1200s and 1300s. Some archaeologists believe that Niani, a site in present-day Guinea, was the capital of Mali. Although the site has extensive **ruins**, excavations suggest that it was **unoccupied** during Mali's most powerful era. The exact location of the capital, as well as the true extent of ancient Mali, remain undetermined.

Arabic and European sources describe the rich and powerful kingdom of Benin in Nigeria, which reached its peak between the 1200s and 1600s. Archaeologists have added details to these written accounts. Their research reveals that the **inhabitants** of Benin City, the capital, worked with copper and built massive earthen walls around important structures.

Archaeological sites along the coast of western Africa include **forts** and castles built by Europeans as they explored and traded in the area in the 1400s and later.

Recent archaeological work has focused on **indigenous** towns and states near these European **outposts**, studying how local Africans responded to contact and trade with Europeans. One of the most fully studied sites is Elmina[3] on the coast of Ghana, the location of the first and largest European trading post in Sub-Saharan Africa. By the 1800s, the African town there had grown to 15,000 or 20,000 inhabitants. Excavations have revealed evidence of **far-flung** trade: European pottery, glass and beads, and fine **ceramics** from China.

3. Eastern Africa

Eastern Africa includes Djibouti, Eritrea, Ethiopia, Kenya, Somalia, Tanzania, and Uganda.[4] Organized archaeological research did not begin in this region until around 1960, though some earlier work was done by colonial officials who collected various artifacts.

Eastern Africa first became famous in the 1960s when dramatic fossil discoveries were made by members of the Leakey Family[5]. These findings cast new light on the earliest human origins in Africa. Other archaeological work has focused on more recent eras in the region's human history.

A key feature of current archaeology in the region is the growing participation of African scientists, students, universities, and museums. Interpretation of the region's history was once largely in the hands of Westerners, but now more local archaeologists and other scholars are studying their own past. In addition, eastern Africa has turned some archaeological sites into tourist attractions and has created local museums to educate schools and communities about their archaeological **heritage**.

Prehistory

Discoveries have made sites in eastern Africa, such as the well-known Olduvai Gorge[6] in Tanzania, centers of **paleoarchaeological** research. **Paleoarchaeology** concerns the study of very old traces of human existence and culture. One area of research is the evolution of the first humans several million years ago. Another is the emergence of the modern human species, **Homo sapiens**.

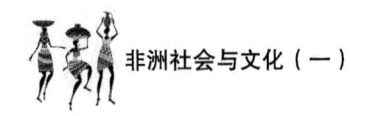

Theories that suggest an African origin for Homo sapiens have focused attention on the Middle Stone Age sites, such as Gadamotta near **Lake Zway** in Ethiopia. The inhabitants of Gadamotta used **obsidian**—glassy, **volcanic** rock that can hold a sharp edge-to manufacture tools more than 200,000 years ago. Other important sites in Tanzania contain stone tools more than 100,000 years old.

Archaeological remains from the Late Stone Age, including small stone tools and rock art, are found at many sites in eastern Africa. At Gamble's Cave and Nderit Drift, near **Lake Nakuru** in Kenya, archaeologists have found blades, **scrapers**, and other tools crafted from obsidian between 13,000 and 9,000 years ago. Sites on the shores of **Lake Turkana** in Kenya have revealed bone harpoons, stone scrapers, grinding stones, and pottery. Hunter-gatherers there ate a wide variety of foods, including crocodile, hippopotamus, fish, and plants. In the **vicinity** of **Lake Victoria**, Africa's largest lake, archaeologists have located relics of a hunter-gatherer population they call the Oltome culture. Among its artifacts are pieces of highly decorated pottery with stamped decorations. The best-known Oltome site is Gogo Falls, which dates from between 4000 and 1000 B.C.

Archaeological evidence suggests that the herding of domestic livestock began in eastern Africa about 4,000 to 5,000 years ago, and many groups in the region still follow a **pastoral** way of life. The most common domesticated animals were cattle, sheep, and goats, though archaeologists have also uncovered bones of camels from sites in Ethiopia and northern Kenya. The earliest indications of farming in the region came from **Lalibela Cave** in the highlands of Ethiopia, which contained traces of beans, **barley** and **chickpeas**. Evidence of domesticated wheat, grapes, and **lentils** has been found at other Ethiopian sites. Although grown in eastern Africa, all these food plants originated in the Near East[7] and would have been introduced to the region.

An economy that combined farming and trading developed rapidly in the Ethiopian highlands starting about 2,500 years ago. Local African communities traded valuable raw materials, such as gold, skins, and **ivory** across the Red Sea to the **Arabian Peninsula**. Several hundreds of years later, Ethiopia became part of a trading network that also crossed the Indian Ocean. These farming communities of Ethiopia are known from archaeological excavations at **Axum**, which eventually developed into a major state.

The first communities to use iron in eastern Africa arose along the shores of Lake Victoria between 2,500 and 1,700 years ago. Archaeologists have not yet identified the origins of these communities, and evidence remains scarce. By about 500 A.D., farmers using iron tools seem to have occupied areas of eastern Africa with **wooded** and wet environments, especially the coastal hills and plains.

Historic era

Early evidence of complex African societies comes from the coast of eastern Africa, where urban communities based on Indian Ocean trading networks were developing by 800 A.D. Some communities built large structures of **timber**, **coral**, and **limestone** and **minted** their own coins. There is evidence of Islam, the religion that originated in **Arabia**. The inhabitants of these urban centers at **Zanzibar** and elsewhere along the coast were the ancestors of the Swahili coastal traders who now live in east African towns such as **Mombasa**.

Fierce debate has **revolved** around the origins of the Swahili coastal communities. Earlier generations claimed that Asian **colonists** had "brought **civilization** to Africa". However, Swahili is a native African language. Archaeologists now believe that the Swahili coastal culture originated in Africa, but that colonists from southern Arabia influenced the culture.

The pattern of peoples and cultures in eastern Africa today is largely the result of events during the past thousands of years. Chief among these events are **migrations** from the north, with waves of livestock—herding people settling in the area. The newcomers developed a **dairy** economy, keeping cattle for milk and sheep and goats for meat.

The past thousands of years also saw the emergence of large population centers around the lakes of eastern Africa.[8] One such center, Bigo, had earthen walls more than 6.2 miles (10 km) long, with **ditches** up to 16 feet (4.9 meters) deep. Some states that appeared in the region later, such as **Buganda** and **Bunyoro**, have survived.

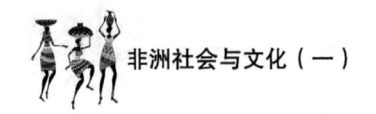

4. Central and Southern Africa

Africa's central and southern regions include Angola, Botswana, Burundi, Central African Republic, Democratic Republic of the Congo, Equatorial Guinea, Gabon, Lesotho, Malawi, Mozambique, Namibia, Republic of the Congo, Rwanda, São Tomé and Principe, South Africa, Swaziland, Zambia, and Zimbabwe.[9] Archaeological sites in these areas contain evidence for the origins and evolution of humans, as well as more recent remains of complex civilizations and trade networks. Research has been **uneven**, however, and many areas remain unexplored.

Prehistory

Archaeologists first uncovered fossils of humanlike australopithecines in South Africa in the 1920s and 1930s. The importance of these discoveries was not immediately recognized, but eventually **paleontologists** realized that australopithecines are the earliest human ancestors. Most likely they lived by gathering wild foods and **scavenging** carcasses killed by large animals. Some of the australopithecine fossils found in the region were individuals killed by animals, and the sites where they were found do not necessarily represent the places where they lived or made tools of stone and bone.

Some archaeological sites in southern Africa, such as Border Cave in Swaziland and **Klasies River Mouth** on the coast of South Africa, contain skeletons of Homo sapiens along with evidence of "modern" behavior such as the development of family groups, food sharing, and the planned use of resources. These sites may be more than 100,000 years old.

Archaeological evidence shows that, during the Late Stone Age, the peoples of central and southern Africa were largely nomadic, moving with the seasons between **mountainous** areas and low-lying lands. They trapped and hunted animals, gathered a wide variety of plant foods, and used **marine** resources such as **shellfish**. They also carefully buried their dead, sometimes placing various objects in the **grave**, and painted complex images on the walls of rock shelters—facts that lead archaeologists to believe that these Stone Age people had a strong sense of the **spiritual world**.

Around 2,000 years ago, the Stone Age way of life began to change in the region. In the drier western areas, domesticated sheep became an important part of the economy. Scientists debate the origins of this **pastoralism**, questioning whether local hunter-gatherers developed livestock herding on their own, or whether pastoral peoples arrived in the region from the north. Researchers agree, however, that the early pastoralists were the ancestors of the **Khoisan**, the indigenous people of southern Africa.

In parts of central and southern Africa with fairly dependable summer rainfall, people adopted a system of mixed agriculture, combining grain farming with livestock raising. Excavation of many ancient villages has shown that this way of life was firmly established by 200 A.D. The villages were linked by the exchange of goods, such as food products, pottery, salt, and iron. They may also have interacted with hunter-gatherers who still followed the Stone Age way of life because stone tools have been found in some village sites.

Historic era

The archaeological picture of central and southern Africa is clearer for the past thousands of years or so. Domestic livestock especially cattle, became very important throughout much of the region. Farming settlements spread into the highlands, where ruins of stone-built communities indicate the existence of large, thriving populations.

By the 1100s A.D., complex states were emerging. **Mapungabwe** and other hilltop towns along the **Limpopo River** in Zimbabwe and Botswana were centers of such states. These societies were organized into different economic and social classes. Their rulers controlled both the local economy and connections with the outside world. These links occurred with traders from Arabia on the coast of the Indian Ocean, where African goods such as gold, ivory, and animal skins were exchanged for foreign items such as glass beads and cotton cloth.

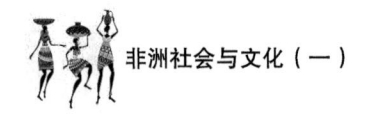

The Mapungabwe state was followed by **Great Zimbabwe**, which flourished until the 1400s. At its peak, Great Zimbabwe probably had a population of more than 10,000 people and included territory from eastern Botswana to near the Indian Ocean. The large stone walls in the center of the town reflected the high status of the ruling class; ordinary people lived in mud and **thatch** houses around the central stone buildings. More than 50 smaller regional centers built in the same style helped maintain the power of Great Zimbabwe.

The Arab traders who linked southern Africa to the Indian Ocean limited their settlements to the coast. European colonists, beginning with the **Portuguese** in the early 1500s, ventured into the **interior**. They were following rumors of vast wealth.[10] Portuguese forts, Dutch trading posts, and British colonial buildings and settlements are the focus of archaeological research into the recent colonial past of southern and central Africa. Many parts of the region, however, are not well-known archaeologically. Much work remains to be done, particularly in the great tropical rain forest that covers much of central Africa. Future research will undoubtedly challenge and change present ideas about the past of central and southern Africa and of the continent as a whole.[11]

III. AXUM(AKSUM)

The Periplus of the Erythraean Sea, a Greek document of the late first century A. D., describes the region ruled from Axum and suggests that the city, located in present-day **Tigray Region**, was already important at that early date. *The Periplus of the Erythraean Sea* also notes that the Red Sea port of **Adulis**, near today's Massawa in **Eritrea**, was part of the **Axumite Kingdom**. Axum engaged in Red Sea **commerce** and trade with the Roman Empire, India, and **Ceylon** (now Sri Lanka). In the first several centuries A.D., Axum dominated the region and thrived on trade and agriculture. Stone palaces had a distinctive architectural style.

In the late third century, the **prophet** Mani[12] wrote that Axum was one of the world's four great kingdoms. King **Ezana** (**reigned** about 303-356A.D.), who was Axum's first **Christian monarch**, called himself king of Axum, Saba, Salhen, Himyar, Raydan, Habashat, Tiamo, Kasu, and the Beja tribes. Saba, Salhen, Himyar, and Raydan refer to two of the **Yemeni** kingdoms and the palaces in their respective capitals. Habashat is **Abyssinia** and Tiamo may be the old Di'amat. Kasu is **Meroë** in the **biblical Kush** in modern Sudan and the Beja tribes still live in Sudan.

In the early 6th century, King Kaleb expanded the Axumite kingdom in Yemen and parts of Arabia. A 6th-century Greek visitor to Axum wrote of a four-towered palace of the king of Ethiopia. Even today, there are impressive remains at Axum, especially the royal tombs and their markers, the **stelae** or **obelisks**. Cut from a type of **granite**, they may represent a kind of **stairway** to heaven for Axum's dead rulers. At the base there are granite plates with carved wine cups for offerings to the **deceased**'s spirit. The Axumites produced their own **coinage** from about the late third

Megalithic obelisks of Axum in Ethiopia
(Photographer: Sun Lihua)

century until the seventh century, when Axum's power began to **wane**. The coins first used Greek and later a combination of Greek and Ge'ez.[13] In the late sixth century, the **Persians** conquered Yemen. Not long later, Axum lost control of the Red Sea trade to the Roman Empire and India. With the rise of Islam in about 640, the Roman or **Byzantine Empire** no longer had access to the Red Sea and Indian Ocean and their ships ended visits to Adulis. Axum became a **doomed** and forgotten place. Muslim states took control of the coastal areas, blocking Ethiopia's foreign trade.

Portuguese **chaplain Francisco Álvares** provided the first extensive description of Axum, having spent eight months in the town during his 1520—1526 visit to

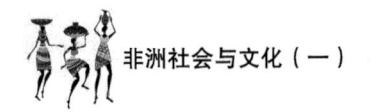

Ethiopia. He documented some structures, especially the original **Saint Mary** of **Zion Church** that probably was destroyed by **Ahmad ibn Ibrahim al Ghazi**. Subsequent visitors to Axum wrote about a town that looked much like it does today. Among the most important ruins are King Ezana's park, King Basen's tomb, King Kaleb's palace, the Mai Shum **reservoir**, the **Pantaleon Monastery**, Saint Mary of Zion Church, Dongar or **the queen of Sheba**'s palace, and the stelae fields. Exciting archaeological work is continuing by the Italian Rodolfo Fattovich and the American Kathryn Bard. Stuart Munro-Hay and David Phillipson have written extensively and **authoritatively** about Axum.

IV. ZIMBABWE RUINS

Justly famous as the site of the largest stone **edifice** built in early Sub-Saharan Africa, Zimbabwe played a **seminal** role in the country's history. It was the original center of monumental stone buildings; the center of the earliest known large-scale state system; and probably the earliest local center of international trade.

1. Description

The ruins, also known as Great Zimbabwe, are located in the Mtilikwe basin, on the southern scarp of the Central Plateau, about 29 km southeast of Masvingo.[14] Their surroundings are **perennially** moist, well-wooded, and filled with granite **outcroppings**, whose natural **exfoliation** provides easily **dressed** building stones. The ruins' **complex comprises** three main groups. On the north is the Hill Ruin (also known as "**Acropolis**"), built **atop** a **kopje** that rises about 100 meters above the rest of the complex. The hill contains a complicated network of **enclosures** separated by **freestanding** walls and natural rock formations. One enclosure contains a natural cave that occasionally **resonates** voices into the lower valley, giving rise to **speculation** that this cave was an early **oracular shrine** that may have provided an original religious basis for the whole complex.

Conical Tower in the Great Enclosure of the Great Zimbabwe
(Photographer: Chen Yong)

About 600 meters **due** south of the Hills' "Western Enclosure" is the famous **Elliptical** Building on the valley floor. This structure has also been popularly called "the Temple", "the Great Enclosure", and other names that reflect modern confusion over the structure's original purpose. Though built later than the Hill Ruin, the Elliptical Building clearly became the complex's most important structure. The overall enclosure is shaped like an irregular **ellipse** more than 250 meters in **circumference**. The great outer wall rises to nearly 10 meters in height, and expands to more than five meters in thickness in places. This wall alone is said to be the largest single precolonial African structure in Sub-Saharan Africa. It contains a greater volume of stones than the entire rest of the complex. Inside the main enclosure are smaller enclosures, a smaller and older wall separated from the eastern outer wall by the narrow "**parallel passage**", and the famed "**conical** tower" at the southern end of the parallel passage.

Between the Hill Ruin and the Elliptical Building is "the Valley Ruins". It contains 10 distinct ruins, half of which were named after 19th-century Europeans by **Richard Nicklin Hall**. These ruins contain most of the architectural features of the Elliptical Building, but each is built on a muchsmaller scale.

Three wall styles have been **discerned** in the complex. The earliest (style "P") features undressed facing blocks arranged in uneven and **undulating** courses. Most of the Hill Ruin is built in this style. A later style ("Q") represents the finest stonework found in the complex and is what was later employed in the best **Khami National Monument** in the west. This style features dressed and carefully matched stone blocks, arranged in closely fitting, even courses, as in the Elliptical Building's outer wall and conical tower. The third style ("R") is regarded as a **degenerate** form of the **intermediate** style. Its walls are built with ill-matched and loosely fitted stones in **uncoursed** rows. An even later period of building has left many walls that are little more than crude piles of stones.[15]

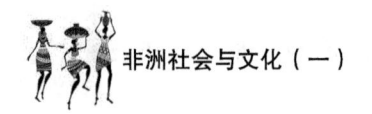

Conical Tower in the Great Enclosure of the Great Zimbabwe
(Photographer: Chen Yong)

Other notable features of the complex include numerous **sandstone monoliths**, including the famous Zimbabwe "birds", **linteled** doorways, stairways, **turrets**, and a particular fine **chevron frieze** atop the Elliptical Building's southeastern outer wall. Most of the enclosures formerly contained **daga** huts, and it is believed that most interior stone wall and dirt floors were once thoroughly **plastered** with daga. Many walls—all of which are **unmortared**—have collapsed, and others have been badly damaged by **overgrown vegetation** and treasure hunters. Considerable rebuilding by late **occupants** of the site and by early 20th-century government workers, the disappearance of almost all daga-work, and damage done by untrained archaeologists have all greatly altered the original appearance of the ruins.

2. History

Attempts have been made to **periodize** the ruins' occupation **sequences**, but these have not yet achieved a **consensus** among archaeologists and historians. Such periodization shave been produced frequently, and sometimes greatly revised, adding to the **bewildering terminology** applied to the country's Iron Age culture history. The general trend in modern **scholarship**, however, has been to **contract** the length of the whole stone-building era to within the first half of the last **millennium**. It is now generally agreed that Zimbabwe was abandoned as a major cultural and political center during the 15th century. Nevertheless, the site still ranks both as the longest-occupied center in the country and as the original stone-building complex.[16]

After a few centuries of very early Iron Age occupation, Zimbabwe seems to have been **unpopulated** until the late 11th century. Stone building began in about the 12th century, and the 13th century saw major **refinements** in metal working, **spinning**, **weaving**, and stone carving. An **elite** minority among the local Karanga people was emerging in the region. By the 14th century, these people were clearly engaging in a profitable gold trade with the east coast, apparently through the port of **Sofala**. Little is known about the nature of this state system, but its rulers were almost certainly receiving **tribute** payments and laborers from a large area, as the immediate region had insufficient resources to support the estimated 2,000 people who **resided** at Zimbabwe during its peak period.

The Elliptical Building is now generally believed to have contained the chief ruler's **residence** and **court**. The Valley Ruins probably housed lesser officials and royal family members, while the **bulk** of the population lived in surrounding, nonstone **dwellings**. The "Zimbabwe Culture" was spread throughout the southern part of the country by the construction of more than a hundred similar, but smaller, stone complexes. These were probably residences of provincial administrators or local **tributary** chiefs.

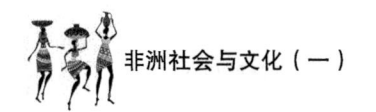

The elaborate and permanent nature of Zimbabwe's buildings was **incompatible** with the essentially **subsistence agriculture** on which the society was based, making its rulers heavily dependent upon tribute and external trade. In the early or mid-15th century the site was suddenly abandoned, perhaps as a response to changing political or commercial circumstances. Furthermore, local forests appear to have been largely **depleted** as a result of heavy use of fire, burned to **accelerate** granite exfoliation for the collection of building stones. It appears possible that the establishment of the **Monomotapa Empire** in the north around this time represented a shift of the Zimbabwe state's power center, a direct connection between these two state systems remains to be proven, however.

After the 15th century, Zimbabwe was cut off from foreign trade and no new building was undertaken by its remaining inhabitants. It is unclear who occupied the site over the next several centuries, but by the early 19th century, the minor Mugabe **chiefdom** was centered near Zimbabwe. This chiefdom had nothing to do with the earlier Zimbabwe rulers, and its people's ignorance of the buildings' origins later contributed to European theories about ancient non-African builders.[17] Zimbabwe is frequently said to have been **sacked** by Mfecane[18] invaders during the 1830s, but there is no evidence that this really happened. By the time Europeans arrived in Zimbabwe in the 1870s, Zimbabwe's buildings were heavily overgrown with vegetation and in a state of advanced **dereliction**.

3. Archaeological Investigation

Karl Mauch became the first European to study Zimbabwe in 1871. He produced the first drawings of the ruins and introduced the first **explicit** theories about their early non-African origins.[19] After the **BSAC** occupied **Mashonaland** in 1890, Europeans recklessly **pillaged** the ruins, despite administrative efforts to protect them. James Theodore Bent was **commissioned** to investigate the site in 1891, but his work was careless and destructive of the **stratigraphical** evidence. The next authorized **excavator**, Richard Nicklin Hall, did even more damage. The first professional archaeologists to excavate were **David Randall-MacIver** and **Gertrude Caton-Thompson**. The only other major excavations were undertaken in 1958 by **Roger Summers** and others. When their work was completed, the government **issued** a 25-year **moratorium** on excavations at Zimbabwe.

V. THE RISE OF THE SWAHILI CULTURE

The rise of the Swahili society and culture dates back to about 800 A.D. when traders from the Arabian Peninsula, **Persia**, China, and India **penetrated** the East African coast. Three primary factors were responsible for the rise of the Swahili culture: trade, religion, and racial **intermarriage**: Over centuries of economic interaction, the indigenous Africans and Arabs along the coast of East Africa intermarried and produced a new and distinct society known as the Swahili. And as a complex inter-regional network of trade evolved and expanded, there occurred a **proliferation** of inter-racial marriages, which led to the emergence of a new culture. The founding of Islam and its spread to Africa in the seventh century also changed the history of East Africa where the coastal people came into direct contact with the religion, its **concomitant** civilization, and **oriental** trade. Over centuries of relations: particularly with the Arabs, a new culture evolved and gradually expanded into the interior.

The **historiography** of East Africa and archaeological evidence suggest that since the first century, the history of the Swahili society has not been **static**, but dynamic. There were economic activities in the region in the pre-Arab period, but commercial changes occurred with the arrival of the Arabs, and by the late 15th century, the Portuguese penetrated and a new dimension was introduced to the economic and political relations of the Swahili states. Swahili, derived from the Arabic word "sawahil" meaning "coast", was the Arabic word for the culture that evolved. Swahili culture has endured and **bequeathed** lasting legacies not only on the people on the coast, but also on a large part of East Africa.

The historical developments in the Swahili states can be **gleaned** through archaeology and numerous written records of the Arab and European geographers, scholars, merchants, and **missionaries** who visited or wrote on the coast between the second and 19th centuries. Paleoanthropologists have indicated that the earliest human beings came from Africa and archaeologists have excavated many sites in eastern and southern Africa to support the emergence of culture in this part of the world. Australopithecines, the earliest humanlike **primates** known to have come from fossil remains in Africa, were found in southern Ethiopia, Kenya, and Tanzania, and the discoveries of Louis and Mary Leakey at the Olduvai Gorge in Tanzania were **testaments** to the **peopling** and development of early civilization in East Africa. While the **interlacustrine** region benefited from the development of agriculture, the coast gained from the growth of trade. Through a slow process, immigration to the coast took place within Africa, especially by the **Bantu-speaking** people, and the population soared because of the thriving economy. The Bantu-speaking people migrated from southern Cameroon, their cradle, by 1000 B. C., **forging** through the Congo forest to **populate** several parts of central, eastern, and southern Africa. They split into two major language families: the Eastern and the Western Bantu. Upon arrival in their different locations, they first interacted with the indigenous people before coming into contact with either the Arabs or Europeans. With time, their language intermixed with Arabic to produce Swahili. Bantu is neither a race nor a culture, but a member of the **Niger-Congo** family of African languages. Speaking over 400 related languages and practicing a common culture, the Bantu developed as an agricultural and technologically advanced people with a complex political system. Aside from speaking related languages, the Bantu also had similar socioeconomic characteristics.

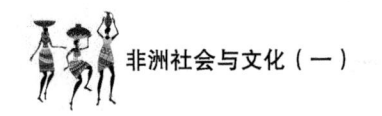

Arab, Chinese, and European writers of early documents about the East African coast had different interests and therefore their information was varied and diverse, though mainly related to commerce and religion. Emphasis was on commerce because the presence of essential articles of trade in East Africa and the Indian Ocean provided a convenient connecting factor. Religion, specifically Islam, was used to **cement** socio-cultural relations. Many of the documents, however, failed to discuss in any significant detail the issue of race relations. This was presumably because race did not create a problem in socioeconomic relations in the Swahili states. The foreign merchants interacted peacefully with the indigenous people with whom they traded.

The earliest written record was *The Periplus of The Erythraean Sea*, a single-authored Greek record, written in the second century. Focusing on the thriving commerce along the coast and supplying detailed information on the scattered urban and market centers that served as ports, the record also mentioned that **customs duties** were paid in several **emporia**. This suggests that a well-structured commercial arrangement evolved between indigenous Africans and foreign merchants. Among the essential articles of trade were gold, **frankincense**, and ivory. The closest information about race in the Periplus was that the Arab merchants "intermarried with East Africans, learned their languages, and exported the **exotic** products of the coast—notably ivory and…slaves". In his analysis of *The Periplus of The Erythraean Sea*, Gervase Mathew believed that the document was "the account of an eyewitness…who traveled on the trade routes of the Indian Ocean".

Another early document was ***The Geography*** of **Ptolemy** written in the fifth century. The author, **Claudius Ptolemaeus** (commonly known as Ptolemy), was a Roman scholar who lived in Egypt during the second century. Among his scholarly works, *The Geography* was the most important: Ptolemy referred to the people in East Africa as "man-eating Ethiopians", suggesting that the people were **cannibals**. Like The *Periplus*, the main theme of *The Geography* was the thriving commerce along the coast, and again like the author of *The Periplus*, Ptolemy described the inhabitants as boat makers and **seafarers**, and mentioned some places such as Opone as an important emporium.

The early inhabitants of the coast have been described in various ways. For example, *The Periplus* described them as very tall people while the Arabs called them Zanjor Biladaz-Zanj (the land of the Black people). *The Periplus* did not identify the different racial groups along the coast and did not specifically refer to the presence of the Bantu-speaking people, but it is certain that the **Nilotic** and

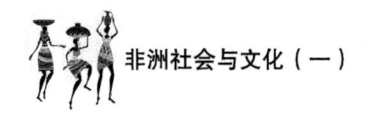

Bantu-speaking peoples had populated East Africa for many centuries before the **advent** of foreigners. Among them were the **Dinker** and **Nuer** in Sudan and **Luo** in western Kenya and Uganda. The dominant group of people were the Bantu who were advanced in agriculture, technology, pottery, and political organization.

The Christian Topography of Cosmas Indicopleutes, written in the mid-sixth century also used the Arabic term "Zanj" to identify the people of East Africa. Cosmas Indicopleutes was a Greek **seafaring** merchant and Christian who travelled to Adulis, which he described as an important port. He did not travel to the southern part of the East African coast, but provided an indication that the Arab merchants controlled trade, intermarried, and spoke local languages.

Numerous written sources in Arabic such as *Kitab al Zanj* were more concerned about the expansion of Islam and the growth of trade than about race relations. *Kitab al Zanj* mentioned Arab influence through two **Omani** brothers. The Omani Arabs became politically influential, especially in Zanzibar until the arrival of the Portuguese. **Joãode Barros**, a Portuguese and the writer of *Decadas da Asia* in the early 16th century, provided information on the immigration of different groups of Arabs to the coast. Because the Arabs were unwilling to compromise their religion by living among **infidels**, they forced the inhabitants to move to the interior. In reference to race and language, **Duarte Barbosa**, a Portuguese **mariner**, identified the people of the coastal city-states as "black men, and men of colour—some speak Arabic, and the rest make use of the language of the **Gentiles** [Bantu language] of the country. It also mentioned the intermarriage that took place among the Arabs thus leading to the establishment of dynasties, especially the Persian **Shirazi** dynasty of **Kilwa**.

Joãode Barros must have derived his information from *The Chronicle of Kilwa*, which credited the founding of Kilwa's Dynasty to seven Persian brothers (the Shirazi Dynasty). The relations between the Persian immigrants and the indigenous inhabitants were **cordial** in spite of their religious differences. *The Chronicle of Kilwa*, like those of **Pate** and **Lamu**, made little reference to race, but mentioned some Swahili-sounding names.

VI. TIMBUKTU

This **trove** of literary treasures is **testimony** to the great intellectual achievements of the scholars of the region. It is changing our notion of Sub-Saharan Africa from being the lands of "song and dance" to a continent with a rich **literary** heritage. Families are now reassembling collections that have been **dispersed** among different branches and building libraries to shelter them or putting them in the hands of expert **caretakers**. Meanwhile African history is being written and rewritten as new **manuscripts** and manuscript collections are brought to light.

For too long Timbuktu has been a place everyone has heard of but cannot find on the map; a place which has been described as more a myth or a word than a living city. Through conservation, **cataloging** and study of its manuscripts, Timbuktu is now being revealed as a city with a rich written history. In the process, our notion of Timbuktu is shifting from it being "the end of the world" to an important historic center of Islamic scholarship and culture.

Founded around 1100., as a seasonal camp for desert nomads, Timbuktu was to develop over the next couple of centuries into a thriving commercial city that was a key **crossroads** for the intellectual, social and economic development of west Africa. Situated on the northernmost bend of the great **Niger River**, between the gold mines in the southern **reaches** of West Africa and the salt mines of the Sahara Desert, it became a major center of **inter-regional** and **transsaharan** trade. An estimated two-thirds of the world's gold came from West Africa in the 14th century, the period in which the **Mali Empire** reached its **zenith**. A substantial proportion of that gold passed through Timbuktu, an important **hub** in the transportation of goods, people, ideas and books.

Timbuktu was an Islamic city from its foundation. Muslim Arabs had extended their control across the whole of North Africa by the end of the seventh century A.D. In the following centuries, Islam and the Arabic language spread deeper into the

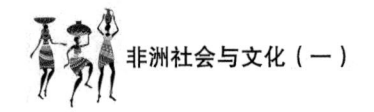

African continent not by conquest but by Muslim traders who **ventured** across the Sahara primarily in search of gold. Thus Arabic became the written language first of tradesmen and travelers and then of scholars and kings. **Diplomatic** and commercial relations between North Africa and **the Niger Bend** and between the Niger Bend and territories further south require communication over great distances. The written word was used to regulate commercial **transactions** (including the slave trade), to **legitimize** authority and even to **instigate** war. Scholarship was thus not only an intellectual and spiritual pursuit, but a means of social and political influence, even at times a matter of life and death. The renowned scholars of the region often came from wealthy trading families; trade created an **affluent** ruling elite whose scholars had the means to purchase books and the time to read and write.

Through trade, conquest and intermarriage, the peoples of black Africa and the Mediterranean mixed, making the Niger Bend one of the most ethnically diverse areas of Africa. Timbuktu had at one time or another been under the political control of almost every ethnic group in the region, each power determined to maintain the security and profits of West African trade routes. But through this **succession** of foreign **overlords**, the scholarly class in Timbuktu exercised considerable **autonomy**. Its learned men constituted the city's ruling elite, serving as **imams** and teachers, **scribes**, lawyers and judges.

Over centuries, Timbuktu gradually lost its **prominence** as a center of long-distance trade as the transsaharan trade routes were **diverted** by the arrival of Portuguese ships along the coast of West Africa and then by the discovery of gold in the Americas. The city has also endured the **vicissitudes** of climate and politics throughout its existence: repeated pillaging and sacking as described by the Timbuktu **chronicler** al-Sadi in the *Tarikh al-sudan*, fires as described by **Leo Africanus**, who visited in the early 16th century; conquest by a succession of west African peoples, as well as by the **Moroccans** and the French, and recently the **Tuareg Uprising** in the last decade of the 20th century and the floods of 1999. All have taken their toll through the centuries. But the independence and **civic** pride of Timbuktu's citizens has ensured the preservation of the city's culture and libraries into the 21st century.

In 1988, Timbuktu and its libraries were listed as a United Nations Educational, Scientific, and Cultural Organization world heritage site.

VII. EARLY NIGERIAN HISTORY

The earliest evidence of civilizations in Nigeria dates back to the Iwo-Eleru rock shelter located near **Akure in Ondo State**. Inside this cave is a skeleton dated about 9000 B.C., in the Late Stone Age. Archeological evidence from the Iron Age is more abundant, particularly from **the Nok**. This civilization was comprised of **agriculturalists** skilled in iron **smelting** who lived between 500 and 200 B.C. Miners in 1943 unearthed numerous clay pots and **terracotta** sculptures used by the Nok. Several notable developments in the 11th century dramatically shaped the cultural landscape and political organization of Nigeria's early peoples.

Social groups in Nigeria did not live in isolation. Instead, they formed **segmented polities**, kingdoms, and empires, particularly around 1000 A.D. Even nomadic peoples, such as the **Fulani**, moved in clearly organized political structures. These early peoples established diplomatic and economic networks that stretched across long distances. For example, **royalty** from **Borno** in the northeastern corner of Nigeria sent 100 camels, 1,130 horses, and 100 articles of clothing to a king in **Borgu** situated in eastern Nigeria. The most studied kingdoms and empires that developed around the 11th century were the **Hausa** Kingdoms and the **Oyo Empire**. According to oral tradition, the Hausa Kingdoms developed from "marriage between Prince Bayajidda of Baghdad and a princess from Daura around the 10th century." One version of the story says their son, Bawo, and his sons established the first several Hausa Kingdoms, which include Daura, Kano, and Katsina, to name a few.

The establishment of early political units, such as the Hausa Kingdoms, however, was not without negotiation or dispute. Land, for instance, was traded, purchased, and stolen. The founder of the town of Ilesha in southwestern Nigeria, according to oral tradition, purchased the site from a chief at Oyo for four slaves (male and female), two cows, one horse, 200 bundles of **cowries**, and 100 **kola nuts**. A kingdom at Kanem, however, was invaded and **dismantled** in 1389 by the nomadic Bulala people who desired the area for their own temporary settlement. The history of Nigeria between 1000 and 1800 included the rise and fall of kingdoms as well as the expansion of long-distance and international trade.

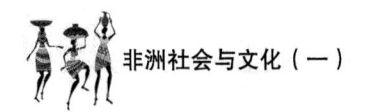

A significant part of trade included the buying and selling of slaves. Nigeria played a major role in the transatlantic slave trade, with seven of West Africa's 13 major slave **depots** located in Nigeria. Roughly 51 percent of all African slaves traded across the Atlantic were from the **Bights of Benin** and **Biafra**. Abolishing the slave trade from the supply side (in Africa) became a major **preoccupation** for European **humanitarians** and, more specifically, missionaries.

1. Nok

The Nok people were agriculturalists who lived between 500 and 200 B.C. in central Nigeria. This civilization has been **heralded** as fairly advanced because of its use of iron and stone materials. The Nok are best known today for their terracotta sculptures, iron **bracelets**, and pottery. There is also evidence that the Nok engaged in the **laborious** task of smelting iron. What little scholars know about the Nok people came from the discovery of their archeological remains during mining activities in 1943. Remains of this society are found in central Nigeria near the city of Jos in Plateau State. Nok art is considered highly sophisticated for its time because of the clay used and the level of detail and design that appears on each piece. Much of the artwork appears to be representations of people and animals. The faces of human sculptures are easily identified as Nok because of the **triangular** eyes, **perforated pupils**, nose, and mouth.

Archeologists have found significant similarities between materials unearthed at Nok and Ile-Ife and Benin. This evidence suggests that the neighboring groups were influenced by the Nok.

2. Ile-Ife

Ile-Ife is the sacred city of the **Yoruba** people, located in **Osun** State. According to oral tradition, Ile-Ife was the cradle of human civilization. It was the final home of **Oduduwa**, the ancestor of Yoruba oba (kings). In the center of town today is a large statue honoring Oduduwa. Archeological evidence, including bronze heads and terracotta sculptures, dates the occupation of Ile-Ife as far back as the 11th century. Ile-Ife had lost its status as the center of Yoruba politics to the Oyo Empire by the 14th century. During the 1980s, Ile-Ife was home to the Ona Artists, who popularized the Yoruba concept of ona (**reverence** for decoration and ornamentation).

Ife head
(Photographer: Han Hong)

3. Benin

Benin was the center of a great Benin Kingdom. Today, it is the modern capital of **Edo State**, located in the **Niger Delta**. A thousand years ago, the people of Benin used the complicated method of lost-wax casting[20] when forging iron tools and **adornments**. Ancient Benin is particularly known for its **bronze statues** and masks, which are displayed in museums around the world. It was also a major center for the trade of ivory and metal works. During the 15th century, Benin was a strong kingdom. According to oral tradition, the Benin people are of Yoruba descent.

4. Benin Kingdom

The Benin Kingdom existed between roughly the 11th and 16th centuries. Its history is divided into two phases, the first being the ogiso (king) dynasty of the Edo-speaking people (also referred to as Bini). According to oral tradition, the second phase was marked by the arrival of Oranmiyan, a Yoruba, from Ile-Ife in the 14th century. After some time, Oranmiyan decided to return to Ile-Ife and left his son, Eweka I, as the ruler. In the 15th century, Benin thrived and expanded, especially under the leadership of Ewuare, who constructed walls around Benin for protection. Ozolua, one of his sons, traveled with Joao Alfonso de Aveiro to Portugal and returned to Benin with luxury items from the Portuguese king. Some Benin people **converted** to **Christianity** and established some churches, such as **Holy Cross Cathedral**. Islam was introduced in the 19th century.

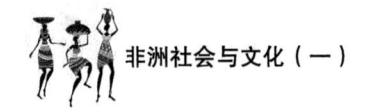

Explanations

［1］**Afar Triangle**：阿法尔三角地带位于非洲东部亚丁湾裂谷、红海裂谷和东非大裂谷交汇处。

［2］**Western Africa includes Mauritania, Mali, Niger, Nigeria, Chad, Cameroon, Benin, Burkina Faso, Togo, Ghana, Côted'Ivoire, Liberia, Sierra Leone, Guinea, Guinea-Bissau, Gambia, and Senegal:** 西非包括毛里塔尼亚、马里、尼日尔、尼日利亚、乍得、喀麦隆、贝宁、布基纳法索、多哥、加纳、科特迪瓦、利比里亚、塞拉利昂、几内亚、几内亚比绍、冈比亚和塞内加尔。

［3］**Elmina:** 距加纳首都阿克拉（Accra）以西130公里处有一座依山傍海的宏伟古堡，这就是加纳最古老，在整个西非地区都赫赫有名的埃尔米纳奴隶堡。起初它是欧洲殖民者掠夺黄金的总部，在奴隶贸易兴起以后，又成为囚禁黑人奴隶、进行奴隶贸易的重要据点。

［4］**Eastern Africa includes Djibouti, Eritrea, Ethiopia, Kenya, Somalia, Tanzania, and Uganda:** 东非包括吉布提、厄立特里亚、埃塞俄比亚、肯尼亚、索马里、坦桑尼亚和乌干达7国。

［5］**the Leakey Family:** "利基家族"主要包括古考古学家、人类学家路易斯·利基（Louis Seymour Bazett Leakey, 1903—1972），他的妻子玛丽·利基（Mary Leakey, 1913—1996），他们的次子，著名古人类学家、环保主义者理查德·利基（Richard Leakey, 1944— ）以及理查德的女儿，古生物学家、人类学家路易斯·利基（Louise Leakey, 1972— ）。自从达尔文提出"猿猴进化成人"的学说，考古学家和人类学家就开始大规模寻找和挖掘早期人类的遗存。利基家族就是其中的佼佼者，是当之无愧的"人类学第一家庭"。从20世纪20年代年至今，这个家族的几代人在东非为发掘和研究早期人类的化石孜孜不倦地工作，在古考古学、古人类学和古生物学等多个领域建树颇多。

［6］**Olduvai Gorge:** 号称"人类摇篮"的奥杜威峡谷位于坦桑尼亚北部，东非大峡谷内。峡谷呈东西走向分布，深约90米，总长近48公里。峡谷

是由剧烈的地质运动和溪流冲刷作用形成的。在过去数百万年中，奥杜威峡谷经历了多次火山喷发和剧烈的地壳变化。

[7] **the Near East**：目前，"近东"一词已经很少使用。近代西方地理学者用"近东"指代"邻近欧洲的东方"。第二次世界大战以后，这个称呼已经基本被"中东"所取代，但两者经常通用："近东"多用在人类文明史方面，"中东"一词则经常出现在国际政治舞台上。

[8] **The past thousands of years also saw the emergence of large population centers around the lakes of eastern Africa**：在过去数千年中，东非大湖周围出现了很多人口非常密集的区域。

[9] **Africa's central and southern regions include Angola, Botswana, Burundi, Central African Republic, Democratic Republic of Congo, Equatorial Guinea, Gabon, Lesotho, Malawi, Mozambique, Namibia, Republic of Congo, Rwanda, São Tomé and Principe, South Africa, Swaziland, Zambia, and Zimbabwe**：中部和南部非洲包括安哥拉、博茨瓦纳、布隆迪、中非共和国、刚果民主共和国、赤道几内亚、加蓬、莱索托、马拉维、莫桑比克、纳米比亚、刚果共和国、卢旺达、圣多美和普林西比、南非、斯威士兰、赞比亚和津巴布韦。

[10] **They were following rumors of vast wealth**：为了找到传说中的巨大财富，他们深入非洲内部。

[11] **Future research will undoubtedly challenge and change present ideas about the past of central and southern Africa and of the continent as a whole**：毫无疑问，未来的研究会挑战并改变人们目前对于中部非洲、南部非洲乃至整个非洲历史的看法。

[12] **Mani**：摩尼（c.216—276）是摩尼教（Manichaeism）创始人和先知。最初他只有两位追随者，随后摩尼及其信徒在波斯北部传教，然后经海路到达印度。摩尼在印度传教期间，杜兰国王（Turan, Shah of India）皈依摩尼教。回到波斯以后，萨珊王朝（Sassanid Empire）国王沙普尔一世（Shapur I the Great）准许他和信徒在萨珊帝国全境旅行和传教。后来摩尼派使徒到罗马和东方传教，摩尼教快速传播，成为一个世界性的宗教，现在已经绝迹。

[13] **Ge'ez**："吉兹语"是生活在埃塞俄比亚高原北部的人曾经使用过的古

代闪族语言，阿姆哈拉语（Amharic）和提格雷语（Tigre）均由吉兹语演变而来。现在，吉兹语仅在埃塞俄比亚基督教堂中使用。

[14] **The ruins, also known as Great Zimbabwe, are located in the Mtilikwe basin, on the southern scarp of the Central Plateau, about 29 km southeast of Masvingo:** 这个废墟就是举世闻名的"大津巴布韦"，距马斯温戈市东南方向约29公里。大津巴布韦遗址坐落在穆蒂利奎盆地当中，位于中央高原南边的陡坡上。

[15] **An even later period of building has left many walls that are little more than crude piles of stones:** 建造时代更晚的建筑现在只剩下一堆残垣断壁。

[16] **Nevertheless, the site still ranks both as the longest-occupied center in the country and as the original stone-building complex**：无论如何，大津巴布韦遗址迄今为止仍然是津巴布韦国内人类定居时间最长的区域，而且遗址从来没有翻建过。

[17] **This chiefdom had nothing to do with the earlier Zimbabwe rulers, and its people's ignorance of the buildings' origins later contributed to European theories about ancient non-African builders:** 这个酋长国和大津巴布韦遗址早期的统治者没有丝毫关联。正是因为酋长国的臣民不了解大津巴布韦遗址的起源，所以欧洲人才提出"遗址并非由非洲人建造"的理论。

[18] **Mfecane**：19世纪20—30年代，为了争夺土地和水源，南部非洲的班图部落之间发生了持续战乱，史称"姆菲卡尼"或者"弃土运动"。

[19] **He produced the first drawings of the ruins and introduced the first explicit theories about their early non-African origins:** 他最早绘制出大津巴布韦遗址，而且率先明确提出"遗址不是非洲人建造的"。

[20] **lost-wax casting:** "失蜡法"是青铜等金属器皿的精密铸造工艺。工匠先用陶土制成模坯，在表面浇一层熔化的蜡，等蜡液冷却凝固后，对蜡模进行加工，在外面涂上陶泥，同时在下部开一个小孔。然后对它进行加热，蜡受热熔化后从小孔中流出，再从小孔向里面注入金属溶液，等溶液冷却以后，敲掉外面的陶土。最后，对铸件进行精雕细琢就大功告成了。

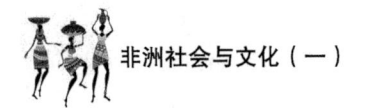

Exercises

I. Read the following statements and decide whether they are true (T) or false (F).

____ 1. Africa's climate became hotter and drier during the Middle Stone Age, producing environmental changes that challenged people to adapt to new conditions.

____ 2. In 1998, archaeologists discovered Africa's oldest boat in Ghana.

____ 3. Evidence of demesticated wheat, grapes, and lentils originated in eastern Africa.

____ 4. Archaeologists now believe that the Swahili coastal culture originated in Africa, but that colonists from southern Asia influenced the culture.

____ 5. Archaeologists believe that Stone Age people in central and southern Africa had a strong sense of the spiritual world.

____ 6. European colonists, beginning with the Spaniards in the early 1500s, ventured into the interior.

____ 7. The great outer wall of the Elliptical Building of the Great Zimbabwe alone is said to be the largest single precolonial African structure in Sub-Saharan Africa.

____ 8. The Bantu-speaking people migrated from southern Cameroon through the Congo forest to several parts of central, eastern, and southern Africa and split into two major language families: the Eastern and the Western Bantu.

____ 9. Christians in Timbuktu constituted its ruling elite, serving as imams and teachers, scribes, lawyers and judges.

____ 10. Arab, Chinese and European writers of early documents about the East African coast had different interests and therefore their information was varied and diverse, though mainly related to commerce and religion.

Unit II Ancient Civilizations in Africa

II. Fill in the following blanks with words that best complete the sentences.

1. Scientific evidence, which began with the study of _____, shows that Africa was the _____ of human beings.
2. During the Early Stone Age in Africa from about 2.6 million years ago, the early beings were believed to hunt _____ and looked for _____ that had been killed by large animals.
3. Archaeological sites along the coast of western Africa include _____ and _____ built by _____ as they explored and traded in the area in the 1400s and later.
4. Eastern Africa has turned some archaeological sites into _____ and has created local museums to educate schools and communities about their archaeological _____.
5. The most common _____ animals were cattle, sheep, and goats, though archaeologists have also uncovered bones of _____ from sites in Ethiopia and northern Kenya.
6. Local African communities traded valuable raw materials, such as gold, skins, and _____ across _____ to the Arabian Peninsula.
7. During the Late Stone Age, the peoples of central and southern Africa were largely _____, moving with the seasons between _____ areas and low-lying lands.
8. In parts of central and southern Africa with fairly dependable summer rainfall, people adopted a system of mixed agriculture, combining _____ with _____.
9. Even today, there are impressive remains at _____, especially the royal tombs and their markers, the _____ or obelisks.
10. The elaborate and permanent nature of Zimbabwe's buildings was _____ with the essentially _____ on which the society was based, making its rulers heavily dependent upon tribute and external trade.

Review and Reflect

✧ What do you think of African civilization?
✧ Why is Africa believed to be the cradle of the humankind?
✧ What accounted for the doom of Axum?

Unit III　Ethnic Groups in Africa

在非洲，"部族"既是个基本的文化单位，又是个政治单位，但绝不用来特指"一个生物学上的特殊群体"。非洲大陆现在至少有1,500个大大小小的部族。其中人口超过2千万的有埃塞俄比亚的阿姆哈拉族、西非的豪萨族、富拉尼族、伊博族、曼德族和约鲁巴族等。

Happy young Afar mothers in Eritrea

(Photographer: Liang Zi)

"There exist a rich variety of ethnic groups within basically all African states and multiculturalism is a living reality. Giving recognition to all groups, respecting their differences and allowing them all to flourish in a truly democratic spirit does not lead to conflict; it prevents conflict."

—International Work Group for Indigenous Affairs

Unit III Ethnic Groups in Africa

> ◎ **Think and Talk**
> ☆ How many ethnic groups are there in China? What are their differences?
> ☆ Which ethnic groups in Africa do you know of? What do you know about them?
> ☆ What is the relationship between different tribes in Africa?

I. OVERVIEW

There are probably at least 1,500 ethnic groups in Africa. They vary in size, in ways of making a living, in their forms of government, in their kinds of family life, and in their religions. Yet all are African and as such are different from other peoples of the world.

Ethnic groups are populations that feel connected by a complex mix of **kinship**, culture, history, and geography. Together, the people in an ethnic group shape their ethnic identity—the sense of belonging to the group and sharing in its culture. Ethnic identity in Africa is as richly diverse as its people, and for most Africans it plays a central role in politics and social life.

Ethnicity—a person's ethnic identity—is not the same thing as race, religion, or language. It is, however, often defined by some or all of these factors. For many Africans, ethnic identity is highly complex and has **multiple** layers. The closest, innermost layer comes from local identity, based on a person's **clan** or village or place of origin. The next level may be a somewhat broader idea of identity, perhaps a sense of being from a particular district.

Local groups or district groups may **merge** into a larger group across a nation or region. Although most of the members of this larger group do not know each other, they may see themselves as having more in common with each other than with people of other ethnic groups. Some of the largest ethnic groups cross national and religious boundaries, but they share similar cultural features, languages, or religious practices that allow them to think of themselves as connected.[1] With all these layers, individual Africans may think of their ethnic identity in different ways. They may present that identity differently in various circumstances.

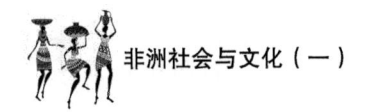

Africa's **tapestry** of thousands of ethnic groups is woven of many **strands**. Some strands can be traced back to the centuries before Europeans conquered Africa and ruled it as colonies. In this **precolonial** period, cultures emerged and mixed as peoples moved about and invaded each other's lands. Other strands developed as a result of European colonial governments that looked for differences among groups and created ethnic categories that often had little meaning for the people themselves. Still other strands are closely linked to political and economic life in modern Africa, in which leaders depend on the backing of their ethnic groups and reward them with power and influence.

Conflict among ethnic groups lies at the root of many civil wars in Africa—sometimes on a horrifying scale, such as the **genocidal** violence that **flared** in Rwanda in the mid-1990s[2]. Yet ethnic identity can **inspire** pride and hope and unite people in groups for effective political and social action. The challenge for many African countries is to balance the **diversity** of ethnicity with equal access to political power, wealth, opportunity and the resources of the nation.[3]

II. WESTERN AFRICA

Ethnicity has always been an important element in the way people identify themselves. In western Africa, however, European colonial powers made ethnic categories more **rigid** than they had been before. The colonial authorities **imposed** strict definitions on western Africa's complex and changeable social structures. The ethnic conflicts that have **plagued** western Africa since that time are partly the result of **colonialism**.

Unit III Ethnic Groups in Africa

1. Ethnic Patterns in the Past

Before conquest by Europeans, western Africa's ethnic groups were rarely separate or **self-contained**. Rather, they belonged to chains of networks of societies with many shifting connections. Even so, Arab geographers made **distinctions** between Arab and African regions, which they called white countries and black countries. Other distinctions existed as well. People in various environments lived differently: **nomadic herders roamed** the deserts, and farmers planted crops in the **savanna** and forests. Meanwhile, merchants, traders, and laborers filled the cities. But even these boundaries between people were **blurred**. In periods of extreme **drought**, the nomadic **Tuareg** of the west African Sahara withdrew to the cities and took up trade and businesses.

Trade, war, and politics brought ethnic groups into contact and even some forms of unity. As states rose to power and expanded their territory, they created new forms of ethnic identity. For example, when the Nupe Kingdom[4] emerged along the banks of **the Niger River** after about 1500, the ethnic group and the state were **identical**. A Nupe was anyone considered a **subject** by the Nupe ruler. On the **fringes** of such states—but still under the state's influence—people lived in societies based on local kinship groups. Over the course of their histories, these societies might be known by several ethnic names as they passed from local organization to state control and back again when the state lost power.[5]

When France and Great Britain explored and colonized western Africa, their **missionaries**, administrators, and social scientists looked for fixed ethnic categories. They **oversimplified** the region's complex ethnicity. They produced maps showing separate ethnic categories with clear boundaries between them. These ethnic categories **hardened** in place as the colonizers identified certain Africans as leaders and developed relationships with them.[6]

This way of regarding ethnic groups suited the French and British strategy of "divide and rule".[7] They found it easier to control people who thought of themselves as many separate populations with separate interests. Based on the **notion** that some groups were racially or ethnically superior to others, the colonial powers gave **favored** groups some degree of self-rule or even control over other groups. In what is now Nigeria, for example, the British regarded the **Fulani** as more advanced than other peoples and allowed them to be governed by their own institutions and **chiefs**.

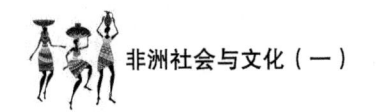

2. Ethnicity Today

Many ethnic conflicts that occur today in western Africa do not represent a return of ancient **hostilities** in the absence of colonialism. Rather, the conflicts are the **legacy** of the colonial era, which invented **artificial** categories, broke up relations among societies, and fostered **resentment** and competition among ethnic groups. In countries such as Benin and Côte d'Ivoire, governments continue to divide and rule their citizens by **reinforcing** the separations between ethnic groups. Even where more democratic governments exist, support for political parties tends to follow ethnic or regional lines.

Colonization was not just a temporary phase. It left a lasting mark on Africa and changed relations between ethnic groups. Western Africa did not return to its precolonial state after independence. Civil wars and ethnic and border conflicts in **Senegal**, **Mauritania**, **Liberia**, **Guinea**, **Mali**, and **Niger** may be signs that the region has entered into a period of redefining itself. The states and borders that the colonial powers put in place are weakening as new social structures and new relations among ethnic groups come into existence.

3. Igbo/Ibo

The Igbo live primarily in southeastern Nigeria and are united by the Igbo language and religion. It is estimated that the Igbo ethnic group's population is roughly 19 million. They are the ethnic majority in Akwa Ibom, Anambra, Cross River, and Rivers State. The origin of the Igbo is uncertain, but some scholars have said they migrated from the **Niger-Benue confluence** to their present location in southeastern Nigeria. The territory dominated by the Igbo is commonly referred to as **Igboland**. Although the Igbo political system is most commonly described as **acephalous**, there are several instances within Igbo society of a **kingship** system.

During the colonial period, the British attempted to establish the administrative practice of indirect rule, which had been successful for them in northern Nigeria. Indirect rule in Igboland, however, initially failed because the British could not identify a chief and **resolved** to appoint an individual to fulfill that role. The Igbo response was the **Aba Women's Riots** of 1929. In May 1966, thousands died during a **massacre resembling genocide**, which sparked the **secession** of the Eastern Region from Nigeria and the Civil War.[8] Today, it is not uncommon to see Igbo war **veterans** sitting along the roadside in **Enugu** collecting donations. The Igbo have developed a reputation as skilled traders and **entrepreneurs**, causing them to travel far from their traditional home in search of business. **Ohaneze Ndigbo** was an important Igbo cultural association. **Notable** Igbo cultural and political figures include Chinua Achebe, Michael Okpara, Nnamdi Azikiwe, and Chukwuemeka Odumegwu Ojukwu.[9]

The Igbo language is part of the **Kwa** language, which is part of the **Niger-Congo family**. It is primarily spoken in eastern Nigeria and in the Niger River basin. When writing, the Igbo use Latin letters, with some **variation**, to express sounds unique to the language. Igbo is a **tonal** language, signifying that the meaning of a word depends on the high or low tone addressed to each **vowel**. There are several dialects of Igbo, for example, Enu-Onitsha Igbo. The translation of this ethnic group's name into English has resulted in two spellings, Igbo and Ibo. Both are widely used and accepted when referring to the language or ethnic group.

The Igbo have practiced their religion since ancient times. They believe that Chukwu (God) created the universe and cohabited with humans. Chukwu created Eri, the **progenitor** of humans, and sent him to a **waterlogged** earth. Eri and Namaku, his wife, arrived in the town of Aguleri, located in present-day Anambra State. A blacksmith was also sent to dry the land with fire. Eri and Namaku had four children—Nri, Aguleri, Igbariam and Amanuke—who are the ancestors of the

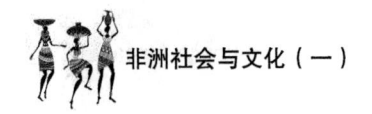

Igbo people. Chukwu assigned the **maintenance** and protection of humans in their daily lives to a **pantheon** of **deities**. Practitioners seek assistance from gods such as Ala, Igwe, and Mbatuku, and give thanks to them through offerings and community festivals. Today, most Igbo practice **Christianity**. They believe very strongly in agbara (spirit), which acts as a strong force to encourage people to do good things.

III. EASTERN AFRICA

Like western Africa, eastern Africa today shows the political and social effects of colonial rule, which imposed artificial divisions on ethnic groups. The colonial powers divided the peoples of Uganda, Kenya, and Tanzania into separate "tribes", usually ignoring the complex relations of marriage and trade between regions and peoples. The word **tribalism** refers to the way of thinking of society along ethnic lines. Many modern scholars have rejected the terms "tribe" and "tribalism" because of their connection with these false and rigid definitions. However, traces of colonial practices remain. People in eastern Africa sometimes use the concept of tribalism to explain differences and conflicts among themselves, even when the differences have more to do with money, land, and resources than with customs or culture.

1. Meanings of Ethnicity

Whether imposed from outside or claimed as one's own, ethnicity divides people into categories. Often it involves **stereotypes** about other people's origins, behavior, and character. It may even suggest that some groups are more "human" than others. The names of some groups indicate that they view themselves as special. Both the **Nuer** and the **Dinka** of southern Sudan call themselves by names that mean "people". The general term for many of the peoples of eastern Africa is **Bantu**, which is a family of languages but also means "people".

One feature of ethnic identity in eastern Africa dates from the 1940s, when some groups that shared culture and language **bonded** together in larger groups using labels that included everyone. In Kenya, for example, the **Nandi**, **Turkana**, and **Pokot** peoples allied themselves under the name **Kalenjin**. Individuals use the name of their small group locally, but in national or political matters they often identify with the more influential Kalenjin—the group to which Kenya's second president, **Daniel arap Moi**, belongs. Another example in Africa is that in Zambia, this process has given rise to "**mega**-ethnic groups" such as the **Bemba**. This name once referred to only one of the many ethnic groups in northeastern Zambia. Today, however, it refers to a **cluster** of groups in northern Zambia that has adopted Bemba as a shared language. The trend toward mega-ethnic groups appears to be continuing.

2. Modern Ethnic Relationships

As in other parts of Africa, ethnic identity in eastern Africa has been changing. More people have gone to live and work in the cities, where different ethnic groups **intermarry**, share cultures, and create new styles. Many people use languages such as English and **Swahili** on occasions rather than their traditional local languages. Political events have also created **upheavals** in ethnic identity. In Rwanda the dominant Hutu waged a **gruesome** genocidal campaign of violence against the minority Tutsi in the mid-1990s. This **tragedy** continues to be felt throughout the region. To **counter** these trends, ethnic leaders often launch cultural **revival** movements or make ethnic awareness a political goal.

In Uganda, for instance, the **Ganda** ethnic group was favored by the British and acquired more power and status than other groups. After Uganda gained independence in 1962, two political parties emerged. One represented the Ganda, while the second had members from many of the country's other ethnic groups. The two parties formed an **alliance**, but within a few years a power struggle **shattered** the alliance, and the party of the Ganda king was banned. The country became deeply divided along lines that were partly ethnic: Ganda versus non-Ganda, southerners versus northerners, speakers of Bantu versus speakers of **Nilotic** languages. During the 1970s,

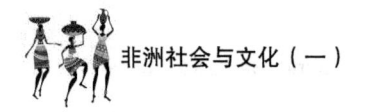

Ugandan leader Idi Amin Dada[10] took advantage of these sharp divisions by explaining his government's failures as the **treachery** of one ethnic group after another.

Kenya is a **striking** example of the problems caused by colonial policies to identify ethnic groups and establish territorial boundaries. The political border that the British created between Kenya and Uganda cuts across ethnic groups linked by language, culture, and history. Kenya's borders with Tanzania, Ethiopia, Sudan and Somalia also **disregarded** ethnic relationships. As a result, artificial differences arose between related peoples.

Tanzania has taken a different approach to ethnicity. The government encourages the use of Swahili, the coastal language, as the national tongue, and people often identify themselves as belonging to several ethnic groups. But although Tanzania's ethnic divisions are not as deep as those of Uganda and Kenya, economic **tensions** tend to **highlight** small differences. For example, the **Chaga**, who live in the foothills of **Mount Kilimanjaro**, have enjoyed success in farming and business. They have faced envy ad **discrimination** from neighboring groups, even though they are very similar to them ethnically.

Swahili women in Tanzania
(Photographer: Sun Lihua)

Stone-built houses on the beach of Zanzibar, Tanzania
(Photographer: Lan Fengyun)

3. Swahili

The Swahili people live in towns and villages along a 1,000-mile stretch of the East African coastline, from Somalia to Mozambique. Many also live on **Zanzibar**, **Pemba**, and **the Comoro Islands** off the coast. The name Swahili, an Arabic term meaning "people of the coast", was given to them by Arabs who conquered the region in the early 1700s. However, the Swahili rarely use this name, preferring to identify themselves by names that refer to individual towns.

The Swahili are Muslims and use both the Arabic and Roman alphabets for writing. Their language, Swahili, belongs to the Bantu family of African languages but includes many words borrowed from Arabic. It has become a common language of trade and communication throughout eastern Africa.

Swahili civilization, unlike that of neighboring African peoples, is urban, **maritime**, and based on commerce. Since they first established towns along the coast before 1000 A.D., the Swahili have been agents in trade between Africa and Asia. Their economy suffered when Great Britain ended the slave trade in the 1800s and more recently when long-distance shipping trade across the Indian Ocean declined. The Swahili are noted for their large, stone-built houses and towns, their elegant clothing and food, and for a high level of literary achievement, especially in poetry.

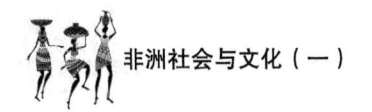

4. Maasai

The Maasai are among the most well-known **indigenous** people in all of Africa, due to their distinctive customs, culture and dress. The Maasai speak Maa, which is a member of the **Nilo-Saharan** language family.

Maasai morans (warriors) in front of their kraal in Tanzania
(Photographer: Lan Fengyun)

The Maasai society **straddles** Kenya and Tanzania with 14-22 sub-tribes, each with distinct appearance, leadership and dialect. The Maasai live in kraals (**manyattas**) arranged in a **circular** manner. The fence around the kraal is made of twigs and sometimes **acacia** thorns, for security against wild animals that **prey** on Maasai **livestock**. The *Inkajijik* (maasai word for "a house") are **oblong** shaped and made of mud, sticks, grass and cow **dung**. It is just about 4-5 feet raised from the ground. The manyatta is not only the dwelling place for the Maasai but symbolically the **warehouse** of Maasai culture. Maasai culture is oiled by **patriarchy** in which men have the **monopoly** of all decision-making processes. However, manyatta is very important and of symbolic value to the woman. The woman is the one who builds the manyatta, sometimes with the help of her co-wives, but in most cases they do it alone. It is what expresses the woman's moral standing in the Maasai society besides being the socializing **crucible**. Women are also responsible for supplying water, collecting firewood, milking cattle and cooking for the family. **Warriors** are in charge of security while boys are responsible for **herding** livestock. During the drought season, both warriors and boys assume the responsibility for herding livestock. The elders are directors and advisers for day-to-day activities. Traditionally, kraals are shared by an extended family. However, due to the new land management system in the Maasai region, it is not uncommon to see a kraal occupied by a single family.

The Maasai are agricultural **pastoralists** whose attachment to animals is a **symbiotic** phenomenon. Their economy revolves around livestock with cattle valued particularly high as a mobile form of wealth, medium of exchange, source of food, symbol of relationship and of sacred significance, however due to increase in population, people no longer follow an extensive pastoral mode of life or restrict their diet to livestock products. Over time, the Maasai people have diversified their economy. They currently engage in both livestock herding and crop farming. Livestock is still the measurement of wealth and signifies one's community status: the more the livestock, the higher the social status. Maasai people have a prayer that says "Meishoo iyiook enkai inkishu o-nkera", which means "May God give us cattle and children". Cattle and children are the most important aspects of the Maasai people.

Traditionally, the Maasai relied on meat, milk and blood from cattle for protein and **caloric** needs. People drink blood on special occasions. It is given to a **circumcised** person, a woman who has given birth and the sick. Blood is very rich in protein and is good for the immune system. However, its use in the traditional diet is decreasing due to the reduced number of livestock and the new land management system.

Ceremonies in Maasai society represent stages in life and **rites of passage**. Traditionally, boys and girls must undergo **initiations** for **minors** prior to circumcision. However, many of these initiations concern men while women's initiations focus on circumcision and marriage.

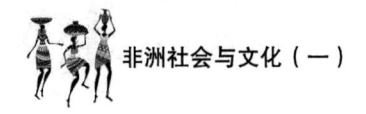

Men will form **age-sets** moving them closer to adulthood. Women do not have their own age-sets but are recognized by those of their husbands. Ceremonies are an expression of Maasai culture and self-determination. Every ceremony is a new stage in life and every Maasai child is eager to go through these vital stages of life.

The Maasai are a people with independent way of thinking, faithful to their kinship and regard their culture with high **esteem**. The society, which has been proud and **self-sufficient**, is also facing many social-economic and political challenges. It's opening up to the world and the cultural practices are becoming less practiced as more people **opt** to go to school.

IV. CENTRAL AFRICA

Colonial administrators of central Africa divided the region into units and considered each unit home to a specific "tribe" with a leadership structure, a unique culture, and centuries of tradition. This practice was no more accurate or effective in central Africa than in other regions.[11] It ignored the flexible, changeable, and evolving nature of ethnic identity. Christian missionaries reinforced this colonial concept as they chose local languages for education and Bible translation and created a structure for the churches' own administrative units. Research in the late 1900s showed that many ethnic names of this region came from colonial practices rather than indigenous African tradition.

Even after independence, some central African politicians and **intellectuals** have continued to reinforce the colonial concept of tribes, which favors certain individuals and groups. However, ethnic identity can also benefit less favored groups by promoting a sense of unity and pride and giving them political influence. Politicians and ethnic leaders with varying interests have tried various approaches, including **sponsoring** ethnic festivals and associations, working to define the histories and **folklore** of ethnic groups, and calling for the return of traditional leadership.

Unit III Ethnic Groups in Africa

1. Multiethnic Societies

Before the colonial era, most African states were multiethnic, that is, they usually had one dominant ethnic group, several other groups, several languages, and a shared culture. The colonial powers remolded ethnicity into a **hierarchical** structure of separate geographical units, each governed by a traditional ruler who served as a colonial official. Today, however, everyday life is multiethnic again, especially in towns but increasingly in rural areas as well.

Although many associations are organized along ethnic lines and designed to promote ethnic identification, numerous **recreational**, sports, and religious organizations resemble society in general and are multiethnic, in them, individuals learn to operate in the wider society. World religions such as Islam and Christianity are perhaps the least ethnically divided institutions in central Africa. Many churches offer services or rituals in more than one language.

Many of the towns of central Africa began as **settlements** created by colonial authorities to meet the needs of government and industry. The towns have been laboratories of multiethnic social life. They have attracted **migrants** of many ethnic backgrounds who speak a variety of languages. Townspeople learn to communicate in a common language, and they share the common experiences of urban life. But many people have complex ties to rural cultures as well.

The region, rather than the individual ethnic group, also shaped politics in central Africa. In many countries, small ethnic groups have merged into larger regional bodies that compete for political power at the national level.

2. Ethnicity and Conflict

A society divided into different ethnic groups does not necessarily produce equal groups with the same amounts of power and status. Some groups may be seen as older, larger, richer, or more advanced than others. Ethnic groups tend to compete, **striving** to improve their positions. When they fail, individuals may try to move into more favored groups by changing their dress, language, or name.

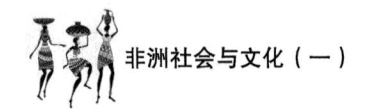

Many Central Africans regard ethnicity as the most important factor in politics, and they tend to view any **disturbance** as an ethnic conflict. Ethnic labels allow complex social, economic, and political issues to be reduced to a simple case of "us against them".[12] In such situations, ethnic identity can harden, and people may be willing to suffer or **inflict** violence on behalf of their ethnic group. In many states in this region, poverty and political disorder have been regarded as ethnic conflicts. This viewpoint has led to bitter **confrontations** and, in some cases, to large-scale violence.

3. Kongo/Congolese

This ethnic group lives in eastern Congo/Zaire, southern Republic of the Congo[13] and northern Angola, near the Atlantic coast. The Kongo people were among the first to come into contact with European explorers, traders and missionaries. The Kongo Kingdom was a flourishing empire in 1482 when **Diogo Cão** first sailed up the mouth of the Congo River and landed in an area near **Boma**, ten years before Christopher Columbus reached America. The kingdom decayed in the 17th century, possibly because of competition between European powers and the rise of the slave trade which upset the balance of power among the various tribes and **chieftaincies**. Nevertheless, the **linguistic** and cultural influence of the group continued to be felt. A **matrilineal** people with a highly organized **judicial** and political **hierarchy**, the Kongo were spread as far east as the plains of **Kinshasa** and their language, **Kikongo**, became one of Congo/Zaire's four national languages.

The Kongo people's access to educational opportunities and their **proximity** to major cities such as Kinshasa and **Matadi** contributed to their large representation in the colonial-era civil service and among the class of developed people. The Kongo were among the earliest and most influential **advocates** of greater personal freedom for Congolese and, later, of independence. They were considered by the colonial authorities to be among the more **radical pro-independence** groups and one of the most anti-Belgium.[14] Their leaders formed the Association des Bakongo in 1950 to protect their culture from influence of the **Ngala** and **Luba**, who began arriving in **Leopoldville** following World War II. The association later became the Alliance des Bakongo (ABAKO) political party which was one of the first groups to **press for** labor rights, political freedoms and, ultimately, independence. ABAKO produced Congo's first president, **Joseph Kasavubu**.

Following independence, the Kongo **cadres** continued to dominate the government and civil service, occupying more than one-third of the administrative positions. **Demographic** studies in the 1980s revealed that up to one-third of the population of Kinshasa traced its origins to the Kongo and one-fifth of these were Kongo of Angolan origin.

V. SOUTHERN AFRICA

For many years, ethnic identity in southern Africa was shaped by **apartheid**, the policy of racial **segregation** that the white government of South Africa adopted to maintain control over the indigenous population. The government used ethnicity to justify its creation of ethnic "homelands" for black people. Many people who opposed apartheid and supported African **nationalism** rejected this approach as racist. To them, ethnicity was created entirely by the racist state to support its aims—property and profit for white people based on the cheap labor and obedience of black people.

Since the end of apartheid in the 1990s, South Africa has had a continuing debate about ethnic identity. Some people believe that as the racist structure of South Africa has been **dismantled**, more authentic forms of ethnicity have emerged. Others still feel that ethnicity is an expression of earlier racist policies and only serves the interests of the ruling class—whether black or while. According to this view, British and Dutch colonists used ethnicity to make black Africans easier to divide, control, and put to work in diamond mines and other white-owned industries. In addition, tribal identities kept people obedient to tribal leaders who were either appointed or influenced by the colonial powers. However, culture is a powerful force, and the fact that ethnic identity was largely invented does not make it a less real part of society.[15]

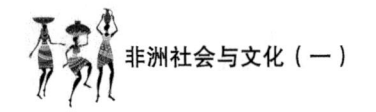

The difficulty of defining ethnicity in southern Africa is illustrated by the **Zulu**. The Zulu State formed in the mid-1800s when many independent **chiefdoms** that shared culture and languages came under the rule of the Zulu king. Even when the Zulu Kingdom united against the British, however, regional **loyalties** remained important, and most subjects of the state did not regard themselves as Zulu.[16] A wider sense of Zulu identity only emerged after about 1920, as a result of changes brought by migrating workers and the decay of the old order. That identity received official recognition through the policy of apartheid when the South African government created a territory called **KwaZulu** as the Zulu "homeland". Since the end of apartheid, some Zulu politicians continue to emphasize the rich Zulu history and to campaign for a self-governing Zulu region or even a fully independent state.

Ethnic identity tends to emerge most strongly when different groups interact and compete for power or resources in southern Africa during colonial times, many indigenous groups were united in their **opposition** to foreign rule and tended to overlook their own differences. After independence, however, ethnic distinctions reappeared as groups struggled for the power once held by colonial administrations. In the same way, Zimbabwe's 2 major ethnic groups, the **Shona** and the **Ndebele**, worked together to defeat the white-dominated government and to win independence. Afterward they came into conflict.

The question of how to balance ethnic and national identity will likely remain a central issue of political life throughout the African continent. In Namibia, for example, the years since independence have brought a number of ethnic **claims** for the recognition of rights to **ancestral** lands or kingdoms as well as a continuing public debate about how to **reconcile** these claims with national unity.

1. Xhosa

The Xhosa are one of South Africa's black ethnic groups. **IsiXhosa** is also one of the Bantu languages spoken in South Africa. There are several subgroups of the Xhosa-speaking population. Each of these groups has a distinct but related **heritage**. At present, about six million isiXhosa speakers reside throughout South Africa, the majority in the Eastern and the Western Cape provinces, as well as fewer in Free State and in KwaZulu-Natal.[17] IsiXhosa is South Africa's second most common language among the black population, after isiZulu, to which it is closely related.[18]

Historically, the Xhosa were part of the South African **Nguni** migration, which moved to the country's southeastern area from the **Great Lakes Region** of present-day Uganda and Rwanda, before the first white settlers' arrival during the 1600s. Due to their cultural, linguistic, economic, and social interactions with other southern African societies and groups, the Xhosa had an open society. For instance, the modern isiXhosa language has large elements of the **Khoikhoi** and **San** languages spoken by the region's original nomadic herders.

The Xhosa first encountered white settlers around **Somerset East** in present-day Western Cape Province in the early 1700s. During the late 1700s, they clashed with the **Boer trekkers** who were migrating inward toward the Xhosa territories from the **Cape Colony**. After more than two decades of territorial conflicts, the Xhosa were pushed east by the British colonial forces during the Third Frontier War from 1811 to 1812. Following this, many Xhosa-speaking clans were forced west by the Zulu, who were expanding their territories during the Mfecane,[19] a period of political instability in southern Africa. The Xhosa's unity and abilities to resist colonial expansion were further weakened by famines and political divisions among themselves. Besides losing their lands to both the Zulu and the European settlers, they also faced restrictions on their political **autonomy** due to the various measures implemented by the British colonial authorities and subsequently by the South African government. Over time, many became **impoverished** and were forced to become migrants and wage laborers in the urban areas or in neighboring countries. IsiXhosa speakers made up a large percentage of workers in South Africa's gold mines.

During the Apartheid Era, many Xhosa were forcefully resettled in the

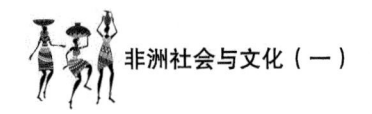

Bantustans of Transkei and Ciskei, which were legally **designated** for them. Furthermore, Xhosa in the Bantustans were systematically deprived of basic social services and employment opportunities. In the cities, like other black South Africans, they were subject to **raids** for failing to obey the **Pass Laws** by not carrying pass books. These homelands were not dismantled until the apartheid regime ended in 1994, and, since then, their living conditions have improved. For example, the Xhosa literacy rate has increased from 30 percent during the apartheid era to around 50 percent in 1996 as primary schools have **instituted** Xhosa language **curricula**. Currently, isiXhosa is one of South Africa's eleven official languages, and there are two isiXhosa radio stations. At least two of South African's three public television stations broadcast partly in isiXhosa. However, many Xhosa are still impoverished because housing and living standards vary among this population. They also face social problems such as high crime rates, broken families, **malnutrition**, and tensions with other black ethnic groups due to competition for scarce resources. Even though the Xhosa are one of South Africa's poorest populations, a minority of them are also the wealthiest. Prominent Xhosa include former presidents Nelson Mandela and Thabo Mbeki, as well as **Reverend** Desmond Tutu.[20]

2. Bushmen

This term, often considered **derogatory**, is used to describe the San, a group of **Khoisan**-speaking hunter-gatherers who live in the **Kalahari Desert**.

The first European encounter with the so-called Bushmen of southern Africa came shortly after Dutch colonists established a settlement on the **Cape of Good Hope** in 1652. The region's **Nama** herders told them about primitive, **foraging** peoples known as the Sonqua, or San. In 1660, Dutch soldier Carl Riebeeck led an army mission into the mountainous regions of the Cape, where he reportedly came upon communities of foragers, whom the Europeans later called Bosjesmen, or Bushmen.

For nearly two centuries, the Bushmen were **vilified** by Europeans, who viewed

Unit III　Ethnic Groups in Africa

them as "wild creatures" who refused to be civilized. European accounts of the time frequently described Bushmen as **mischievous bandits lurking** on the **peripheries** of human settlement. During the 17th and 18th centuries, these perceptions were used to justify **Afrikaner** efforts to **exterminate** the people they called "the lowest race on the earth". Between 1785 and 1795 alone, Afrikaner settlers are reported to have killed at least 2,500 San and taken **captive** at least another 700. European missionaries were unconcerned with the mass killings because Bushmen were seen as "dogs", whose existence threatened human civilization.

By the mid-19th century, however, European views of Bushmen had changed. Now the Bushman was cast as the "noble **savage** and hunter", **eternally** childlike and **attuned** to nature. Europeans marveled at Bushmen's "timeless existence", and scientists claimed they represented the missing link to primitive society. **Archaeological** research on rock paintings of hunting scenes in South Africa's mountain ranges provided evidence for the theory that the Bushmen had not changed in thousands of years.

The San people in the Kalahari Desert in southern Africa
(Photographer: Sun Lihua)

In the 20th century, the image of the primitive Bushman has been reinforced by photographs, films, and written works. In 1925, the Denver African Expedition

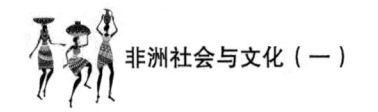

catered to American audiences hungry for **Tarzan**-type images by bribing San people to pose for **shots** that emphasized their "**exotic** primitiveness". Later, **ethnographic** films such as **Marjorie Shostak**'s *Nisa* supported these ideas by lending a **pseudoscientific** authority to popular images of the Bushmen.

In the late 20th century, Western images of the Bushmen, while as far **removed** as ever from the reality of San life, have become even more commercially valuable. In 1978, Afrikaner film director **Jamie Uys** struck gold with *The Gods Must Be Crazy*, a popular film that reinforced notions of the happy but primitive Bushmen. In Botswana, the government deliberately **propagates** the Bushmen myth. In the **Central Kalahari Game Reserve**, the biggest tourist attraction was once the Bushmen themselves. In 1996, however, the government of Botswana threatened to remove those Bushmen who did not conform to "traditional" Bushmen hunting and gathering techniques and who had acquired cattle herds and other un-Bushmen-like assets. By 2002, the last of the Bushmen had been **evicted** from the reserve and **forcibly** resettled in camps and newly built villages.

Supporters of the government's policy argue that the San hunting-and-gathering lifestyle is no longer **viable**, and point to improvements in the villages over the Bushmen's former nomadic existence. **Critics** argue that resettlement camps are **rife** with **alcoholism**, **depression**, and a rising incidence of AIDS. They also claim that the Bushmen were not forced off the land for their own good, but rather because the land contains valuable diamond deposits. In 2006, a Botswana court held that the government's actions were an **unconstitutional infringement** on Bushmen's rights. Though, as of 2009, the Bushmen are legally entitled to return to the reserve, the government of Botswana has thus far not allowed them to do so.

Explanations

［1］**Some of the largest ethnic groups cross national and religious boundaries, but they share similar cultural features, languages, or religious practices that allow them to think of themselves as connected**：非洲一些最大的部族甚至跨越了国家和宗教的界限。但是相似的文化特征、语言和宗教活动使部族成员之间产生了认同感。

［2］**…the genocidal violence that flared in Rwanda in the mid-1990s**：发生在1994年4月初至6月中旬之间的"卢旺达大屠杀"（Rwandan Genocide）又称"卢旺达内战"（The Rwandan Civil War），是胡图族（Hutu）针对图西族（Tutsi）以及胡图族温和派进行的有组织的种族大屠杀，共造成80—100万人死亡。

［3］**The challenge for many African countries is to balance the diversity of ethnicity with equal access to political power, wealth, opportunity and the resources of the nation**：很多非洲国家目前面临的共同挑战是：在兼顾部族多样性的同时，让本国所有部族都能平等地行使政治权利，分享财富、发展机遇以及国家的资源。

［4］**Nupe Kingdom**：据说是忒叟尔德（Tsoede）创立了努佩王国。努佩人生活在尼日尔河（the Niger River）和卡杜纳河（Kaduna）之间的盆地上。大多数努佩人信奉伊斯兰教，还有一些信仰传统宗教。

［5］**Over the course of their histories, these societies might be known by several ethnic names as they passed from local organization to state control and back again when the state lost power**：在发展过程中，这些社会的氏族名称可能发生过变化，自治时期用氏族名称，隶属于某个王国的时候就用王国的名称，王国衰亡以后又重新采用了氏族名称。

［6］**These ethnic categories hardened in place as the colonizers identified certain Africans as leaders and developed relationships with them**：当殖民主义者选择某些非洲人来管理其他非洲人，并且和前者发展关系的时候，部族分类就固定下来。

[7] **This way of regarding ethnic groups suited the French and British strategy of "divide and rule":** 上述对待部族的方式便于英法殖民者对他们的非洲殖民地"分而治之"。

[8] **In May 1966, thousands died during a massacre resembling genocide, which sparked the secession of the Eastern Region from Nigeria and the Civil War:** 1966年5月,尼日利亚爆发了一起种族灭绝性质的大屠杀事件,数千人丧生,生活在尼国东部地区的伊博人因此退出联邦,尼日利亚内战爆发。

[9] **Notable Igbo cultural and political figures include Chinua Achebe, Michael Okpara, Nnamdi Azikiwe, and Chukwuemeka Odumegwu Ojukwu:** 伊博族著名文化和政治人物包括钦努阿·阿契贝(知名作家,代表作《瓦解》*Things Fall Apart*),迈克尔·奥克帕拉(政治领袖,1959—1966年间担任尼日利亚东部地区总理),纳米迪·阿兹奇维(著名民族主义者,尼日利亚首任总统)和楚库埃梅卡·奥杜梅古·奥朱古(军官、政治家,1967—1970年间,尼日利亚东部的伊博人脱离联邦政府,成立比夫拉共和国(Biafra),奥朱古担任共和国元首)。

[10] **IdiAminDada**:伊迪·阿明·达达是乌干达第三任总统(1971—1979)。他行伍出身,历任各级军职,1965年被任命为陆军司令。1971年,他发动军事政变,推翻了米尔顿·奥博特(Milton Obote)政权。他在任职期间将8万亚洲人驱逐出境,迫害和屠杀国内的阿乔利族(Acholi)、兰吉族(Lango)和其他部族的成员。1978年,乌干达民族主义者在坦桑尼亚的支持下发动乌坦战争(The Uganda-Tanzania War),次年推翻阿明政府。阿明逃亡国外,先后隐居在利比亚和沙特阿拉伯,直至2003年去世。

[11] **This practice was no more accurate or effective in central Africa than in other regions:** 无论在中非地区还是在非洲其他地区,这种做法都不正确,也无法产生预期效果。

[12] **Ethnic labels allow complex social, economic, and political issues to be reduced to a simple case of "us against them"**:有了部族标签以后,人们就倾向于把复杂的社会、经济和政治问题简单地归咎于"我族"

和"他族"之间的矛盾冲突。

[13] **eastern Congo/Zaire, southern Republic of the Congo:** Congo/Zaire是刚果民主共和国（Democratic Republic of the Congo），简称刚果（金），旧称扎伊尔共和国（1971—1997）；Republic of the Congo是刚果共和国，简称刚果（布）。

[14] **They were considered by the colonial authorities to be among the more radical pro-independence groups and one of the most anti-Belgium:** （比利时）殖民政府认为：刚果族是支持刚果独立、反对比利时殖民统治最激进的部族之一。

[15] **However, culture is a powerful force, and the fact that ethnic identity was largely invented does not make it a less real part of society:** 主要由人为炮制出的族群身份并不能削弱文化所具有的强大力量。

[16] **Even when the Zulu kingdom united against the British, however, regional loyalties remained important, and most subjects of the state did not regard themselves as Zulu:** 即便在祖鲁王国团结一致反抗英国人的时候，王国内部不同地区的人们依然效忠于自己的酋长，王国的大多数臣民并不认为自己是祖鲁人。

[17] **At present, about 6 million isiXhosa speakers reside throughout South Africa, the majority in the Eastern and the Western Cape provinces, as well as fewer in Free State and in KwaZulu-Natal:** 目前，南非大约有600万人说科萨语，他们主要生活在南非东开普省、西开普省，在奥兰治自由邦和夸祖鲁–纳塔尔省也有一些。

[18] **IsiXhosa is South Africa's second most common language among the black population, after isiZulu, to which it is closely related:** 对于南非黑人而言，科萨语是仅次于祖鲁语的第二大语言，而且这两种语言密切相关。

[19] **Mfecane:** "姆菲卡尼"是19世纪20年代至30年代，为了争夺土地和水源，南部非洲的班图各部落之间发生的持续战乱，又称"弃土运动"。

[20] **Prominent Xhosa include former presidents Nelson Mandela and Thabo Mbeki, as well as Reverend Desmond Tutu:** 著名的科萨族人物包括南非前总

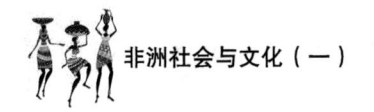

统纳尔逊·曼德拉和塔博·姆贝基、以及南非大主教德斯蒙德·图图。

Exercises

I. Read the following statements and decide whether they are true (T) or false (F).

_____ 1. Africa's tapestry of thousands of ethnic groups is woven of many strands formed in precolonial period, colonial period or modern times.

_____ 2. Trade, war, and politics brought ethnic groups into contact and even some forms of unity in western Africa before the conquest by Europeans.

_____ 3. The many ethnic conflicts that occur today in western Africa represent a return of ancient hostilities before the colonial era.

_____ 4. The political border that the French created between Kenya and Uganda cuts across ethnic groups linked by language, culture, and history.

_____ 5. Swahili civilization, unlike that of neighboring African peoples, is urban, maritime, and based on agriculture.

_____ 6. In Maasai society, the man is the one who builds the manyatta, sometimes with the help of other men, but in most cases they do it alone.

_____ 7. Kikongo is one of Congo/Zaire's four national languages.

_____ 8. The Xhosa are one of Nigeria's black ethnic groups.

_____ 9. The living conditions of Xhosa have improved after the apartheid regime ended in 1984.

_____ 10. It's claimed that Bushmen were not forced off the land for their own good, but rather because the land contains valuable gold deposits.

II. Fill in the following blanks with words that best complete the sentences.

1. Ethnic groups are populations that feel connected by a complex mix of _____, culture, history, and _____.

2. Ethnic identity can _____ pride and hope and _____ people in groups for

Unit III   Ethnic Groups in Africa

effective political and social action.

3. The ethnic conflicts that have plagued western Africa are partly the result of _____.

4. Tanzanian government encourages the use of _____, the coastal language, as the _____ tongue, and people often identify themselves as belonging to several ethnic groups.

5. The Swahili are noted for their large, _____ houses and towns, their _____ clothing and food, and for a high level of _____ achievement, especially in poetry.

6. Maasai economy revolves around livestock with _____ valued particularly high as a mobile form of wealth, _____ of exchange, source of food, symbol of relationship and of _____ significance.

7. Even after independence, some central African politicians and intellectuals have continued to _____ the colonial concept of tribes, which _____ certain individuals and groups.

8. In South Africa, tribal identities kept people _____ to tribal leaders who were either _____ or _____ by the colonial powers.

9. Besides losing their lands to both the _____ and the _____ settlers, the Xhosa also faced restrictions on their political _____ due to the various measures implemented by the British colonial authorities and subsequently by the South African government.

10. Critics argue that resettlement camps for the Bushmen are rife with _____, _____, and a rising incidence of _____.

Review and Reflect

✧ What are the reasons for and consequences of tribalism?
✧ What do you think of the work of missionaries in Africa?
✧ What can be done to better protect indigenous groups in Africa?

Unit IV　Colonization of Africa

19世纪末以前，非洲只有少数地区处于欧洲殖民统治之下，主要集中在沿海地区、尼罗河流域和刚果河流域。但是19世纪末至20世纪初的"瓜分非洲狂潮"彻底改变了这一状况，只有埃塞俄比亚和利比里亚两国基本保持了独立。经过艰苦卓绝的斗争，非洲各国在20世纪中叶以后陆续取得独立。多年的殖民统治使他们伤痕累累：传统文化与社会土崩瓦解、教育水平低下、基础设施简陋、产业发展单一、贸易渠道被切断等。另一方面，很多新政府腐败独裁，领导不力。尽管有了新起点，但是非洲大陆的发展道路依旧曲折而漫长。

Maria Ernestina, the last known ex-slave died in 1974

(Photographer: Sun Lihua)

"We have been giving away mountains and rivers and lakes to each other, only hindered by the small impediment that we never knew exactly where they were."

—Lord Salisbury, Prime Minister of the UK from the middle 1880s to the early 1900s

> **Think and Talk**
> ☆ What is colonialism in your eyes?
> ☆ What do you think is the difference between colonialism and imperialism?
> ☆ Have you heard of "The Berlin Conference"? What do you know about it?

I. THE SCRAMBLE FOR AFRICA[1]

In nearly all African countries nowadays, at least one of the official languages used in government, education, and mass media is a European language, which is a **relic** inherited from the history of colonization.

In the history, Western European powers have colonized nearly all parts of the African continent, except Liberia and Ethiopia, **culminating** in the notorious period of "the Scramble for Africa" between the late 19th century and the early 20th century. And a wave of **decolonization** took place in the middle of 20th century, in which colonized peoples **agitated** and struggled for independence and colonial powers were forced to withdraw their administrators and forces from Africa.

1. Introduction

"The Scramble for Africa" (also known as "the **Partition** of Africa" or "the Conquest of Africa") was the invasion, occupation, colonization, and **annexation** of African **territory** by European powers during the period between 1881 and 1914. In 1870, only 10% of Africa was under European control; while by 1914 it was 90%, with only Ethiopia and Liberia still remaining independent.

The Berlin Conference[2] of 1884 regulated European colonization and trade in Africa. Consequent to the fierce political and economic **rivalries** among the European empires, in the last quarter of the 19th century, the partitioning of Africa was how the Europeans avoided warring among themselves over Africa. The last 59 years of the 19th century saw the transition from "informal **imperialism**" by military influence and economic dominance, to the direct rule of the colonies.

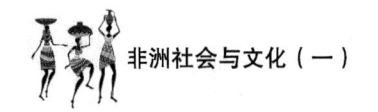

2. How Did the Scramble for Africa Happen?

The Portuguese had been the first Europeans to firmly establish their **settlements**, trade posts, permanent **fortifications** and **ports of call** along the coast of the African continent in the 15th century. There was little interest in and less knowledge of the African inland for some two centuries **thereafter**.

European exploration of the African **interior** began in earnest at the end of the 18th century. By 1835, Europeans had generally mapped most of northwestern Africa. In the middle decades of the 19th century, the most distinguished European explorers were David Livingstone[3] and H. M. Stanley[4], both of whom mapped the vast areas of southern Africa and central Africa.

Arduous expeditions in the 1850s and 1860s by **Richard Burton, John Speke** and **James Grant** eventually located the great central lakes and the source of the Nile. By the end of the 19th century, Europeans had **charted** the Nile from its source, traced the courses of the Niger, **Congo** and **Zambezi River**, and realized the abundant resources of Africa.

Even as late as the 1870s, European powers still controlled only 10% of the African continent, and all their territories being near the coast. The most important **holdings** were Angola and Mozambique, held by Portugal; the Cape Colony,[5] held by the United Kingdom; and Algeria, held by France.

"The Scramble for Africa" in the late 19th century was so intense that there were fears that it could lead to inter-imperialist conflicts and even wars. To prevent this, the German **chancellor** Otto von Bismarck **convened** a diplomatic summit of the European powers. This was the famous "Berlin Conference", held from November 1884 to February 1885, on which Western European powers divided Africa and its resources into political partitions. The conference produced a treaty known as the "*Berlin Act*", with **provisions** to guide the conduct of the European imperialist competitions in Africa.

By 1905, control of almost all African soil was claimed by Western European governments, with the only two exceptions being Liberia (which had been settled by African-American former slaves) and Ethiopia (which had successfully resisted colonization by Italy). Britain and France had the largest holdings, but Germany, Spain, Italy, Belgium, and Portugal also had their own colonies. As a result of colonialism and imperialism, Africa lost not only its **sovereignty**, but also control of its natural resources like gold, diamond and rubber, etc. Europeans often justified their cruel colonization using the concept of the "White Man's Burden", "Civilized Mission", an **obligation** to "**civilize**" the peoples of Africa.

Technological advancement facilitated European overseas expansionism. Industrialization brought about rapid advancement in transportation and communication, especially in the forms of steam **navigation**, railways, and **telegraphs**. Medical advances also were important, especially medicines for tropical diseases. The development of **quinine**, an effective treatment for **malaria**, enabled vast expanses of the tropical areas to be accessed by Europeans.

3. Two Relatively Independent States: Liberia and Ethiopia

Relatively, there are two countries in Africa which are considered to have been barely colonized in history. The real situation, however, is much more complicated and still open to debate.

Slaves bound by chains (**Photographer: Sun Lihua**)

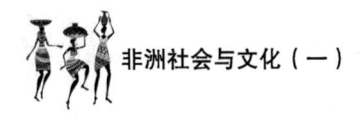

Liberia

Liberia was a colony for just over 17 years before **partial** independence was achieved through the declaration of a **commonwealth** in 1839. True independence was declared eight years later on 26 July 1847. The American Colonization Society (ACS) created the Cape Mesurado Colony on the **Grain Coast** in 1821. This was further expanded into the Colony of Liberia in 1824. The American Colonization Society was an organization initially run by white Americans who believed there was no place for free blacks in the US. Its **administration** was later taken over by free blacks.

The Republic of Liberia, beginning as a settlement of the American Colonization Society, declared its independence on July 26, 1847. The United States did not recognize Liberia's independence until during the American Civil War on February 5, 1862. Between January 7, 1822 and the American Civil War, more than 15,000 freed and **free-born** Black Americans from the United States and 3,198 **Afro-Caribbeans relocated** to the settlement. The black American settlers carried their culture with them to Liberia. The Liberian **constitution** and flag were modeled after the United States. In January 3, 1848, **Joseph Jenkins Roberts**, a wealthy free-born black American from **Virginia** who settled in Liberia, was elected as Liberia's first president after the people **proclaimed** independence. Liberia maintained and kept its independence during the European colonial era.

Ethiopia

In the 1880s, Italy failed to take **Abyssinia** (as Ethiopia was then known) as a colony. In 1935, **Mussolini** ordered a new invasion and in the following year Abyssinia was **annexed** by Italy. In the same year, the country was **merged** with **Eritrea** and Italian Somalia to form "Italian East Africa". Emperor **Haile Selassie** made an **impassioned** appeal to **the League of Nations** in 1936, gaining support from the US and Russia. But many League of Nations members, including Britain and France, recognized Italian colonization. It was not until 1941, when Selassie was restored to the Ethiopian **throne**, that independence was regained in Ethiopia.

A painting depicting Ethiopian resistance to Italian invasion
(Photographer: Han Hong)

Ethiopia derived **prestige** with its uniquely successful military resistance during the late 19th century Scramble for Africa, becoming the only African country to defeat European colonial power and retain its sovereignty. Subsequently, many African nations adopted the colors of Ethiopia's flag following their independence. Ethiopia was also the first independent African member of the 20th century League of Nations and the United Nations.

II. COLONIALISM VS IMPERIALISM

Colonialism is not a modern phenomenon. World history is full of examples of one society gradually expanding by incorporating **adjacent** territory and settling its people on newly conquered territory. The ancient Greeks set up colonies as did the Romans, the **Moors**, and the **Ottomans**, to name just a few of the most famous examples. Colonialism, then, is not restricted to a specific time or place. Nevertheless, in the 16th century, colonialism changed decisively because of technological developments in navigation that began to connect more remote parts of the world. Fast sailing ships made it possible to reach distant ports and to **sustain** close ties between the center and colonies. Thus, the modern European colonial project emerged when it became possible to move large numbers of people across the ocean and to maintain political sovereignty in spite of geographical **dispersion**. Thus the term colonialism is usually used to describe the process of European settlement and political control over the rest of the world, including the Americas, Australia, and parts of Africa and Asia.

The difficulty of defining colonialism stems from the fact that the term is often used as a **synonym** for imperialism. Both colonialism and imperialism were forms of conquest that were expected to benefit Europe economically and strategically.

Neck-chains to chain the slaves
(Photographer: Sun Lihua)

The term colonialism is frequently used to describe the settlement of North America, Australia, New Zealand, Algeria, and Brazil, places that were controlled by a large population of permanent European residents. The term imperialism often describes cases in which a foreign government administers a territory without significant settlement; typical examples include the Scramble for Africa in the late 19th century and the American **domination** of **the Philippines** and **Puerto Rico**. The distinction between the two, however, is not entirely consistent in the **literature**. Some scholars distinguish between colonies for settlement and colonies for economic **exploitation**. Others use the term colonialism to describe **dependencies** that are directly governed by a foreign nation and contrast this with imperialism, which involves indirect forms of domination.

Colonialism is a practice of domination, which involves the **subjugation** of one people to another. One of the difficulties in defining colonialism is that it is hard to distinguish it from imperialism. Frequently the two concepts are treated as synonyms. Like colonialism, imperialism also involves political and economic control over a dependent territory. The **etymology** of the two terms, however, provides some clues about how they differ. The term colony comes from the Latin word "colonus", meaning "farmer". This root reminds us that the practice of colonialism usually involved the transfer of population to a new territory, where the arrivals lived as permanent settlers while maintaining political **allegiance** to their country of origin.[6] Imperialism, on the other hand, comes from the Latin term "imperium", meaning "to command". Thus, the term imperialism draws attention to the way that one country exercises power over another, whether through settlement, sovereignty, or indirect mechanisms of control.[7]

The confusion about the meaning of the term imperialism reflects the way that the concept has changed over time. Although the English word imperialism was not commonly used before the 19th century, **Elizabethans** already described the United Kingdom as "the British Empire". As Britain began to acquire overseas dependencies, the concept of empire was employed more frequently. Imperialism was understood as a system of military domination and sovereignty over territories. The day to day work of government might be exercised indirectly through local **assemblies** of **indigenous** rulers who paid **tribute**, but sovereignty rested with the British.

Ruins of Bagamoyo, a trading port for slave trade, Tanzania
(Photographer: Sun Lihua)

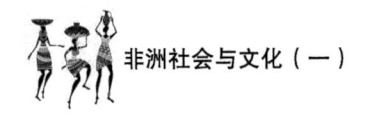

III. MOTIVATIONS OF THE COLONIZATION OF AFRICA BY EUROPEAN POWERS

The European imperialist push into Africa was motivated by three main factors: economic, political, and social. In the 19th century, the **imperatives** of capitalist industrialization—including the demand for sources of raw materials, the search for markets and profitable investment **outlets**, **spurred** the European scramble, the partition, and the eventual conquest of Africa. Thus the primary motivation for European **intrusion** was economic.

But other factors played an equally important role in the process. The political **impetus** derived from the inter-European power struggle and competition for **preeminence**. Britain, France, Germany, Belgium, Italy, Portugal, and Spain were competing for power. One way to demonstrate national preeminence was through the **acquisition** of territories around the world, including Africa.

The social factor was the third major element. As a consequence of industrialization, major social problems grew in Europe: unemployment, poverty, homelessness, social **displacement** from rural areas, and so on. These social problems developed partly because not all people could be absorbed by the new capitalist industries. One way to resolve this problem was to acquire colonies and export this "surplus population". This led to the establishment of settler-colonies in Algeria, Tunisia, and southern African countries such as South Africa, Namibia, Angola, Mozambique, Zimbabwe and Zambia.

Thus it was the **interplay** of these three factors that led to "the Scramble for Africa" and the **frenzied** attempts by European commercial, military, and political forces to declare and establish a **stake** in different parts of the continent—the declaration of **exclusive** claims to particular territories for trade, the **imposition** of **tariffs** against other European traders, and claims to exclusive control of waterways and commercial routes in different parts of Africa.

IV. ORIGIN OF THE MODERN STATES OF AFRICA

During the Scramble for Africa at the end of the 19th century, European powers staked claims to virtually have the images of the entire continent. At meetings in Berlin, Paris, London and other capitals, European statesmen and **diplomats bargained** over the separate **spheres** of interest they intended to establish here. Their knowledge of the vast Africa **hinterland** was slight. **Hitherto** Europeans had known Africa more as a coastline than a continent; their presence had been confined mainly to small, isolated **enclaves** on the coast used for trading purposes; only in Algeria and in southern Africa had more substantial European settlement taken root.

The map used to carve up the African continent were mostly inaccurate; large areas were described as **terra incognita**. When marking out the **boundaries** of their new territories, European negotiators frequently resorted to drawing straight lines on the maps, taking little or no account of the **myriad** of traditional **monarchies**, chiefdoms and other African societies that existed on the ground.[8] Nearly one half of the new **frontiers** imposed on Africa were **geometric** lines, lines of **latitude** and **longitude**, other straight lines or **arcs** of circles.[9]

In some cases, African societies were ripped apart: the **Bakongo** were partitioned between French Congo, Belgian Congo and Portuguese Angola; **Somaliland** was carved up between Britain, Italy and France. In all, the new boundaries cut through some 190 culture groups. In other cases, Europe's new colonial territories **enclosed** hundreds of diverse and independent groups, with no common history, culture, language or religion. Nigeria, for example, contained as many as 250 **ethno-linguistic** groups. Officials sent to the Belgian Congo eventually identified six thousand chiefdoms there.

Some kingdoms survived **intact**; the French retained the monarchy in Morocco and Tunisia; the British ruled Egypt in the name of a dynasty of foreign monarchs founded in 1811 by an **Albanian mercenary** serving in the **Turkish** army. Other kingdoms, such as **Asante** in the Gold Coast[10] (Ghana) and **Loziland** in

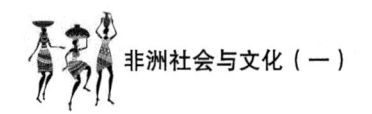

Northern Rhodesia (Zambia) were merged into larger colonial units. Kingdoms that had been historically **antagonistic** to one another, such as **Buganda** and **Bunyoro** in Uganda, were linked into the same colony. New territories were established across the great divide between the desert regions of the Sahara and the belt of tropical forests to the south—Sudan, Chad and Nigeria—throwing together Muslim and non-Muslim peoples in **latent** hostility.

As the **haggling** in Europe over African territory continued, land and peoples became little more than pieces on a **chessboard**. Britain traded the North Sea island of **Heligoland** with the Germans for **Zanzibar**, and parts of northern Nigeria with the French for fishing rights off **Newfoundland**. France exchanged parts of Cameroon with Germany in return for German recognition of the French **protectorate** over Morocco. By the time the Scramble for Africa was over, some 10,000 African **polities** had been **amalgamated** into forty European colonies and protectorates.

Thus were born the modern states of Africa.

On the ground, European rule was enforced both by treaty and by conquest. From their enclaves on the coast, officials moved ever deeper into the interior to proclaim the changes agreed in the **chancelleries** and country **mansions** of Europe. The task was a prolonged one: French claims extended over about 3.75 million square miles; those of Britain over about two million square miles. Many treaties were **duly** signed. The **Basuto** king, **Moshoeshoe**, fearful of the **encroachment** of white settlers into his mountain **terrain** in southern Africa, appealed for the protection of Queen Victoria, **imploring** that his people might be considered "**fleas** in the Queen's blanket". Several of his neighbours—the **Tswana** chiefdoms of **Bechuanaland** (Botswana) and the **Swazi**—followed suit.

V. TYPES OF COLONIAL ADMINISTRATION

By 1900, much of Africa had been colonized by seven European powers—Britain, France, Germany, Belgium, Spain, Portugal and Italy. The European powers set about establishing colonial state systems. The colonial state was the machinery of administrative domination established to facilitate effective control and exploitation of the colonized societies.

Partly as a result of their origins in military conquest and partly because of the racist **ideology** of the imperialist powers, the colonial states were **authoritarian** and **bureaucratic** systems. Because they were imposed and maintained by force, without the **consent** of the governed, the colonial states never had the effective **legitimacy** of normal governments. Second, they were bureaucratic because they were administered by military officers and **civil servants** who were **appointees** of the colonial power. While their forms of administration varied, partly due to the different national administrative traditions and specific imperialist ideologies of the colonizers and partly because of the political conditions in the various territories that they conquered.[11]

1. Indirect Rule

In Nigeria, the Gold Coast in West Africa, and Kenya, Uganda, **Tanganyika** in East Africa, for example, Britain organized its colonies at the central, **provincial**, and regional or district levels. There was usually a **governor** or **governor-general** in the colonial capital who governed along with an appointed **executive council** and a **legislative** council of appointed and selected local and foreign members. The governor was responsible to the colonial office and the colonial secretary in London, from whom laws, policies, and programs were received. He made some local laws and policies, however. Colonial policies and **directives** were implemented through a central administrative organization or a colonial **secretariat**, with officers responsible for different departments such as **Revenue**, Agriculture, Trade, Transport, Health, Education, Police, Prison, and so on.

The British colonies were often subdivided into provinces headed by provincial **commissioners** or residents, and then into districts headed by district officers or district commissioners. Laws and policies on taxation, public works, forced labor, mining, agricultural production, and other matters were made in London or in the colonial capital and then passed down to the lower administrative levels for enforcement.

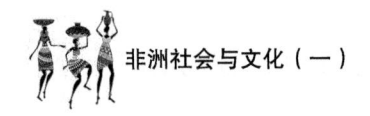

Italian colonial ruins in southern Ethiopia
(Photographer: Du Fengyan)

At the provincial and district levels, the British established the system of local administration popularly known as indirect rule. This system operated **in alliance with** preexisting political leaderships and institutions. The theory and practice of indirect rule is commonly associated with Lord **Frederick Lugard**, who was the first British high commissioner for northern Nigeria and later governor-general of Nigeria. In the **Hausa/Fulani emirates** of northern Nigeria, he found that they had an established and functional administrative system. Lugard simply and wisely adapted it to his ends. It was cheap and convenient.

Despite attempts to portray the use of indirect rule as an expression of British administrative genius, it was nothing of the sort. It was a **pragmatic** and **parsimonious** choice based partly on using existing functional institutions. The choice was also partly based on Britain's unwillingness to provide the resources required to administer its vast empire. Instead, it developed the **perverse** view that the colonized should pay for their colonial domination. Hence, the choice of indirect rule.

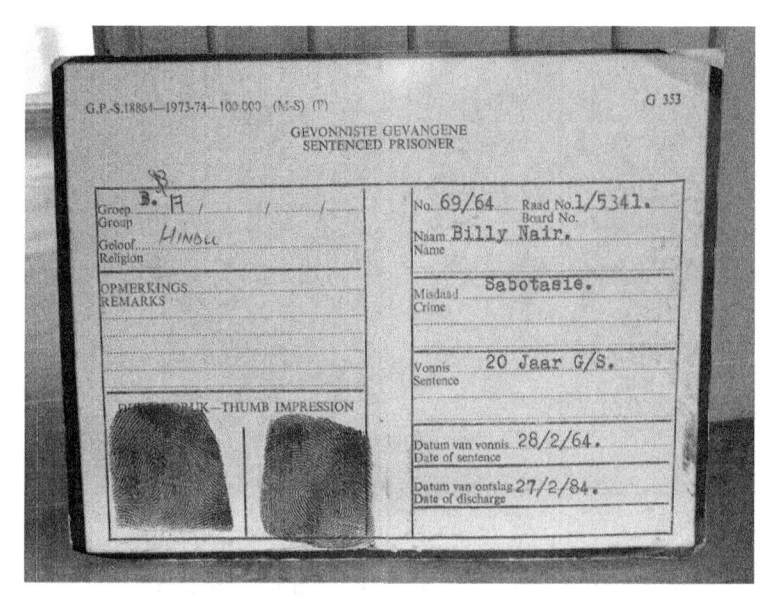

An ID card of a sentenced prisoner during the Apartheid
(Photographer: Sun Lihua)

The system had three major institutions: the "native authority" made up of the local ruler, the colonial official, and the administrative staff; the "native **treasury**", which collected revenues to pay for the local administrative staff and services; and the "native courts", which **purportedly** administered "native law and custom", the supposedly traditional legal system of the colonized that was used by the courts to **adjudicate** cases.

In general, indirect rule worked fairly well in areas that had long-established centralized state systems such as chiefdoms, **city-states**, kingdoms, and empires, with their functional administrative and **judicial** systems of the government. But even here the fact that the ultimate authority was the British officials meant that the African leaders had been **vassalized** and exercised "authority" at the mercy of European colonial officials. Thus the political and social **umbilical cords** that tied them to their people in the old system had been broken. Some **astute** African leaders **maneuvered** and ruled as best they could, while others used the new colonial setting to become **tyrants** and **oppressors**, as they were responsible to British officials ultimately.

The House of Slaves, Gorée Island, Dakar, Senegal
(Photographer: Chen Yong)

In the **decentralized** societies, the system of indirect rule worked less well, as they did not have single rulers. The British colonizers, unfamiliar with these novel and unique political systems and insisting that African "natives" must have **chiefs**, often appointed licensed leaders called **warrant** chiefs, as in **Igboland**, for example.

2. Assimilation

The French, for their part, established a highly centralized administrative system that was influenced by their ideology of colonialism and their national tradition of extreme administrative centralism. Their colonial ideology explicitly claimed that they were on a "civilizing mission" to lift the **benighted** "natives" out of **backwardness** to the new status of civilized French Africans.[12] To achieve this, the French used the policy of assimilation, whereby through **acculturation** and education and the fulfillment of some formal conditions, some "natives" would become evolved and civilized French Africans.[13] In practice, the **stringent** conditions set for citizenship made it virtually impossible for most colonial **subjects** to become French citizens.

For example, potential citizens were supposed to speak French fluently, to have served the French **meritoriously**, to have won an award, and so on. If they achieved French citizenship, they would have French rights and could only be tried by French courts, not under **indigénat**, the French colonial **doctrine** and legal practice whereby colonial "subjects" could be tried by French administrative officials or military commanders and sentenced to two years of forced labor without due process. However, since France would not provide the educational system to train all its colonized subjects to speak French and would not establish administrative and social systems to employ all its subjects, assimilation was more an imperialist political and ideological **posture** than a serious political objective.[14]

In terms of the actual administrative system in its various African colonies—Algeria, Tunisia, and Morocco in north Africa, and Senegal, French Guinea, French Sudan, **Upper Volta**, **Dahomey**, and others in West Africa, and Gabon, **Congo-Brazzaville**, Ubangi-Shari in Central Africa—the French used a system of direct rule. They also created **federations** in West Africa and Central Africa. In the colonial capitals, the governors were responsible to the minister of colonies in Paris. Most laws and policies were sent from Paris, and the governors who ruled with general councils were expected to enforce them in line with France's **centralist** traditions. The colonies were also subdivided into smaller administrative units.

While France tried to maintain this highly centralized system, in some parts of its colonies where it encountered strongly established centralized state systems, the French were compelled to adopt the policy of association, a system of rule operating in alliance with preexisting African ruling institutions and leaders. Thus it was somewhat like British indirect rule, although the French still remained committed to the doctrine of assimilation. In the association system, local governments were run with African rulers whom the French organized at three levels and grades: provincial chief, district chief, and village chief. In practice, the French system combined elements of direct administration and indirect rule.

In general, the French administrative system was more centralized, bureaucratic, and **interventionist** than the British system of colonial rule. The other colonial powers—Germany, Portugal, Spain, Belgium, and Italy—used varied administrative systems to facilitate control and economic exploitation. However, no matter the system, they were all **alien**, authoritarian, and bureaucratic, and **distorted** African political and social organizations and undermined their moral authority and political legitimacy as governing structures.

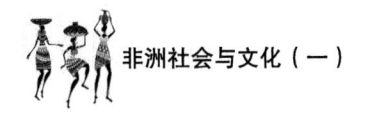

VI. DECOLONIZATION OF AFRICA

The decolonization of Africa was almost as fast as the more famous Scramble to colonize Africa had been. Between 1956 and 1963, 29 African states gained their independence, and 17 of those countries became independent in 1960. How can we account for this rapid flight from Empire?

1. World War II

The **cataclysm** of World War II exhausted Europe economically and socially. While the **Britons** were among the victors of the war, they would endure **rationing** until 1950, and much of Europe was receiving aid from the United States.

This did not mean they were ready to **renounce** imperialism—far from it. The war had once again proven to Europe the vital importance of colonies, but as the difficulties **mounted**, Britain, France, and Belgium would find the financial and political costs of imperialism to be too high.

Robben Island where Mandela was imprisoned during Apartheid
(Photographer: Sun Lihua)

During the war, Britain had also signed *the Atlantic Charter*[15]—a document drafted in opposition to **Nazi** Germany's conquests that proclaimed the rights of people to self-determination. After the war, anti-colonial **nationalists** quickly seized upon these **clauses** demanding that Britain respect its own declaration. Finally, many colonized Africans had served in the war, and the **veterans** who returned home to unemployment and colonial racism soon joined the voices calling for decolonization.

2. Anti-Colonialism and the Anti-Imperial Superpowers

The growing anti-colonialism in Africa was part of a global push for decolonization. In 1947, India and Pakistan achieved their independence, and from that point forward, the days of empire were numbered—or at least, the years of modern European imperialism were numbered. Nationalists across Southeast Asia and Africa were pushing for greater **autonomy** and soon, freedom.

These movements gained strength from each other, and together wore down European will and means.

The new superpowers of the world, the United States and the Union of Soviet Socialist Republics (**U.S.S.R.**) were also anti-imperialist—at least in theory. Both countries were arguably empires themselves, but both were undeniably guided by anti-imperialist ideologies and would eventually oppose the overseas empires of Europe.

3. African Nationalists and Revolutionaries

For decades, African nationalists had been pushing for a greater role in colonial governance, and their efforts paved the way for decolonization, particularly in several British and French colonies.

Independence though also owed much to violent revolutionaries and anti-colonial warfare. Two of the more famous examples are the **Mau Mau Uprising** in Kenya and **the Algerian War of Independence.** Wearied by warfare from World War II, European voters were increasingly uneasy with the brutal force needed by that point to hold onto colonies, and **suppression** was also expensive. Wars and uprisings made the colonial governments far more willing to work earnestly with moderate nationalists to find a way forward.

4. Neocolonialism

More **cynically**, the growing willingness of France, Britain, and Belgium to entertain thoughts of decolonization was also tied to the realization that there would be many ways to profit from these territories even after independence. As the push for decolonization grew, the imperial powers began looking to a future when they could still **wield** economic power in their former colonies without formally ruling them.[16]

5. Movement toward Independence

The Union of South Africa was formed and became virtually self-governing in 1910. Egypt achieved a measure of sovereignty in 1922, and in 1925 **Tangier**, previously attached to Morocco, was made an international zone. At the end of World War II, a rise in international trade spurred renewed exploitation of Africa's resources. France and Britain began campaigns to improve conditions in their African holdings, including access to education and investment in **infrastructure**. Africans were also able to pressure France and Britain into a degree of self-administration. Belgium and Portugal did little in the way of colonial development and sought greater control over their colonies during this period.

A poster calling for struggle for freedom on Robben Island
(Photographer: Sun Lihua)

In the 1950s and 1960s, in the face of rising nationalism, most of the European powers granted independence to their territories.

VII. THE POST-COLONIAL PERIOD

In the early post-colonial period, the most pressing problems facing new African states were the need for aid to develop natural resources, provide education, and improve living standards; threats of **secession** and military **coups**; and shifting alliances among the states and with outside powers. Recognizing that unity and cooperation were needed, African nations established the Organization of African Unity (**OAU**) in 1963 in **Addis Ababa**, Ethiopia. African nations were also forced to form alliances based on the Cold War politics of the USSR, the United States, Cuba, and other countries in order to receive badly needed aid. This period saw the **overthrow** of democratic forms of government and numerous coups resulting in the establishment of military **regimes** and single-party governments.

Beginning in the late 1960s and continuing through the mid-1970s, a severe drought **desiccated the Sahel region**. The resulting famine, disease, and environmental destruction caused the death of thousands of people and forced the southward migration of additional hundreds of thousands to less affected areas.

From 1975 into the 21st century, Africa continued to experience political, social, and economic **upheaval**. The post-independence era has also been marked by a rise in nationalist struggles. Wars in Sudan, Ethiopia, and Somalia continued, and political instability in these nations continued. Civil war in Ethiopia resulted in the birth of a new country, **Eritrea**; in 1998—2000, the two nations fought a bloody border war. The conflict between North and South Sudan largely ended with a peace agreement in 2005, and in 2011 South Sudan voted to become an independent nation. Other conflicts within Sudan, most notably in **Darfur** but also elsewhere, continued to **fester**.

South African blacks led an enduring struggle against white domination, with frequent **confrontations**, such as **the Soweto Uprising** in 1976, leading to government **repression** and escalating violence. Throughout the 1980s, the international community applied pressure in the form of economic **sanctions** in order to induce the South African government to negotiate with the African National Congress (**ANC**). In 1989, newly elected state President **F. W. de Klerk** promised democratic reforms that would phase out white **minority** rule, and in 1992 the legal **underpinnings** of Apartheid[17] were largely **dismantled**. Consequently, South Africa's black majority participated in the country's first fully democratic elections in 1994, which brought Nelson Mandela[18] and the African National Congress to power.

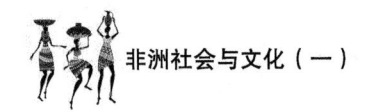

Other African nations began to introduce democratic reforms in the late 1980s and early 1990s that included **multiparty** elections; transitions to democratically elected leadership have taken place in countries such as Mali, Zambia, Benin, and Malawi. Political instability and civil **strife** continued to **plague** several regions of the continent into the late 1990s, most notably Liberia and Sierra Leone in West Africa and Congo, Rwanda, and Burundi in the Great Lakes Region.[19] Peace treaties signed in Liberia (1997) and Sierra Leone (1999) between those countries' governments and **insurgents** promised some hope of stability.

In Rwanda in 1994 a **Hutu**-led government that provoked ethnic tensions leading to the **genocide** of nearly one million persons was overthrown by **Tutsi**-led forces; by 1997 there was a growing war between the Rwandan army and Hutu **guerrilla** bands. Also in 1997, 30 years of **dictatorial** rule in **Zaïre** were brought to an end, and the country's name was changed to the Democratic Republic of the Congo (**DRC**). The new government was soon threatened, however, by **mutinous** troops who assumed control of large areas of the country; a cease-fire was signed in 1999, but **unrest** continued in parts of Congo in subsequent years. Nigeria **ushered in** a new government in 1999 with the first democratically elected president since 1983. Several African countries made positive **strides** in managing **market-oriented** economic reform in the 1990s, most notably Ghana, Uganda, and Malawi.

In 1992—1993, the worst African drought of the 20th century and numerous civil wars were the primary causes of a famine that spread across portions of **Sub-**

Saharan Africa and most severely affected the nations of Somalia and Mozambique. The **scourge** of AIDS has continued to pose a major health threat to many African nations, as a lack of economic resources often has prevented an effective response. Warfare, poverty, and hunger continue to present significant challenges in Africa, where ethnic tensions and political instability, along with the resulting economic **disruption**, still **afflict** many countries.

Mindful of the Organization of African Unity's relative ineffectiveness in dealing with these issues and seeking an organization with greater powers to promote African economic, social, and political integration, African leaders established the African Union (AU),[20] which **superseded** the OAU in 2002. The AU has proved somewhat more effective than OAU, but has had difficulty in successively confronting and resolving serious political crises (and sometimes civil wars) in Somalia, Madagascar, Zimbabwe, and other nations.

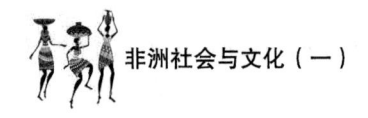

Explanations

[1] **The Scramble for Africa:** "瓜分非洲"。欧洲殖民者从15世纪起开始入侵非洲。在19世纪中期,他们在沿海地区和大河入口处建立的零星据点仅占非洲总面积的10%左右。19世纪70年代以后,欧洲列强掀起了瓜分非洲的狂潮。19世纪晚期,除埃塞俄比亚和利比里亚勉强维持独立以外,非洲基本被瓜分完毕。帝国主义侵略给非洲带来空前的破坏和灾难:政治方面,绝大多数国家和地区丧失了主权和独立;殖民统治给后殖民时代非洲的很多矛盾冲突埋下伏笔;经济方面,非洲人民失去大片土地,人口锐减;丰富的资源被掠夺;农业与家庭手工业相结合的自然经济开始瓦解;许多地区被迫种植某种单一的经济作物,造成经济畸形发展;社会方面,非洲原有的社会结构受到严重冲击,部落组织和酋长统治逐渐崩溃;非洲被卷入资本主义世界体系,新的经济因素和阶级结构产生。

[2] **The Berlin Conference:** "柏林会议"通常是指在德国首都柏林举行的列强瓜分非洲的会议。会议在1884年11月至1885年2月期间召开,由德国首相俾斯麦(Otto von Bismarck)主持。与会国包括15个国家:东道主德意志帝国、大英帝国、法兰西第三共和国、俄罗斯帝国、奥匈帝国、美利坚合众国、意大利王国、西班牙帝国、葡萄牙帝国、奥斯曼帝国、荷兰殖民帝国、比利时王国、瑞典王国、丹麦王国和挪威王国。会议名义上是解决刚果河流域的归属问题,实际上讨论更多的是列强瓜分非洲的一般原则。通过此次会议,各列强在非洲的势力范围得到初步确认,为日后帝国主义列强完全瓜分非洲提供了合法性。

[3] **David Livingstone:** 大卫·利文斯通(1813—1873)是英国探险家、传教士、维多利亚瀑布(Victoria Falls)和马拉维湖(Lake Malawi)的"发现者",也是非洲探险的最伟大人物之一。

[4] **H. M. Stanley:** 亨利·莫顿·史丹利爵士(Sir Henry Morton Stanley, 1841—1904)是英裔美籍探险家、记者,以其在非洲的冒险经历以及寻找英国传教士大卫·利文斯通的事迹而闻名于世。此外,他也曾探索、开

发过刚果地区。

[5] **the Cape Colony:** 开普殖民地位于南非境内，包括开普敦（Cape Town）及其邻近地区。在1806年至1910年期间，开普殖民地隶属于大英帝国。

[6] **This root reminds us that the practice of colonialism usually involved the transfer of population to a new territory, where the arrivals lived as permanent settlers while maintaining political allegiance to their country of origin:** 这个词根提醒我们，"殖民主义"通常意味着"人们迁移到新的土地上，但是定居下来的新移民在政治上依然效忠于自己的母国"。

[7] **Thus, the term imperialism draws attention to the way that one country exercises power over another, whether through settlement, sovereignty, or indirect mechanisms of control:** 因此，"帝国主义"一词意味着"一个国家利用各种手段对另一个国家行使权力，包括移民、控制主权或者间接控制。"

[8] **When marking out the boundaries of their new territories, European negotiators frequently resorted to drawing straight lines on the maps, taking little or no account of the myriad of traditional monarchies, chiefdoms and other African societies that existed on the ground:** 欧洲殖民者通常使用直线来绘制殖民地之间的边界，几乎没有考虑现实存在的、数量众多的非洲传统社会结构——君主国、酋长国、以及其他社会形态等。

[9] **Nearly one half of the new frontiers imposed on Africa were geometric lines, lines of latitude and longitude, other straight lines or arcs of circles:** 在欧洲殖民主义者绘制的非洲国界线中，几乎一半都是简单的几何线条、与经线或纬线平行的直线、其他直线以及弧线。

[10] **the Gold Coast:** "黄金海岸"是加纳共和国的旧称。成立于1821年的黄金海岸是英国在西非几内亚湾沿岸的一个殖民地，因当地盛产黄金而得名。1957年，英属黄金海岸宣告独立，成立加纳共和国，是非洲最早实现独立的国家之一。

[11] **While their forms of administration varied, partly due to the different national administrative traditions and specific imperialist ideologies**

of the colonizers and partly because of the political conditions in the various territories that they conquered: 然而欧洲殖民者管理殖民地的方式各不相同，部分原因是他们的治国传统和帝国主义意识形态不同，部分原因是被征服殖民地的政治生态千差万别。

[12] **Their colonial ideology explicitly claimed that they were on a "civilizing mission" to lift the benighted "natives" out of backwardness to the new status of civilized French Africans:** 法国人的殖民思想非常清楚：他们认为自己肩负着"使命"——要帮助愚昧无知的非洲人摆脱落后局面，成为"文明的"非裔法国人。

[13] **To achieve this, the French used the policy of assimilation, whereby through acculturation and education and the fulfillment of some formal conditions, some "natives" would become evolved and civilized French Africans:** 为了达到这个目的，法国殖民者采取了同化政策——通过文化适应、教育、以及其他手段，让非洲人成为"先进的、文明的"非裔法国人。

[14] **However, since France would not provide the educational system to train all its colonized subjects to speak French and would not establish administrative and social systems to employ all its subjects, assimilation was more an imperialist political and ideological posture than a serious political objective:** 然而，由于法国既没有意愿为殖民地人民提供学习法语的教育体制，又没有意愿在行政和社会体制中为他们提供就业机会，因此，与其说法国的同化政策是一个严肃的政治目标，不如说它是帝国主义在政治方面和思想意识方面的惺惺作态。

[15] ***The Atlantic Charter***：《大西洋宪章》是美国总统罗斯福和英国首相丘吉尔在1941年8月14日共同签署的联合宣言。苏德战争（the Russo-German War）爆发后，第二次世界大战范围扩大，美英两国迫切需要表明本国对法西斯侵略的态度，向世人阐明自己进一步协调反法西斯战争的战略。《宪章》宣布的八点原则被美英两国标榜为重建战后世界和平和秩序的政策依据，它体现了资产阶级民主政治的一般原则，贯彻了罗斯福在1940年1月提出的所谓"四大自由"的精神。《大西洋宪章》是英美

立场折衷的产物，其中美国的主张得到了更多的反映。

[16] **As the push for decolonization grew, the imperial powers began looking to a future when they could still wield economic power in their former colonies without formally ruling them:** 由于去殖民化运动的声势日益高涨，帝国主义国家对于殖民地的未来有了新的设想——即便不再直接统治前殖民地，但是他们依然可以利用自己的经济实力对其加以掌控。

[17] **Apartheid:** "种族隔离"特指1948—1994年期间，南非白人政府在国内推行的种族隔离政策：按照种族、人群被分成白人与非白人（包括黑人、印度人、马来人、及其他混血民族），在政治、经济等方方面面受到区别待遇。根据该制度，一个人的种族背景决定了他拥有的权利：欧洲白人拥有至高无上的权力和地位；而非裔、亚裔与混合血统者则受法律制约，参与国家政治事务以及改善自身经济状况的机会极其有限。在推行种族隔离政策的后期，迫于国际舆论与贸易制裁，以及南非国内日益高涨的反种族歧视的呼声和斗争，南非白人政府在1994年废除了臭名昭著的"种族隔离"制度。

[18] **Nelson Mandela:** 1918年7月18日，纳尔逊·曼德拉出生在南非东开普省特兰斯凯（Transkei, the Eastern Cape）一个科萨（Xhosa）部落酋长家庭。1944年，曼德拉加入南非非洲人国民大会党（非国大，ANC）。1948年，支持种族隔离政策的南非国民党（National Party）赢得大选，曼德拉开始积极投身政治。1961年，他创建了非国大的军事组织"民族之矛"（Umkhonto we Sizwe）。1962年，曼德拉被捕入狱，南非政府以"煽动罪"和"非法越境罪"判处他5年监禁。1964年6月，他又被指控犯有"企图以暴力推翻政府罪"，刑期改为无期徒刑。虽然备受迫害和折磨，但他始终没有放弃反对种族主义，建立平等、自由的新南非的坚强信念。由于国际社会对南非实行严厉的经济制裁；另一方面，南非人民反对种族歧视的斗争如火如荼，内外交困的南非白人政府于1990年解除隔离，实现民族和解。当年2月10日，南非总统德克勒克宣布无条件释放曼德拉。次日，曼德拉终于重获自由。出狱后，曼德拉放弃了武装斗争的方式，转而支持调解与协商，并在推动多元族群民主的过渡时期挺身而出。1994年5月9日，在南非首次多种

族大选中，曼德拉成为南非历史上首任黑人总统（1994—1999）。因为致力于消除种族歧视，1993年曼德拉荣获诺贝尔和平奖。他是"南非国父"，在南非人民心中享有崇高的地位，被亲切地称为"马迪巴（Madiba）"（"马迪巴"是曼德拉的科萨族名字）。他还著有《漫漫自由路》（*Long Walk to Freedom*）一书。

［19］**the Great Lakes Region:**（非洲）大湖地区指的是非洲中东部、东非大裂谷周围的一些国家，即维多利亚湖（Lake Victoria）、坦噶尼喀湖（Lake Tanganyika）、尼亚沙湖（Lake Nyassa）、图尔卡纳湖（Lake Turkana）、艾伯特湖（Lake Albert）和基伍湖（Lake Kivu）等湖泊的周边地区，包括布隆迪、刚果民主共和国、肯尼亚、卢旺达、坦桑尼亚、乌干达六国。东非大裂谷在形成的过程中，造就了该地区众多的湖泊。非洲大湖地区的总人口约为1.07亿，是世界上人口密度最大的地区之一，同时也是非洲自然资源分布最密集的地区。非洲大湖地区最主要的语言是斯瓦希里语。

［20］**the African Union (AU)：**"非洲联盟"简称"非盟"，总部设在埃塞俄比亚首都亚的斯亚贝巴，包含54个非洲会员国，是集政治、经济和军事于一体的全非洲性质的政治实体。非盟前身是1963年5月25日在埃塞俄比亚首都亚的斯亚贝巴成立的"非洲统一组织"（简称"非统"）。2002年7月8日，非统组织在南非德班召开了最后一届首脑会议。9日至10日，第一届非盟首脑会议宣布非盟成立，至此，非盟正式取代了非统组织。

Exercises

I. Read the following statements and decide whether they are true (T) or false (F).

____ 1. In the modern era, Western European powers colonized nearly all parts of the continent, except Kenya and Ethiopia.

____ 2. The Berlin Conference of 1884 regulated European colonization and trade

Unit IV　Colonization of Africa

in Africa.

_____ 3. The British had been the first Europeans to firmly establish settlements and trade posts along the coast of the African continent in the 15th century.

_____ 4. As a result of colonialism and imperialism, Africa lost not only its sovereignty, but also control of its natural resources like gold, diamond and rubber, etc.

_____ 5. Technological advancement facilitated European overseas expansionism. Industrialization brought about rapid advancement in transportation and communication, especially in the forms of steam navigation, railways, and telegraphs.

_____ 6. Before the Scramble for Africa, European powers' knowledge of the vast Africa hinterland was slight. Hitherto Europeans had known Africa more as a coastline than a continent.

_____ 7. When marking out the boundaries of their new territories, European negotiators frequently resorted to drawing straight lines on the maps, taking little or no account of the myriad of traditional monarchies, chiefdoms and other African societies that existed on the ground.

_____ 8. The British used the policy of assimilation, whereby through acculturation and education and the fulfillment of some formal conditions, some "natives" would become evolved and civilized British Africans.

_____ 9. In South Africa in 1994, a Hutu-led government that provoked ethnic tensions leading to the genocide of nearly one million persons was overthrown by Tutsi-led forces.

_____ 10. Mindful of the Organization of African Unity's relative ineffectiveness in dealing with these issues and seeking an organization with greater powers to promote African economic, social, and political integration, African leaders established the African Union (AU), which superseded the OAU in 2002.

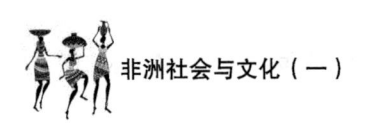

II. Fill in the following blanks with words that best complete the sentences.

1. "The Scramble for Africa" (also known as "the _____ of Africa" or "the _____ of Africa"), was the invasion, occupation, colonization, and annexation of African territory by European powers during the period between 1881 and 1914.

2. In 1870, only _____ percent of Africa was under European control; by 1914, it was _____ percent.

3. In the middle decades of the 19th century, the most distinguished of the European explorers were _____ and _____, both of whom mapped the vast areas of southern Africa and central Africa.

4. In the 1880s, _____ failed to take Abyssinia (as _____ was then known) as a colony.

5. The term colony comes from the Latin word "colonus", meaning "farmer". This root reminds us that the practice of colonialism usually involved the transfer of _____ to a new territory, where the arrivals lived as permanent _____ while maintaining political allegiance to their country of origin.

6. Imperialism, on the other hand, comes from the Latin term "imperium", meaning "to command". Thus, the term imperialism draws attention to the way that one country exercises power over another, whether through _____, _____, or _____ of control.

7. The European imperialist push into Africa was motivated by three main factors: _____, _____, and _____.

8. While Britain organized its colonies at the central, provincial, and regional or district levels, the French, for their part, established a highly _____ system.

9. Between 1956 and 1963, _____ African states gained their independence, and 17 of those countries became independent in the year _____.

10. South Africa's black majority participated in the country's first fully democratic election in 1994, which brought _____ and _____ to power.

Unit IV Colonization of Africa

Review and Reflect

- As to his attitude towards African natives, Christopher Columbus made the following two remarks. How do you understand them and what is your comment on them?

    "They ought to make good and skilled servants, for they repeat very quickly whatever we say to them. I think they can very easily be made Christians, for they seem to have no religion. If it pleases our Lord, I will take six of them to Your Highness when I depart, in order that they may learn our language."

    "I could conquer the whole of them with 50 men, and govern them as I pleased."

- As to the legitimacy of colonialism, what do you think of the following so-called "civilizing mission" put forward by the westerners?

    "The legitimacy of colonialism has been a longstanding concern for political and moral philosophers in the Western tradition. At least since the Crusades and the conquest of the Americas, political theorists have struggled with the difficulty of reconciling ideas about justice and natural law with the practice of European sovereignty over non-Western peoples. In the 19th century, the tension between liberal thought and colonial practice became particularly acute, as dominion of Europe over the rest of the world reached its zenith. Ironically, in the same period when most political philosophers began to defend the principles of universalism and equality, the same individuals still defended the legitimacy of colonialism and imperialism. One way of reconciling those apparently opposed principles was the argument known as the "civilizing mission", which suggested that a temporary period of political dependence or tutelage was necessary in order for "uncivilized" societies to advance to the point where they were capable of sustaining liberal institutions and self-government."

- As to New Colonialism, the African American Ayesha Fleary made the following remark. How do you understand it and what is your comment on it?

    "Bill Gates is another weapon of Colonialism and domination in the ongoing war against African people."

Unit V　African Religions

当代非洲的主要宗教包括伊斯兰教、基督教和非洲传统宗教。基督教和伊斯兰教先后传入非洲以后，都经历了本地化，与传统宗教相互影响、相互渗透的过程。传统宗教是非洲黑人固有的、具有悠久历史和广泛社会基础的宗教，它对非洲社会生活方方面面的影响仍然根深蒂固。

Prayers outside Church of Saint George, Lalibela, Ethiopia early on a Sunday morning
(Photographer: Han Hong)

"For Africans, religion is quite literally life and life is a religion. They do not know how to exist without religion, and religion is in their whole system of being."

—John Samuel Mbiti, Kenyan-born Christian religious philosopher and writer

◎ Think and Talk

☆ Are you religious? What do you think is the value of a religion?

☆ What do you think is the predominant religion on African continent?

☆ Do you know anything about African traditional religion?

Unit V   African Religions

I. AFRICAN TRADITIONAL RELIGION

Before **missionaries** brought **Christianity** to Africa, each tribe had its own religious beliefs and practices, collectively called African Traditional Religion (ATR). ATR is essential to understand the past on which the present stands. It is also **imperative** to mention ATR since religion **permeates** all areas of life in Africa. In Kenya, although those who follow ATR are only 1.6 percent, it plays a significant part in people's lives since even **Christians revert** back to ATR in times of life crisis.

1. Elements of African Religion

Although there are as many indigenous religions as different societies in Africa, these religions share many common features and beliefs. Their beliefs deal with the relation of humans to the **divine** and with communication between the human world and the spirit world. African religions also share many ideas with world religions such as **Judaism** and **Buddhism**. Yet certain aspects of African faiths differ from those of most world religions.

Gods and spirits

Most African religions acknowledge the existence of a supreme **deity** who created the world and then, in most cases, retired from dealing with **earthly** affairs. This deity is usually male and often rules with a female earth goddess or mother goddess. As in the Christian and Muslim faith, the supreme being of African religions possesses **attributes** that define him as the opposite of humans—**immortal**, all powerful, all knowing, and incapable of error.[1] However, while the God of Christians and Muslims is concerned about all humans, the supreme deity of African religions generally cares only for the people of a particular society.

In some African religions, the supreme deity continues to have dealings with humans after creating the world. More often this duty falls to a host of lesser spirits or **mystical** beings. Generally considered living aspects of the supreme deity, these spirits may hold power over humans, who are usually unaware of them. The spirits have no shape or form and cannot be detected unless they wish to be. They are often associated with a **sacred** site, which may serve as their dwelling place or **shrine**. A major **distinction** from one African religion to another is that each has its own unique set of spirits.

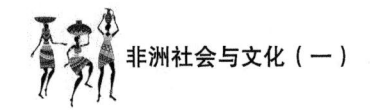

Ancestors are considered a special type of spirit in many African religions, and ancestor worship plays an important role in various **rituals**. Not all **deceased** individuals become ancestors. Individuals must be selected for the honor and then receive proper funeral **rites**. The individuals chosen vary from one society to another but may include men who have fathered children and women who were the firstborn in their families.[2] Meanwhile, Africans offer prayers and **sacrifices** to ancestors to protect the living and punish those who harm or are disloyal to the family groups or **clans** of **descendants**.

Myths

All African religions feature myths, which are stories that are used to explain the nature of the society and of the universe. Myths tell about the creation of the world, **ancestral** origins, historical events and heroes. Many Africans regard myths as representing basic truth, though they may be **clothed** in **fanciful narratives**. What matters is that myths help explain the past and present, resolve moral and social issues, and provide a **cosmology**—an account of the structure and purpose of the universe.

Creation myths are an essential part of African religions. All share a basic pattern: a supreme deity creates the world from nothing, sacred figures appear and use magic or divine power to form the society, and then humans appear and create the earthly history of a group. The creation story emphasizes the separation between humans and the divine, which is often represented by the division between the earth and the sky. This separation occurs because of the **wickedness** of humans, which causes them to break up into many cultures and languages and lose their divine nature.

Other common African myths deal with the relationship between humans and animals and the differences in the natures of men and women. Many of these myths serve to explain and **justify** the **distribution** of power and authority among humans and other living things.[3]

Like the myths of other cultures, African myths help to explain the world and human society, making the world more **predictable** and controllable. However, the deeper meaning of the myths may be available only to individuals who have the special training or insight needed to communicate with the world of the spirits.

Evil and witchcraft

All African religions contain notions of evil, which may take the form of sudden illness or death, unexpected failure, or bad dreams or visions. Believed to originate outside the individual, these forms of evil may affect the body and eventually cause it to break down and **disintegrate**. The occurrence of evil may be unexpected, may spring from a sense of guilt, or may be punishment for **antisocial** actions.

Africans use **divination** to explain and combat forms of evil and to identify its source—either spirits or other humans. The spirit world is usually considered the source of "predictable" **misfortune**, that is, punishment for misdeeds or the result of personal actions.[4] In such cases, the evil is removed through sacrifice. Unjust or unexplained misfortune is typically blamed on humans known as **witches** and **sorcerers**.

In all African societies, witchcraft and **sorcery** usually express jealousy and hatred between rivals, and it is assumed that the victim and **evildoer** know one another. **Remedies** for the problem are based on this **rivalry** and may include forcing the accused person to withdraw the evil or misfortune. The evildoer may be punished or even killed, especially if accused of witchcraft or sorcery on many occasions. Frequent accusations against an individual are usually a sign of a long-standing unpopularity in the group. Belief in witchcraft and sorcery occurs among urban Africans as well as among rural folk.

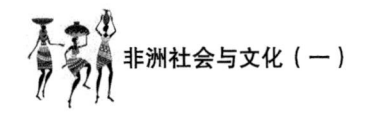

2. Religious Practices and Prohibitions

Contact and communication between the living and the nonliving are at the heart of almost all African religions. Communication between humans and the spirit world can be led by human **intermediaries**—such as priests, **diviners**, or **prophets**—in the form of prayer, visions, **prophecies**, and sacrifice. It can also be **initiated** by spirits through **possession** of humans.[5]

Sacrifice and rituals

Sacrifice is a way to purify the community or an individual through ritual. Often performed on a regular basis, sacrifices are usually conducted to remove **contamination** caused by existing conditions. The most common regular sacrifices are **rites of passage**, which are rituals performed at important moments of **transition** in a person's life.

African rites of passage usually occur at birth, marriage and death; on **initiation** into secret societies (often associated with reaching a certain age); and on achieving an important position such as that of king or priest. In rites of passage, the person being initiated is typically separated from the everyday world both physically and symbolically. This period of **seclusion**, which may be long or short, is marked by symbolic **reversal** of the normal order—such as wearing forbidden clothes or eating forbidden foods. It may also involve performing actions such as wild dancing or working oneself up into an **ecstatic** state to show closeness to the source of divine and spiritual power.

In addition to regular sacrifices, special purification sacrifices can be performed at any time to heal individuals struck down by sickness, physical or psychological harm, moral impurity. Such sacrifices often include killing and feasting on an animal that is blessed and identified with the person for whom the sacrifice is being performed. **Slaughtering** and cooking the animal carried away the person's sin or sickness. By eating the animal's flesh together, the community symbolically renews the **communal** bond that was disrupted by the pollution of the affected individual.

Possession and divination

Communication between the living and nonliving may also occur through possession, a condition in which a spirit or ancestor takes control of a living person. Possession is seen as a mystical link between the person being possessed and the spiritual agent that takes control. When a person with no special religious status is possessed, it is seen as a sign that he or she has been chosen by the spirits and linked to their world. Individuals with professional skill or knowledge may be able to convince a spirit to possess them through dancing, **hyperventilation** (become dizzy by rapid breathing), or the use of drugs. Although either men or women may be possessed, the majority who reach this state are women. Well-known examples include the **bori cult** of northern Nigeria and the **zar cult** of northeastern Africa, in which women possessed by spirits form cult groups around the particular possessing spirits. The possessed person often does not recall the experience. As with sacrifice, one effect of possession is the purification of the victim and a change of status, such as being removed from certain family or social obligations.

Another form of communication with the spirit world is the practice of divination. Diviners, the men and women who perform divination, are believed to speak for spiritual forces. They may explain past misfortunes or **foretell** likely future events. Many diviners act as **mediums**, communicating with spirits through possession or **trance**. The mediums often wear clothing or eat foods that symbolize the "wilderness" that is the source of their special knowledge. Other diviners interpret physical signs, such as animal tracks or the arrangement of items in a basket, as spiritual messages. A type of divination called

A Luo diviner in Meru, Kenya
(Photographer: Han Hong)

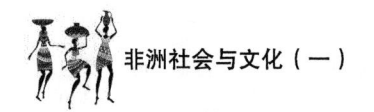

oracle consultation is sometimes used to determine guilt. In consulting an oracle—usually a material object or a place thought to contain spirits—the diviner asks it to respond to a series of yes-or-no questions to reveal a person's guilt or innocence.[6]

Religious reform

African history is filled with the appearance of prophets who have come from outside the community to reform or reshape a society and its religion. The **upheaval** caused by European colonization of Africa inspired many prophets who promoted political as well as religious change, including some who led their followers into battles for independence. In recent times, prophets have drawn heavily on ideas and symbols from Islam and Christianity. Many prophets have founded new Christian churches that focus on African concerns, including healing, well-being, material success, and long life. Others have **merged** ideas from indigenous and foreign faiths into religious groups that are unique to Africa.

3. Animal Symbols

Animal symbolism plays an important role in African religion, appearing in both myths and rituals. In parts of central and southern Africa, the **python** represents the being from which the world was created. Other creatures, such as the **praying mantis** in the myths of the San people of southern Africa, play the role of creator as well. Among the **Tabwa** people of the Democratic Republic of the Congo (**Kinshasa**), the **aardvark** is a living symbol of the contradictions and puzzles of human existence. It was also a symbol for the ancient Egyptians, who originally pictured their god **Seth** as an aardvark. Cats feature prominently in mythology as symbols of the seasons, of day and night, and of life and death.

4. Characteristics

Regarding the basic characteristics of ATR, firstly, it is primarily **holistic**. In ATR there is no distinction between the sacred and the **secular**. According to an

African **theologian**, Africans are "**notoriously** religious". To ignore these traditional beliefs, attitudes, and practices can only lead to a lack of understanding African behaviors and problems. Religion is the strongest element in traditional background, and exerts probably the greatest influence upon the thinking and living of the people concerned.

Secondly, ATR is communal. It is not for the individual primarily, but for the community. **Sociability**, relationship, participation, and sharing are the central moral imperatives of African religion, and the unity of community is of **paramount** importance.

II. HISTORY OF CHRISTIANITY IN AFRICA

Christianity first arrived in North Africa, in the 1st or early 2nd century A.D. The Christian communities in North Africa were among the earliest in the world. Legend has it that Christianity was brought from **Jerusalem** to **Alexandria** on the Egyptian coast by **Mark**, one of the four **evangelists**, in 60 A.D. This was around the same time or possibly before Christianity spread to northern Europe.

Once in North Africa, Christianity spread slowly west from Alexandria and east to Ethiopia. Through North Africa, Christianity was embraced as the religion of **dissenters** against the expanding **Roman Empire**. In the 4th century A.D., the Ethiopian King **Ezana** made Christianity the kingdom's official religion. In 312 A.D., Emperor **Constantine** made Christianity the official religion of the Roman Empire.

In the 7th century, Christianity retreated under the advance of Islam. But it remained the chosen religion of the Ethiopian Empire and persisted in pockets in North Africa.

In the 15th century, Christianity came to Sub-Saharan Africa with the arrival of the Portuguese. In the south of the continent, the Dutch founded the beginnings of the **Dutch Reform Church** in 1652.

In the interior of the continent, most people continued to practice their own religions undisturbed until the 19th century. At that time, Christian **missions** to

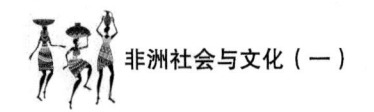

Africa increased, driven by an antislavery **crusade** and the interest of Europeans in colonizing Africa. However, where people had already **converted** to Islam, Christianity had little success.

Christianity was an agent of great change in Africa. It **destabilized** the **status quo**, bringing new opportunities to some, and undermining the power of others. With the Christian missions came education, literacy and hope for the disadvantaged. However, the spread of Christianity paved the way for commercial **speculators**, and, in its original **rigid** European form, denied people pride in their culture and ceremonies.

Although missionaries had been actively **preaching** the **Gospel** for many centuries, statistics show that by the end of 1900, only about 10% of the African population had accepted Christianity. In the 20th century—mostly in the last few decades—this radically changed. Statistics now show that more than 60% of the African population in south of the Sahara consider themselves to be Christians. With the dawn of the 21st century, Christianity is still the fastest growing religion in Africa.

1. Gospel to Africa

The first "**messenger**" of the Gospel in Africa is possibly the Ethiopian official who was **evangelized** and **baptized** on the road between Jerusalem and **Gaza**. Although the Bible does not mention it, legend has it that the official returned to his country, where he established the first Christian Church in Africa.

Nubia[7]

It is interesting to note that although many people accept this as the beginning of the modern Ethiopian church, experts claim that the region then known as Ethiopia and the country as we know it today are not the same. According to them, the official actually came from Nubia (situated in the territory known today as Sudan) and it was in this region that he established the 1st church.

During the 6th century, the Church in Nubia experienced a **phenomenal** growth period after several missionaries were sent to the region. Over time, Nubia became a

predominantly Christian kingdom. With the expansion of Islam (by 710 A.D., large part of northern Africa was ruled by Islamic Arabs), clashes between Nubia and the Muslims became more frequent. By 1000, Nubia was divided into two kingdoms—a northern (Makuria) and a southern (Alwa) kingdom. In 1275, the capital of Makuria was captured by the Egyptians. The Muslims **victimized** the Christian populations in almost every African country that they conquered and by the 17th century, most of the Christians had converted to Islam to such a degree that the Nubian church had disappeared.

It is interesting to note that Sudan, although it was declared an Islamic state in 1983, is still divided between an "Islamic" north (65% of the population) and a "Christian" south (23% of the population).

Abyssinia

The first missionary who preached the Gospel in **Abyssinia** (the modern state of Ethiopia) was Ferments. In the fourth century, he traveled to India and had to work as a slave in the administration of King Axiom, the ruler of Abyssinia. During his term as a slave, he preached the Gospel of Christ to the Abyssinians and was later set free and allowed to start a church. He started off as the **pastor** of the church, but later (356 A.D.) became **bishop**.

A priest of rock-hewn Biete Maryam (Roman Catholic Church), Lalibela, Ethiopia, demonstrating the cross of the church
(Photographer: Sun Lihua)

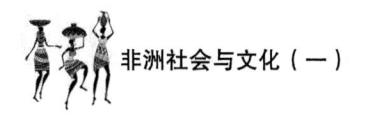

The Church in Ethiopia was different from other churches in the early centuries in that it remained relatively strong despite efforts to destroy it. These attempts included conquests by the Muslims, efforts to unify **the Coptic Church** with **the Roman Catholic Church** and **persecution** by the **Marxist** government between 1974 and 1987. The result is that today 65% of the Ethiopian population are Christian. The Coptic Church of Ethiopia is still the largest group. Approximately 58% of the country's total population of 63 million people belong to the Coptic Church.

2. Missionary Work in Parts of Africa

In West Africa (1420—1780)

While Christianity grew in Europe and large parts of northern Africa and even in the east, the rest of Africa continued to practice their traditional beliefs for many centuries. Developments in shipping and **exploratory** voyages to discover new worlds assisted the Church in its efforts to reach **hitherto** neglected parts of the African continent.

Between 1421 and 1445, **Prince Henry the Navigator commissioned** at least ten voyages in an attempt to find an **alternative** route to India. During similar efforts at the same time and later, Portuguese sailors made contact with various tribes along the coast of West Africa. In 1462, the **Pope** in Rome appointed a missionary **prefect** to promote missionary work in West Africa.

The Portuguese missionaries experienced their first major breakthrough in 1492 when Manikongo, King of the **Bakongo** tribe (in the region that today forms part of the southern regions of the Republic of the Congo and northern Angola), and many of his followers converted to Christianity. His **successor**, Alphonso, declared the Congo a Christian kingdom and many of his **subjects** went to study the priesthood and government administration in Portugal.[8]

Various factors, including the fact that the Portuguese bought slaves from the Angolans just south of the Congo and that many slaves were **abducted** from the Congo, led to the decline of the Church in the Congo. By 1700, Christianity had disappeared from this region.

In 1750, Thomas Thompson from the Society for the Propagation of the Gospel (**SPG**) in England became the first **Protestant** missionary on the west coast of Africa. He worked in the coastal regions of modern-day Ghana, but had to return to England after four years because of bad health. One of his converts, Philip Quaque, returned with him to further his studies. Quaque became the first African to be **ordained** as a preacher in **the Anglican Church**. He was also the first African who was accepted by the SPG and sent out as missionary to work among his own people in West Africa.

The Christian Church and many of its missionaries played an important role in restricting and later abolishing slavery worldwide. In 1787, a group of British Christians founded a settlement for freed slaves—**Freetown**—on the west coast of Sierra Leone. Missionaries from the Church Mission Society (**CMS**) and later also from the Wesleyan Methodist Missionary Society (**WMMS**) achieved some success early in the 19th century, not only with the spreading of the Gospel to tribes and groups in these regions, but also in the establishment of schools, a university college and various indigenous Christian churches.

In East Africa (1560—1700)

The first missionary to work in East Africa was one Da Silveira who landed on the east coast of modern-day Mozambique in 1560. He continued on foot inland to work among the **Monomotapa** tribesmen. Muslim traders, who bought gold from the King of the Monomotapa, convinced him that Da Silveira was a clever witch doctor who wanted to place a curse on him through baptism.[9] Soon afterwards the King ordered Da Silveira killed through **strangulation**.

Other missionaries followed in Da Silveira's footsteps and in 1652, the King of Monomotapa was baptized as a Christian. Nevertheless, no other major breakthroughs followed and Christianity faded when the missionaries left the area.

Between 1500 and 1700, various Portuguese missionary groups moved northwards on the coast of East Africa, but their efforts to evangelize these regions were not successful. Some success was achieved in **Mombasa** (modern-day Kenya), but by 1700, when the Portuguese **stronghold** on East Africa started to slip, the Roman Catholic Church's work on the eastern coast of Africa came to a halt.

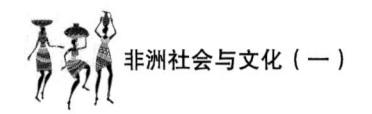

3.Two Famous Protestant Missionaries

The first Protestant missionary station in East Africa was established in Mombasa in 1844 by **Johann Ludwig Krapf**, a German missionary working for The Church Mission Society. In 1846, another missionary from CMS, **Johannes Rebmann**, joined Krapf and together they undertook various missionary **expeditions** into the interior. In 1848, Rebmann became the first European to catch a glimpse of **Mount Kilimanjaro**, the highest mountain in Africa. However, tropical diseases and hostile tribes prevented them from achieving any real success.

Krapf and Rebmann paved the way for other CMS missionaries who settled in East Africa in 1876 and who eventually established a missionary station in **Buganda** (modern-day Uganda). In 1879, the London Missionary Society (**LMS**) established two missionary stations on the east coast of **Lake Tanganyika** (the western region of modern-day Tanzania), where many tribes and groups were eventually reached with the Gospel.

From the south, the well-known Scottish missionary **David Livingstone**, who was sent to Africa in 1840 by LMS, launched various missionary expeditions. Livingstone was at first stationed in **Kuruman**, but slowly moved north and eventually explored the entire southern Africa as well as parts of central Africa, including modern-day Angola, Botswana, Zimbabwe, Zambia, Mozambique, Malawi and Tanzania. From 1851 until his death in 1873, Livingstone not only explored places never before seen by any other European, for example **Victoria Falls**, but he also shared the Christian message with thousands of indigenous tribe members who had never heard the Gospel before.

As a direct result of Livingstone's explorations and pioneering work, the Livingstonia Missionary Station was established on the western shore of **Lake Malawi** in 1876. In the same year, **the Church of Scotland** also established missionary posts along the lake, including the **Bandawe Missionary Station**, where many missionaries died of **malaria** and other tropical diseases shortly after their arrival.

Biography of Johann Ludwig Krapf

Johann Ludwig Krapf (1810—1881) was a German missionary in East Africa, as well as an explorer, **linguist** and traveler.

Vision in Ethiopia

Krapf's first posting was to Ethiopia, where he worked from 1837 to 1842, when he was forced to return to Cairo. Here he made his first long overland journey, and armed already with some knowledge of **Ge'ez** and **Amharic**, he set out to master the **Cushitic** speech of the **Oromo** people, the dominant people throughout much of central and southern Ethiopia. His first publications date from this period, with translations of the *Gospels of John and Matthew* into Oromo. In 1842 his pioneering linguistic achievements were recognized when he was awarded an **honorary doctorate** at **Tübingen University**. He became obsessed with the idea that the Oromo, whom he described as "the most intellectual people of eastern Africa", were the key to the evangelization of the continent, and when driven out of Ethiopia, he determined to reach them via Mombasa. *The Journal of the Rev. Messers Isenberg* and *Krapf, Missionaries of the Church Missionary Society*[10] was published in 1843. It consists of edited **extracts** from Krapf's journals with much shorter additions from Isenberg's letters, and although not in the first rank of writings on Ethiopia, it contains valuable information about the **theological controversies** that were raging in the Ethiopian church at that date, as well as about the people and politics, and the land itself and its geography.

The Mombasa years

Having experienced the **imperviousness** of the **Ethiopian Orthodox Christians** to his Protestant and **Pietist** interpretations of **Scripture**, and their unreadiness for a **reformation**, he turned to the Oromo, convinced that they were the key to the

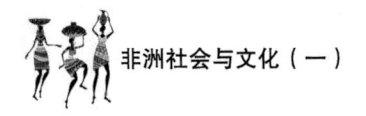

conversion of Africa. When his position became intolerable in Ethiopia because of political **machinations**, he made his way down the east coast of Africa to **Zanzibar** and then across to Mombasa, in order to try to reach the Oromo by another route. Yet oddly he stayed in and around Mombasa for years, not seeming to realize that his inland journeys would not take him anywhere near the Oromo, who lived far to the north. The idea that they would be the key to the evangelization of Africa proved to be pure **fantasy**.

A new phase of missionary activity

The move back to Germany marked the beginning of a new phase of Krapf's missionary activity, not his retirement from it. He became an adviser to others on mission work in eastern Africa, making several further visits to Africa in this connection, of which the 1853 visit to Ethiopia in connection with **Bishop Gobat**'s mission was the first. In the years that followed he did what he could to raise support in Germany for this mission. The most significant of his African visits was that to East Africa in 1862 to help Thomas Wakefield of **the United Methodist Church** to found a mission there. He chose a site for the mission at Ribe, not far from Rabai, and it was both men's hope that this mission would be a stepping stone to the Oromo. Indeed, Methodist missionaries did make contact with some of the more **southerly migrant** Oromo, but this was not the breakthrough that had been hoped for. The Methodist Church in Kenya dates back to this pioneer mission. Several **Lutheran** missions that took up work in East Africa, including the **Bavarian Evangelical** Lutheran Mission founded in response to his death, owed something to the inspiration of his life and work.[11] These later missions were to work under colonial rule, which broke open the **self-containment** of precolonial societies that had proved such a barrier to Krapf and his companions.

A final visit to Ethiopia

A final visit to Ethiopia took place in 1867—1868, when Krapf accompanied the expedition led by **Sir Robert Napier**, which ended in the **Battle of Magdala**.

Krapf was forbidden to engage in **evangelism**, though it was accepted that he might discuss religion with the Ethiopians if they raised the subject. Presumably he agreed to go with the expedition because he could not resist the opportunity of seeing Ethiopia once again, but he had to be **invalided** back to Germany after only three months. A second major activity of these years was his work on languages and translation and the task of seeing translations of Scripture through the press, a topic that occupied so much of his later **correspondence**. His linguistic range was extraordinary, including two of the **Semitic** languages of Ethiopia (Amharic and **Tigrinya**), a Cushitic language (Oromo), **Maasai**, which is often classified as **Eastern Nilotic**, and several **Bantu** languages. His observations on these and on the relationships and contrasts between them laid a basis for further **ethnographic** studies. Translations into Oromo, **Kiswahili**, and **Kikamba** had appeared in the 1840s.

Biography of David Livingstone

Livingstone was a Scottish missionary and one of the greatest European explorers of Africa, whose opening up the interior of the continent contributed to the "Scramble for Africa".[12]

David Livingstone was born at Blantyre, south of **Glasgow** on 19 March 1813. At 10, he began working in the local **cotton mill**, with school lessons in the evenings. In 1836, he began studying medicine and **theology** in Glasgow and decided to become a missionary doctor. In 1841, he was posted to the edge of **the Kalahari Desert** in southern Africa. In 1845, he married Mary Moffat, daughter of a fellow missionary.

Livingstone became convinced of his mission to reach new peoples in the interior of Africa and introduce them to Christianity, as well as freeing them from slavery. It was this which inspired his explorations. In 1849 and 1851, he travelled across the Kalahari, on the second trip **sighting** the upper **Zambezi River**. In 1852, he began a four-year expedition to find a route from the upper Zambezi to the coast. This filled huge gaps in western knowledge of central and southern Africa. In 1855,

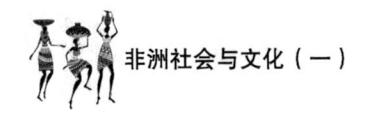

Livingstone discovered a spectacular waterfall which he named "Victoria Falls". He reached the mouth of the Zambezi on the Indian Ocean in May 1856, becoming the first European to cross the width of southern Africa.

Returning to Britain, where he was now a national hero, Livingstone did many speaking tours and published his best-selling ***Missionary Travels and Researches in South Africa*** (1857). He left for Africa again in 1858, and for the next five years carried out official explorations of eastern and central Africa for the British government. His wife died of malaria in 1862, a bitter blow and in 1864 he was ordered home by a government unimpressed with the results of his travels.

At home, Livingstone **publicized** the horrors of the slave trade, securing private support for another expedition to central Africa, searching for the Nile's source and reporting further on slavery. This expedition lasted from 1866 until Livingstone's death in 1873. After nothing was heard from him for many months, **Henry Stanley**, an explorer and journalist, set out to look for Livingstone. This resulted in their meeting near Lake Tanganyika in October 1871, during which Stanley uttered the famous phrase: "Dr. Livingstone, I presume?" With new supplies from Stanley, Livingstone continued his efforts to find the source of the Nile. His health had been poor for many years and he died on first May 1873. His body was taken back to England and buried in **Westminster Abbey**.

4. Missionary Work during Colonialism (1880—1914)

While missionaries were often the first Europeans to explore the unknown regions of Africa and to make contact with tribes living in these areas, they were soon to be followed by other Europeans who were interested in obtaining the wealth of Africa. The race to conquer Africa's wealth reached its peak in the 19th century. In 1879, indigenous leaders ruled approximately 90% of the continent. By 1900, this all changed when almost the entire African continent was **annexed** by Western colonial rulers, including Britain, Germany, France, Belgium, Portugal, Spain and Italy.

5. Church and Missions in Africa Today

The inside of St. Paul's Cathedral, Embu, Kenya

(Photographer: Du Fengyan)

The Christian Church in Africa enjoyed growth **unprecedented** in the 2000-year-old history of Christianity. Statistics showed that by 1900, there were approximately eight million Christians (10% of the entire population) in Africa. Over a period of a hundred years, this figure has increased dramatically. By 2002, 351 million people (approximately 48% of Africa's population and 60% of the population south of the Sahara) considered themselves to be Christians.

The modern Church in Africa comprises 15,000 different **denominations** and groups, of which 13% are Protestant, 10% Independent, 4% Anglican, 15% Roman Catholic and 6% Orthodox Christians. While the population growth on the continent is on the decline, Christianity is still growing at a rate of 2.8% **per annum**. Protestantism is growing fastest (4.2%), with Independent Churches second (3.9%) and the Anglicans third (5.2%).

III. HISTORY OF ISLAM IN AFRICA

According to Arab oral tradition, Islam first came to Africa with Muslim **refu-**

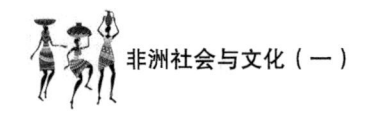

gees fleeing persecution in the Arab **peninsula**. This was followed by a military invasion, some seven years after the death of the prophet **Mohammed** in 639 A.D., under the command of the Muslim Arab General, **Amr ibn al-Asi**. It quickly spread west from Alexandria in North Africa (the **Maghreb**), reducing the Christians to pockets in Egypt, Nubia and Ethiopia.

Kaole Ruins, Bagamoyo, Tanzania, the remnant of one of the oldest mosques in East Africa
(Photographer: Sun Lihua)

Islam came to root along the East African coast sometime in the eighth century, as part of a continuing dialogue between the people on the east coast and traders from **the Persian Gulf** and **Oman**. Like early Christianity, Islam was **monotheistic**, that is, Muslims worship only one God.

Islam was a modernizing influence, imposing a consistent order among different societies, strengthening powers of government and breaking down ethnic loyalties.

Unlike Christianity, Islam tolerated traditional values, allowing a man to have more than one wife. For many, this made conversion to Islam easier and less upsetting than conversion to Christianity.

In the early centuries of its existence, Islam in Africa had a dynamic and **turbulent** history, with reforming movements and dynasties clashing and succeeding each other. Gaining power depended on securing trade routes into gold-producing areas in Sub-Saharan Africa. Islamic rulers expanded north as well as south. In the last quarter of the 11th century, Islam dominated the **Mediterranean** world.

In the 14th century, **the Black Death** came from Europe and seriously **undermined** the social and economic life of North Africa, or the Maghreb, as it is known. However, Islam remained the dominant religion.

From the 16th to the 19th century, much of the Maghreb was under **Ottoman** rule. By the 1880s, Islam had taken root in one third of the continent.

IV. CHRISTIANITY AND ISLAM IN ETHIOPIA

Christianity and Islam have peacefully co-existed in Ethiopia for centuries. According to tradition, a group of Arab followers of Islam endangered of persecution by local authorities in **Arabia** took **refuge** early in the seventh century in the **Aksumite Kingdom** of the Ethiopian Christian highlands: these people were well-treated and permitted to practice their religion as they wished. Consequently, the prophet Mohammad concluded that Ethiopia should not be targeted for **jihad**. In those days, Ethiopian Christian rulers felt no doubt, however, that Islam would be **subservient** to Christianity.

Holy Trinity Cathedral in Addis Ababa, Ethiopia
(Photographer: Han Hong)

Since this time, Christian-Islamic relations have remained generally **cordial**.

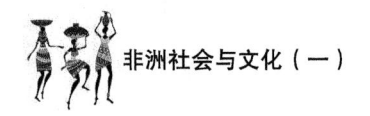

of course, there were some occasional clashes between Muslims and Christians, the invasion of **Gragn**, the **Khedive** of Egypt and the **Mahdist** were basic examples.[13] But it is natural that when more than one religion exists, the relationship between them could be competitive or cooperative. Thus, relatively the relationship between Christians and Muslims seemed to be cooperative, but nowadays this relationship becomes competitive.

Regarding the historical dispute, the Islamic threat to Ethiopia became more serious in the first half of the 16th century when **Ahmad ibn Ibrahim al-Ghazi** (known as the "Gragn the left-handed") **rallied** a diverse group of Muslims in a jihad designed to end Christian power in the highlands. Aided by forces coming from the Ottoman **Turkish**, Gragn defeated the Ethiopian emperor and conquered most of the Ethiopian highlands. Moreover, during this period, many Turkish and Arab adventures from the south Arabian Peninsula joined the mission. In the process, he destroyed a number of Ethiopia's centers of Christian civilization. Ahmad Gragn and his followers were **dazzled** at the extent of the riches of the Church, and at the **splendor** of Ethiopian Christian culture at the time. As the most important **repository** of the cultural heritage of Christian Ethiopia, the Church was a special target for the destructive **furies** of the **Imam**. Ahmad Gragn's **chronicler** outlines a large number of cases in which beautiful churches were pulled down, their riches **plundered**, and holy books burnt to ashes, and the clergy **massacred**. In this way, the rich material and spiritual culture attained by **medieval** Ethiopia was almost completely destroyed in not more than a decade.

During the invasion, Ethiopian Christians were in a state of fear and tension. With the tension of forced conversion, Christians had a psychological life-and-death struggle, putting their identity at a crossroads and losing a remarkable sense of confidence. As a result, most people rejected their faith and favored the invaders. But there were some people who stood against the interest of the invaders. Apart from the forced conversion, a number of people were killed, a number of religious scholars were massacred. The religious scholars of the Orthodox Church have been said to have had **reputed** wisdom and holiness, these people were massacred, they were **ruthlessly** murdered. It was not until 1543 that Ethiopia raised a large army that defeated the Muslims and killed Gragn. Thousands of Muslims and Christians lost their lives in these wars.

Murals at Bebre Berhan Selassie, the only church that survived the fire by Madists in 1888, Gondar, Ethiopia
(Photographer: Han Hong)

In addition to the invasion of Ahmad ibn Ibrahim al-Ghazi, in 1875 the Khedive of Egypt organized a force, including several officers from both sides of the American Civil War, designed to conquer Ethiopia's Christian kingdom.[14] Marching into the highlands from the Red Sea coast, the Ethiopians defeated them decisively. Moreover, the last major, organized threat from Islam occurred in 1888, when the forces of the **Mahdi** in the Sudan **sacked** the former capital **Gondar** and burned many of its churches. In the following year, the Ethiopians defeated the Mahdist troops at **the Battle of Metema** on the Ethiopian-Sudanese border. This history reflects Christian-Muslim competition for control over the Ethiopian highlands.

In the 20th century, three internal developments **revived** Christian concerns about Islam; these were the case of **Lij Iyasu**, the Italian invasion and the Eritrean Liberation Front (**ELF**). Upon the death of Emperor **Menelik** in 1913, his grandson, Lij Iyasu, inherited the **throne**. Iyasu was pushed aside after three years, having made what the Christian leadership considered too many **overtures** to Muslims, renewing concerns that followers of Islam might try to assume power. Following its invasion of Ethiopia in 1936, Italy took a number of measures that favored Muslims at the expense of Christians, a policy that led to some incidents that Christians did not soon forget. For example, in Muslim areas, the Italians replaced **Amhara** judges with **Qadis**; they appointed new Muslim **chiefs** and created two new **governorships**. This was intentionally made to divide the unity of the nation. In 1961, the Eritrea Liberation Front began an armed struggle to create an independent Eritrean state. A largely Islamic movement, the ELF, drew its fighters from Muslim **nomadic** tribes, and its leaders called for a jihad against Christian Ethiopia. Leadership of the Eritrean independence movement subsequently shifted to Christians who continued to hold the upper hand when Eritrea became independent in 1993.

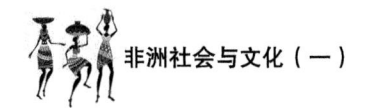

Despite a relatively peaceful history, incidents of religious conflicts arose in Ethiopia with the fall of the Derg Government[15] in 1987. That is, nowadays, there are occasional clashes between Christians and Muslims in some areas of the country. Some of the religious conflicts that have captured people's attention in the near past include the conflicts happening in **Jimma**, **Kemise** and **Harar**. In these conflicts, Christians were massacred and injured; they **emigrated** from their homeland and sought refuge in the nearby towns. In those areas, Christians have faced religious persecutions including forced conversion to Islam, **marginalization**, **verbal** violence and many other harsh modes of treatment. Although forgiveness is encouraged for peaceful co-existence, the bitter encounters experienced by those Christians should not be left unrecorded.

Explanations

[1] **As in the Christian and Muslim faith, the supreme being of African religions possesses attributes that define him as the opposite of humans—immortal, all powerful, all knowing, and incapable of error:** 与基督教的"上帝"和伊斯兰教的"真主安拉"一样，非洲传统宗教中的最高神也具有凡人没有的属性：他长生不老，无所不能，无所不知，从不犯错。

[2] **The individuals chosen vary from one society to another but may include men who have fathered children and women who were the firstborn in their families:** 不同社会选择祖先崇拜对象的标准各不相同。但是在很多社会中，后继有人的男子和排行老大的女人可能会成为被推崇的祖先。

[3] **Many of these myths serve to explain and justify the distribution of power and authority among humans and other living things:** 很多这类神话的作用就在于解释为什么人类和其他生物之间存在着力量和权威的差别，并且说明这些差异的合理性。

[4] **The spirit world is usually considered the source of "predictable" misfortune, that is, punishment for misdeeds or the result of personal actions:** 人们通常认为："可以预测的"不幸是灵魂世界对作恶者的惩罚，正所谓"恶有恶报"。

[5] **It can also be initiated by spirits through possession of humans:** 通过灵魂附体的方式，活人和逝者也可以接触和沟通。

[6] **In consulting an oracle—usually a material object or a place thought to contain spirits—the diviner asks it to respond to a series of yes-or-no questions to reveal a person's guilt or innocence:** 在向一个神谕（通常是一件物体，也可能是被认为灵魂出没的地方）问卦时，占卜者会问一系列是或否的问题，然后根据得到的卦来判定一个人是否有罪。

[7] **Nubia:** "努比亚"是古代非洲最伟大的文明古国之一，历史可以追溯到公元前2000年以前。

[8] **His successor, Alphonso, declared the Congo a Christian kingdom and many**

[8] of his subjects went to study the priesthood and government administration in Portugal：在他的继任者阿方索宣布基督教为刚果国教以后，很多刚果臣民去葡萄牙学习如何当牧师，以及如何管理政府。

[9] Muslim traders, who bought gold from the King of the Monomotapa, convinced him that Da Silveira was a clever witch doctor who wanted to place a curse on him through baptism：向莫诺莫塔帕国王购买金子的穆斯林商人设法让国王相信：狡猾的巫医达·西尔维拉想趁国王受礼的时机对他下咒语。

[10] The Journals of the Rev. Messrs Isenberg and Krapf, Missionaries of the Church Missionary Society：《英国海外传道会传教士艾森伯格牧师和克拉普夫牧师的日志》

[11] Several Lutheran missions that took up work in East Africa, including the Bavarian Evangelical Lutheran Mission founded in response to his death, owed something to the inspiration of his life and work：约翰·路德维希·克拉普夫的人生经历和忘我工作激励着若干在东非传教的路德教会，其中包括在他去世以后，为纪念他而成立的巴伐利亚福音路德教会。

[12] Scramble for Africa："瓜分非洲"。欧洲殖民者从15世纪起开始入侵非洲。19世纪70年代以后，欧洲列强掀起了瓜分非洲的狂潮。19世纪晚期，除埃塞俄比亚和利比里亚勉强维持独立以外，非洲基本被瓜分完毕。帝国主义殖民统治给非洲带来了空前的破坏和灾难。

[13] Of course, there were some occasional clashes between Muslims and Christians, the invasion of Gragn, the Khedive of Egypt and the Mahdist were basic examples：当然，穆斯林和基督徒之间偶尔也会发生矛盾，典型的例子有"征服者"艾哈迈德·伊本·伊布拉欣·阿尔-加齐领导穆斯林入侵阿比西尼亚；埃及总督率部企图征服信奉基督教的埃塞俄比亚王国；以及苏丹马赫迪的军队洗劫贡德尔，焚烧教堂。

[14] ...in 1875 the Khedive of Egypt organized a force, including several officers from both sides of the American Civil War, designed to conquer Ethiopia's Christian kingdom：为了征服埃塞俄比亚这个基督教王国，1875年，埃及总督组织了一支队伍，其中就有几位在"美国内战"中，为南方或者北方效力的军官。

[15] **Derg Government:** "德格"是"埃塞俄比亚武装部队、警察和地方后备军协调委员会"的简称。1974年初，一批埃塞少壮派军官发动政变，推翻了海尔·塞拉西一世（Haile. Selassie）政权，废黜帝制，成立临时军事行政委员会。"德格"的统治一直持续到1987年。13年间，数万反对者未经审判和监禁被执行死刑。

Exercises

I. Read the following statements and decide whether they are true (T) or false (F).

____ 1. Communication between the living and nonliving can occur through either human intermediaries or possession.

____ 2. In different parts of Africa, both python and praying mantis play the role of creator.

____ 3. Dogs feature prominently in mythology as symbols of the seasons, of day and night, and of life and death.

____ 4. The basic characteristic of African traditional religion is secular.

____ 5. The Christian Church and many of its missionaries played an important role in restricting and later abolishing slavery worldwide.

____ 6. Johann Ludwig Kraph was convinced that the Oromo were the key to the evangelization of the African continent.

____ 7. After David Livingstone died on 1st May 1873, his body was taken back to England and buried in Westminster Abbey.

____ 8. Both Christianity and Islam tolerated traditional values, allowing a man to have more than one wife.

____ 9. In Ethiopia, relatively the relationship between Christians and Muslims seemed to be competitive, but nowadays this relationship becomes cooperative.

____ 10. The rich material and spiritual culture attained by medieval Ethiopia was almost completely destroyed in not more than a decade by the forces of the Mahdi in the Sudan.

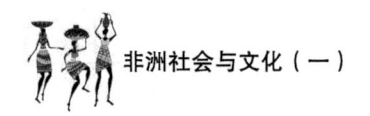

II. Fill in the following blanks with words that best complete the sentences.

1. While the God of Christians and Muslims is concerned about all humans, the _____ deity of African religions generally cares only for the people of a _____ society.
2. Africans use _____ to explain and combat forms of evil and to identify its source—either spirits or other humans.
3. _____ and _____ between the living and the nonliving are at the heart of almost all African religions.
4. The social unrest caused by European _____ of Africa inspired many prophets who promoted political as well as religious change, including some who led their followers into battles for _____.
5. In the 19th century, increased Christian missions to Africa were driven by an antislavery _____ and the interest of Europeans in _____ Africa.
6. With the dawn of the 21st century, _____ is still the fastest growing religion in Africa.
7. Sudan, although it was declared an Islamic state in 1983, is still divided between an "_____" north (65% of the population) and a "_____" south (23% of the population).
8. In 1855, _____ discovered a spectacular waterfall which he named "Victoria Falls".
9. The modern Church in Africa comprises 15,000 different _____ and groups, of which 15% are Roman Catholic, 13% Protestant, 10% _____, 6% Orthodox, and 4% Anglican Christians.
10. In some places in Ethiopia, Christians have faced religious persecutions including forced _____ to Islam, _____, _____ violence and many other harsh modes of treatment.

Unit V African Religions

Review and Reflect

- What are the causes of Islamic fundamentalism in Africa?
- What do you think of the work of European missionaries in Africa?
- Do you think different religions can co-exist peacefully?

Unit VI　Festivals and Values in Africa

对于非洲人而言，节日庆典举足轻重。非洲各国都有大大小小、名目繁多的节日。受地域、部族、历史、宗教、文化等因素的影响，非洲各地的节日习俗各不相同。在非洲人的传统观念中，世界和人类是如何产生的？他们有怎样的宇宙观和世界观？他们有哪些普遍价值观？

The Reed Dance Ceremony—an annual cultural event in Swaziland
(Photographer: Liang Zi)

"A human presence among all of these, a feature on the face of our native land thus defined, I know that none dare challenge me when I say—I am an African!"

—Thabo Mbeki, former President of South Africa (1999—2008)

◎ Think and Talk

☆ Which African festivals do you know of?

☆ What do you know about African initiation ceremony?

☆ Do you personally know some Africans? What are their attitudes toward life?

Unit VI Festivals and Values in Africa

I. FESTIVALS

1. Overview

Festivals have long been at the center of African cultural and social life. At the core of African social experience and **indigenous** knowledge systems are ceremonial events designed to mark critical moments such as the birth of a child, **puberty** or **initiation** into adulthood and secret society,[1] marriage, and death. Since precolonial times, many Africans have celebrated Eid al-Fitr[2] and Eid al-Kabir,[3] Muslim gift-giving festivals that they embraced following the 19th-century West African Islamic **jihads**. **Calendric** times are also marked by agricultural seasons, or **taboo** periods for the consumption of certain food products to celebrate, **ritualize**, and privately or publicly mark the moment, with suitable **observances** to either pay **homage** to an individual, or impress the significance of the dead and living members of the community.

Ethiopian New Year celebration
(Photographer: Sun Lihua)

The **esoteric** and sacred rituals displayed in African festivals have been documented in early 19th century European explorers' **chronicles**, **missionary**

145

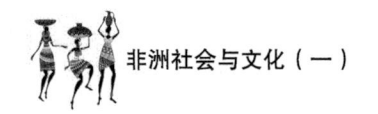

reports, and films, as well as classic and **contemporary ethnographies** of Sub-Saharan Africa. These accounts provide a **diachronic** view with which to compare the meanings and ways in which present-day festivals are celebrated, allowing for a better appreciation of the specific function that individual members of the community may perform their capacity as **priests**, **devotees**, **mediums**, or musicians with an audience, and the **designated** public arenas—a sacred **grove**, a courtyard, a market place, and so on—where such activities are staged.

Preparation for Ethiopian Christmas
(Photographer: Sun Lihua)

The nature and scale of the celebration of many festivals are reflected and shaped by the occupation and social organization of the community. The rank and social status of an individual is not lost in the seating arrangement at the festival durbar (exhibitions and gathering);[4] the role the individual plays in the ritual performances, ranging from the family harvest and **ancestral** ritual ceremony, to the hunter and blacksmith **masquerades** of the so-called **stateless** people, to the large-scale **chiefly** durbars associated with sacred **kingships**, has likewise not gone unnoticed.

In West Africa, the Poro[5] (society of the sacred grove) initiation ceremony of the **Senufo**—the Côte d'Ivoire and Burkina Faso people, famous for their prestigious display for large audiences and funeral rituals—reveals the male-female **complementarity** in that society. The **mythical** ancient woman reported as central to the Senufo **ideological** core and religion symbolizes "**bipartite deity**" and "nurturing". She is **entrusted** with the ceremony via the intimate involvement of young girls in every stage of the preparation of this male secret society festival designed to help shape the intellect, moral character, and skill of each succeeding generation and **age set**. That women are accorded such a central role in Poro initiation is a reflection of Senufo thought regarding the nature of deity and family, which is of **cosmological** and social order. In Senufo **cosmogony**, the woman represents an institutionalized expression of the deeply rooted concept of twinship, and the deep respect for her is dramatized by the formal daily gestures that people extend to her. This is especially seen during the Poro Festival, when a Poro junior blacksmith **adorned** in a mask dances to pay homage to the female member of his **lineage**; the act of touching her shoulder secures him her blessings.

Furthermore, the **sequences** of ritual performance, **procession**, costume, and eating of meals during the Incwala,[6] Odwira,[7] and Kundun Festivals[8] celebrated by the **Swazi**, **Asante/Akuapem**, and **Ahanta**, respectively, with a long history of **polities**, serve to reveal both the power of the king or **chief**, and the splendor and wealth of the state he represents. During the Incwala celebration, as with the Odwira of the **Akan** of Ghana, a week or more of celebrations involves a series of ritual activities, **culminating** in the natural, social, and cosmological **purification** and renewal of the powers of the king, kingships, and the nation.

An essential and enduring feature of African festivals is ritual practice, the content of which deals with **libations**, mythical themes, and creation **narratives**. This is exemplified by the Bagre Festival celebrated by the **Dagaaba** of northern Ghana and southwestern Burkina Faso. Not only does the Bagre Festival address **historiographic** and cosmological constructions, but it allows this oral society to capture the sense and meaning of the historical past that still has relevance to their daily lives at the present times. As sites for cultural production and popular culture, festivals offer an opportunity to hear and see the ordinary people's creativity in music, oral **lore**, and **visual art**. The rituals and accompanying music and dance represent African art and theater, which are invariably linked to the African religious outlook. For example, religious and theatrical elements come alive in the **mockery duel** preceding the Ekpe[9] dance of the **Efiks** of Nigeria.

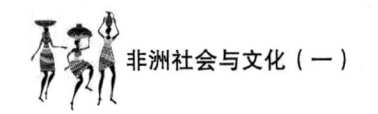

The dynamic nature and wide variety of festivals that Africans celebrate across time and space defy previous attempts to classify them into fixed categories and **genres**.[10] Although **differentiation** into royal or sacred kingship, religious or secular holidays, masquerades, and colonial and national festivals is a useful characterization, they provide a far too static image of African celebratory activities and self-representations.

As with other aspects of African life experience, the intent and modes of festival celebration have been significantly shaped and affected by colonialism, modernity, and Western instruments. Even as many Africans continue to conceive of their festivals as **primordial** ancestral traditions, it is appropriate to view them as **constitutive** of the continent's "invented traditions".

In the postcolonial era, several "**neotraditional** festivals" have **proliferated**, assuming new meanings and political dimensions. These **mediate** and serve as points of **contestations** and exchange among cultural traditions at the local and regional levels and between local communities and national governments. Following the examples of the First Festival of Black Arts[11] and Nigeria's Second World Black and African Festival of Arts and Culture[12] organized in Senegal and Nigeria, respectively, in recent years other states, including Ghana, have undertaken to organize and plan national and yearly **pan-African** festivals in response to pan-Africanist revival and "self-discovery" of Africans in the **diaspora** and to attract **heritage tourists** to their nation.

II. GENERAL TYPES OF AFRICAN FESTIVALS

African royal festivals and religious ceremonies have been documented for several centuries, figuring prominently in early Western travel writing, colonial **expositions**, museum displays, **ethnographic** films and **monographs**, and more recently in national dance and theater performances. The 19th century **Christian** missionaries often portrayed such festivals as **heathen** practices that catered to "primitive" instincts, illustrating the **depravity** of savage **idolatry**.

Throughout the 20th century, however, this limited perspective yielded to a more informed appreciation of the religious meanings, social values, and historical **dynamics** of such rituals and festivals as they continued to develop in a range of African societies and under a variety of colonial and postcolonial conditions, including the expansion of Christianity and Islam. Due mainly to modern **anthropological** studies, which have investigated the cultural forms of indigenous African festivals while focusing on their sociopolitical functions, we can better appreciate their central role as mechanisms not only of social regulation and reproduction but also of social disruption and change.

No reliable definition or **typology** of African festivals exists, in part because of their complexity—they perform multiple social and religious functions—and also because they change over time, often mixing and blending genres. Festivals wax and wane, they remember and forget, they **improvise** new themes and repeat old **dogmas**. This is important to emphasize because there has been a tendency on the part of scholars and **practitioners** alike to portray indigenous festivals as fixed traditions, handed down by the ancestors since the beginnings of mythical time. If, in principle, celebrants presume rigid **fidelity** to the ways of their ancestors, in practice they can innovate substantially, modifying festivals to fit changing circumstances and even using festivals to promote social and political change. With this **fluidity** and flexibility in mind, we can identify a number of general festival forms and processes in Africa.

1. Royal Rituals

Firstly, we can identify royal rituals or festivals of sacred kingship as a genre associated with political centralization throughout Sub-Saharan Africa, particularly in the historic kingdoms and empires of the western **Sahel** and **littoral**, and down through central and southern Africa, following the waves of **Bantu** migrations that formed the **Lovedu**, **Tsonga**, **Nguni**, Swazi, and **Zulu** polities. In West Africa, **illustrious** examples include the Odwira Festival among the Asante of Ghana and the **Shango** Festival of the **Yoruba** in Nigeria, both of which ensure natural, social, and cosmological renewal through the ritual purification and empowerment of the sacred king.

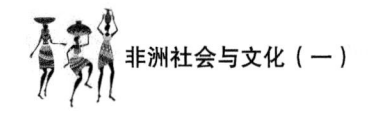

Usually associated with transitions between seasons, harvests, and agricultural cycles, such festivals are often called "new **yam**" or first-fruits ceremonies and operate according to a logic—first identified by **Sir James Frazer**—whereby agricultural productivity and social well-being are associated with the king's sacred body, which must remain physically and ritually healthy for the kingdom to thrive. In southeast Africa, the royal Swazi Incwala Festival has become a well-known ritual of sacred kingship. Ritual idioms of **fecundity** and the restoration of cosmological balance are really about politics, making sacred kingship a rich focus for the study of political symbolism.

2. Masquerade

Secondly, we can distinguish masquerades as a generic form of African festival. Although they can combine with the celebration of sacred kingship, they more often stand apart, representing lineage-based spirits of the dead, as in Yoruba Egungun[13] Festivals; spirits associated with age grades, as in **Bamana puppet** masquerades in Mali or **Afikpo** masks in Nigeria; or spirits associated with secret societies and voluntary associations, such as masquerades of the Liberian Poro Society, of Yoruba hunters' associations, and of canoe houses among the **riverine** groups of **the Niger Delta**. Whereas royal rituals are generally associated with cosmological renewal, masquerades are usually oriented toward **placating** the dead, controlling **witchcraft**, and **ostracizing malefactors** in the community through ritually **sanctioned** accusations or **parodic** displays of **antisocial** behavior.[14]

Masquerades also play an important role in the organization and representation of gender relations, since their membership associations are often **segregated** by sex, as in the male Poro and female **Sande** societies, and because their performances portray gender **stereotypes**, as in Gelede[15] **caricatures** of warriors, brides, drummers, and prostitutes. Because of their overtly **mimetic** routines, masquerades often incorporate figures of power and value from national and global arenas into their costumes and masked superstructures. Some Gelede masks feature Europeans and airplanes. In the Hauka possession **cult** among the **Songhai** of Niger, masked dancers embody the power of colonial officers—adding Nigerien military officers to their spirit **pantheon** when the army came to power.

3. Muslim Festivals

Thirdly, we can consider Muslim festivals as a **bona fide** festival form associated with the Islamic **emirates** of West Africa, combining political **pageantry** with religious feasting and gift exchanges between the **sovereign** and his **subjects**. **Subjugated** and **converted** by Islamic jihad (holy wars) in the 19th century, these kingdoms incorporated elements of preconquest ritual into the annual **Sallah Festival**, performed on the Muslim high holidays of Eid al-Fitr and Eid al-Kabir. During the Sallah, the ruling **emir** ritually negotiated the rank and status of his **vassal** chiefs and **courtiers** by distributing gifts and kola nuts[16] in lavish public displays. **Mobilizing** thousands of spectators, the Sallah features a vast procession of political and religious officials on horseback, surrounded by **retinues** of drummers and praise singers. The point of the Sallah, called the jafi salute, dramatizes the loyalty of the **mounted** warriors as they charge toward the emir in a **mock** attack, stopping short, weapons drawn, to proclaim **fealty** to their commander.

4. Colonial Festivals

Fourthly, colonial festivals should be included in our survey of African festival types, given their historical role in establishing colonial authority by incorporating Africans into wider administrative structures and by inspiring **allegiance** to the symbols and centers of the colonial powers. In the British colonies, **Empire Day** provided a festive celebration of colonial rule, mobilizing the native authorities as collective bodies engaged in competitive school sports, with food and prizes distributed by the district officer.

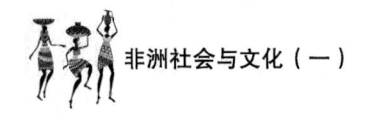

Although **secular** in function, the British **Crown** was **sanctified** by the formal reading of the king or queen's message, followed by **throngs** singing "*God Save the King/Queen*". Another such ceremony of imperial incorporation was the durbar, a colorful **spectacle** of mounted officers and soldiers in which chiefs and emirs were invested with **insignia** that identified them as agents of the Crown, clearly organized into status grades and ranks. Although durbars were performed to mark special events like the **coronation** of **King George V** in 1911 and the Prince of Wales's visit to **British West Africa** in 1925, they came to celebrate the **rank and file** of native administration under indirect rule.

5. National Festivals

Fifth are national festivals, state-sponsored festivals of arts and culture that emerged with the cultural nationalism of African Independence Movements and developed into **affirmations** of post-colonial nationhood. Performed at all levels of political organization, from the local district or province to the nation-state, these festivals adapt traditional ritual and masquerade performances for a more secular stage and general public, thereby weaving different ethnic identities and traditions into a modern national culture. Occasionally such festivals are organized on an international scale, celebrating global dimensions of blackness and **Africanity**, as in Nigeria's Second World Black and African Festival of Arts and Culture (FESTAC'77) held in 1977.

III. INITIATION

In traditional Africa, virtually all aspects of society involve initiation. Initiation rites are carried out for the purpose of admitting people into a new class, organization, or status. Initiation ceremonies are also carried out as people move from one stage of their lives to another. In this respect, age determines the type and nature of initiation ceremonies that are carried out. Some initiation ceremonies are also sex or **gender specific**. In this connection, female initiation ceremonies are sometimes different from the male. Africans believe that an individual exists in three different **teleological realms**: the world of the ancestors, that of the living, and that of the generation unborn. Age is very significant because it represents the movement from one stage of life to another. Initiation ceremonies are carried out as an individual moves from one stage of existence to another.

1. Initiation of the Newborn Baby

At birth, a lot of rituals are carried out to initiate a newborn baby into the world of the living. New babies are not considered members of the family until all traditional rites are carried out. Initiation at birth involves **consultation** with the **oracles** and the gods, and performance of different types of spiritual **cleansing**. The oracles have the power of revealing the destiny of the child, so part of initiation at birth is knowing the personality the child is going to take in future. The parent might also be given guidelines on how to bring the baby up and avoid troubles. **Naming ceremonies** in some cultures involve carrying the new baby to the family, **clan**, or village **shrine** to determine if the baby truly belongs to the members of the family.

Sowei Mask in Sande Society, Sierra Leone
(Photographer: Han Hong)

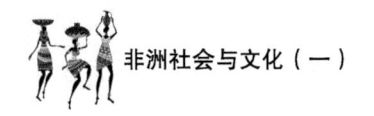

2. Adolescent Initiation

Adolescent initiation involves the passage from childhood to adulthood. This **rite of passage** varies from culture to culture. It is between the age of 12 and 16 among the **Ngulu** of East Africa. Adolescent initiation is also a classic example of age- and gender-specific type of initiation. The initiation rites of boys and girls are carried out separately. During this period, girls are taught the secret of marriage, **domesticity**, and how to be excellent mothers. Among the **Bemba** of southern Africa, Chisungu is the name given to female puberty rites. That of men is called Chisungun. In most cultures, **circumcision** is carried out during puberty rites. Girls below the traditionally accepted age of puberty are not taught how to have sex or take care of men's emotional and physical needs. For boys, the success at initiation determines the admission into some associations, such as age grades and, of course, the class of potential husbands. Marriage cannot take place without adolescent-oriented initiation, because virtually all aspects of traditional marriage practices are revealed during this period. Age governs the nature of information people are expected to acquire. Initiation rites are the only traditionally accepted methods of revealing the aspects of the life of the society that adults are expected to know.

3. Initiation of the Dead

The world of the living leads to the world of the dead or of the ancestors. The rituals carried out for the dead are meant to initiate the dead into the world of the ancestors. The transition from the world of the living to that of the ancestors is therefore not complete without rituals. The spirits of the dead that have not been initiated into the world of the ancestors are capable of affecting the **well-being** of the community. This is because the **corpse** belongs to neither the realm of the ancestors nor that of the living. His or her spirit will be at the crossroads—roaming about with no **entity** to **commune** with. A situation of this nature is capable of **infuriating** the dead, who could start **tormenting** the living by appearing harmfully in their dreams or even in the real world. Among the Yoruba of modern southwestern Nigeria, proper burial of the dead is considered a responsibility the living owe the dead. The type of burial rites is sometimes determined by the cult to which the dead ones belonged. For instance, **adherents** of **Ogun** cannot bury advocates of **Obatala**, and **vice versa**. Burying the dead in accordance with his or her faith plays a significant factor in the corpse's passage/transition into the ancestral world and the nature of the relationship he or she would establish with the living.[17]

IV. COSMOLOGY AND WORLD VIEW

Most African traditional cosmological myths present the **Supreme Being** as the Creator of all things in heaven and on earth. African creation stories vary, however, in content from one culture to another. Common to all is the notion of the Supreme Deity as the Creator **par excellence**. The creative power of the Supreme Being is often reflected in the different names with which this Being is called. For instance, the **Mende** of Sierra Leone call this Being **Ngewo**. The name carries the meaning of "the Eternal One who rules from above", and in that capacity the Being through whom all things came into being. The Akan and **Ga** of Ghana call Him **Nyame** and **Nyonmo**, respectively, meaning the "bright, glorious things", or simply put, "the God of fullness or God of satisfaction".

The names of praise and attributes **accorded** Nyame among the Akan throw more light on His nature and character as the Creator par excellence. Notable among these are Odomankoma ("the Author of all things") and Borbore ("**Excavator**", "Originator" "Inventor" "Carver" "**Hewer**", or "Creator", among other translations). Among the Mende, Ngewo created the earth and all things therein and created the first couple—a man and a woman. The **Tiv** tribe conceive of God as the Great **Carpenter** who carved the world, bringing out of it different types of shapes and forms. However, while the Yoruba tribe see **Olorun** (the Supreme Being) as the Creator par excellence, it is believed that He did this through the agency of Orisa-nla (the archdivinity).

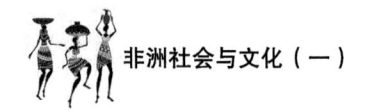

Virtually all African cosmologies agreed that there was originally a smooth relationship between the Supreme Being and human beings and that heaven was very close to the earth, but that this was later interrupted as a result of an offense from one human being or the other which resulted in the withdrawal of heaven, the **abode** of God, from the earth. One tradition traces it to an act of misconduct on the part of a woman who constantly knocked the heaven with her **pestle**. Another links the cause of separation to the misconduct of a man who misbehaved to the Supreme Being after eating too much food.

The Asante of Ghana, for instance, trace the withdrawal of God (with the sky heaven) from the human world to a woman (a type of the **biblical** Eve), who, "pounding the national food (fufu[18]) constantly, went on knocking against Him (God) with her long pestle". When this became unbearable to God, He decided to move His abode up higher. In a desperate attempt to reach Him, the children of the woman, by the advice of their mother, embarked on the construction of a "Tower of **Mortals**" (a kind of Biblical "Tower of Babel"[19]). But this **crumbled** and killed many of them, as a result of which the survivors gave up their task.

The myth of the Manianga of the western part of the Democratic Republic of the Congo locates the distortion of the sweet **communion** between God and human beings in the action of the first man, Mahungu. Mahungu, according to the myth, at first lived very close to God, and God satisfied him with every good thing. However, he later began to take God for granted. Consequent upon this, God became angry with his laziness and failure to keep His confidence. Therefore "God withdrew from the earth and no longer intervened in human affairs". Death, in the Manianga's view, in contrast with Christian and Muslim thought, is far from being a punishment consequent upon human misconduct, but something later introduced by God as a **benevolent** act of **salvation** for human beings from the helplessness and misery caused by the sin of the first man, Mahungu.

Besides these two accounts, there are other variations. The Mende of Sierra Leone in their own myth attribute the separation between God and humanity to human **insatiable** demands, which wearied Ngewo. For fear that they might soon wear Him out, He secretly withdrew His abode far away from theirs one night while the people were sleeping. For the **Bambuti** and the **Meru**, the separation was caused by a pregnant woman's irresistible desire to eat the forbidden fruit of a tree called tahu.

African world view gives prominence to the existence and activities of spirits. Belief in the world of spirits is widespread among all African tribes. Africans generally have a strong belief in the existence of **divinities**/spirits who **predated** human existence. A number of them are believed to be good, while others are wicked spirits (demons); some are widely worshipped, while others are of local importance. The actual number of these spirit beings is not known with precision. They are all believed to be "children" of the Supreme Being, simply because they derived their beings from Him from time **immemorial**, and serve His purpose directly or indirectly in His governance of the world.

In all, African cosmological myths and world views present the Supreme Being as the Ultimate Reality, the First **uncaused** Cause, from and through whom all other beings derived their existence. He is believed to be the Sustainer of all things, and to whom all must return at the end. Apart from the human world, where human beings are made the crown of God's creation, there is also the world of spirits, where God reigns supreme and from where He directs the affairs of the worlds, with the divinities/spirits acting as His ministers-in-council.

V. PERSONHOOD

What is it like to be a person in Africa? What does it entail? A person is an agent whose actions are recognized as meaningful—not as senseless, disconnected fragments of raw behavior—by other persons within the same social **milieu**. As a social and historically situated phenomenon, personhood is both structural and historical, immediate and **processual**, **unilinear** and **multilinear**, **incremental** and **reversible**, collective and individual, objective and subjective, embodied and **disembodied**, fixed and fluid.

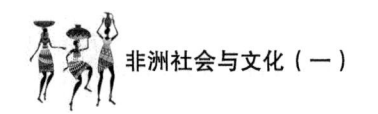

The word "person" derives from the Latin "persona", originally referring to a character in a drama, a mask, then applied to a human being. To be a person is to be seen and view oneself from outside in relation to other persons within a given social context. It is common in Africa to hear persons introducing themselves in terms of their ethnicity, clan, lineage, age grade, **caste**, residential unit, and ritual cult. These same persons are also likely to belong to and identify with historically recent, extralocal organizations, often Christian churches and national political parties. Within each group, persons have rights and obligations, are held **accountable** for their actions, and are subject to sanctions. Not all these identities are kin-based, local, and traditional, but all are constitutive of the social field of personhood.

In addition to being grounded in society and history, personhood in Africa is also processual, incremental, multilinear, and reversible. Personhood happens to people in increments as they walk through the stages of life and pursue different biographical careers. Persona are not born persons, they become persons. Some individuals are temporarily or permanently excluded from personhood. The Kel Ewey **Tuareg** do not take their children and former slaves seriously because in their view they are not (yet) persons. In Uganda, **Lugbara** women, children, and strangers are referred to as afa (things), because they lack the sense of **jural** responsibility.

Other individuals in Africa become persons—gendered persons—at naming initiations, and other critical **junctures**, but proceed thereafter on a long multilinear journey toward fuller degrees of personhood. Becoming married, bearing children, securing one's livelihood, and holding ritual or political offices are among the most common **requisites** of full personhood. Not all people **delineate** their biographies as keenly and explicitly as the **Gusii** of Kenya, who follow "life plans" and try hard to be on "schedule", but few would deny that life should be lived according to shared ideals. Some succeed and attain full personhood. Others see their personhood diminish or vanish altogether, temporarily or permanently. Childless women are repeatedly described as lesser persons. Successful entrepreneurs see their dynamism wane under the attack of jealous or wronged others, not always human. In the case of witches, the state of non-personhood is often irreversible, and one dies socially before one dies physically.

It goes without saying that rules, codes of behavior, representations, social roles, and other **normative** aspects of social life are always subjectively **apprehended**—viewed from inside at the same time that they are viewed from outside. And even though subjective, emotionally charged experiences can never be relived and re-experienced by others or even captured as experience by other subjects, they are always given an outer expression, if not always in public verbal description, then in culturally shared forms of self-expression.

A wedding in Lalibela Churches, Ethiopia
(Photographer: Han Hong)

Equally widespread is the cultural **objectification** of **selfhood** as a component of personhood. Persons in Africa are often described as comprising, in addition to physical bodies, such **immaterial** components as doubts, souls, the shadow cast by one's own body, and breath. It is these components, frequently one's shadow or a soul, which serve as **instantiations** of selfhood and individual agency, here understood as **elusive** and vulnerable qualities. To borrow an expression from the **Bakongo** of the Democratic Republic of the Congo, in interpersonal situations of **asymmetry** or **divergence**, one fears that one's shadow may be stepped upon.

But selfhood in Africa is not the **prerogative** of interpersonal asymmetry. The relationship between father and son among the Bakongo, a **matrilineal** people, and, **inversely**, the relationship between the descendants of a common ancestress in the patrilineal **Tallensi** of Ghana are interesting cases of symmetrical bonding and **self-deployment**. These relationships suggest that personhood and selfhood constitute a single field of contrasting but **complementary modalities** of experience that emerge or recede in particular sociological **niches** and contexts of interaction.

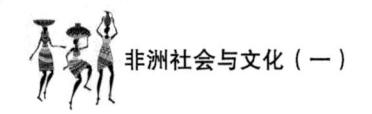

Personhood in Africa is also an embodied phenomenon. The **Iteso** and **Taita** of Kenya locate strong emotions in the heart and reserve the head for public knowledge, Whereas the Uduk feel in the liver and think in the stomach. The **Dinka** word for "self" is gwop (body), and "I myself" is literally "I body". It comes perhaps as no surprise that in some cultures people express their apprehension toward globalized forms of political and economic **encroachment** by means of **perturbing** stories in which their bodies are turned into commodities. The **Haya**, for example, fear that their blood be stolen and sold in the urban centers of Tanzania and cross the border.

One often assumes that persons are human beings endowed with the **cognitive** capacity of self-awareness. Yet personhood, humanness, and self-awareness do not always **coincide**. In Africa, the **prototype** of full personhood is not a living human being, but an ancestor, a disembodied agency, and many "persons", including trees, **totemic** animals, and material objects, are endowed with nonhuman bodies and lack self-awareness. What is more, personhood is fluid. Across the expanse of south Central Africa, the **Luvale** and related peoples personify their divination baskets to learn the cause of misfortune, disease, and death. The **Lobi** of Burkina Faso establish relationships with their many tila, best described perhaps as material representations of certain spirits.

While these **ontological** flows generate vitality, creativity, and transformative capacity, they also present many risks of their own. Ill-intentioned others may **appropriate** one's sweat, shadow, **excretory** products, nail **parings**, hair, photographs, or the sound of one's name with grave consequences to one's vitality, health, and agency. Spirits of all kinds rise to the head of the living, dispossessing their hosts of their sense of self and person. Some **Kuranko** men in Sierra Leone change their shapes into that of elephants to destroy the crops and kill the **livestock** of their worst enemies.

Unit VI Festivals and Values in Africa

Silver anniversary of a couple in Botswana
(Photographer: Sun Lihua)

Far from being a fixed ontological category, personhood is a dynamic force field, an **agentive** capacity, a coping strategy, a weapon, a project, an opportunity, and a risk. It is firmly grounded in society, politics, history, cosmology, and symbolism. And it advances and recedes across ontological boundaries according to the **exigencies** and uncertainties of interpersonal life as lived in Africa.

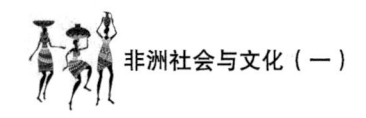

Explanations

[1] **secret society:** 秘密社团或组织，他们的活动和内部运作方式不为外界所知。社团经常举行一些秘密仪式来加强成员与成员之间、成员与会社之间的联系。

[2] **Eid al-Fitr:** "开斋节"(Eid al-Fitr，阿拉伯语)又称"肉孜节"（波斯语Ruzi）或"小节"，是伊斯兰教主要节日之一。开斋节与"宰牲节"并称为伊斯兰教两大节日。伊斯兰教法规定，穆斯林成年男女在伊斯兰教历每年9月（Ramadan，俗称"斋月"）封斋1个月，每日从黎明前到日落后，禁绝饮食、房事和一切非礼行为，以省察己躬，洗涤罪过。根据伊斯兰教先知穆罕默德关于"尔等见新月封斋，见新月开斋"的训谕，每年斋月始于伊斯兰教历9月初新月的出现，于教历10月初见到新月时结束。

[3] **Eid al-Kabir:** "古尔邦节"又称"宰牲节"，是伊斯兰教传统节日，通常在伊斯兰教历的12月10日举行。依照传统，穆斯林在古尔邦节这天清晨沐浴更衣，到清真寺做礼拜、上坟缅怀先人。节前，穆斯林家家户户打扫干净，制作各种糕点，烤馕，做新衣裳，为节日做好准备。从清真寺做完礼拜之后，穆斯林就回到家里杀牛宰羊，煮肉做饭，施舍穷人，招待来宾。青年男女有说有笑，载歌载舞，开展各种庆祝活动，节日期间洋溢着欢乐的气氛。庆贺节日的形式多种多样，各地互有异同。

[4] **The rank and social status of an individual is not lost in the seating arrangement at the festival durbar (exhibitions and gathering):** 节日聚会的座次安排体现了在座每个人的等级和社会地位。

[5] **Poro:** 坡罗社是一个纯男性秘密社团，主要存在于塞拉利昂、利比亚、几内亚和科特迪瓦等非洲国家。与之相对的是女性秘密会社——桑德社（Sande Society）。

[6] **Incwala Festival:** 东南非国家斯威士兰王国（Swaziland）的一种古老仪式，一般在每年11月到第二年1月之间举行，持续一个月左右，届时有各种丰富多彩的庆祝活动。

[7] **Odwira Festival:** 奥德韦拉节是西非加纳的一个传统节日，它起源于阿克罗崩王国（Akropong）1826年在卡塔满苏（Katamansu）一役中打败了"不可战胜的"阿散蒂军队，通常每年9月举行。在奥德韦拉节期间，人们要彻底打扫城镇，重头戏是清洗祖先遗留下来的凳子。

[8] **Kundun Festival:** 西非加纳一个盛大的传统节日。一般在薯类收获的季节举行，人们通过这个节日来感谢上帝慷慨赐予他们的食物。为了驱赶妖魔鬼怪，老百姓穿上特殊服饰，带上面具，敲起非洲鼓载歌载舞。他们还会向上苍祈福，并且洒酒祭祖。节日持续一周时间，每天的庆祝内容和参与人群都有所不同。

[9] **Ekpe:** 流行于尼日利亚等国的一个秘密社团。人们在这个社团的节庆仪式上表演面具舞。

[10] **The dynamic nature and wide variety of festivals that Africans celebrate across time and space defy previous attempts to classify them into fixed categories and genres:** 非洲节日不但各具特色，而且还与时俱进。因此，企图将非洲节日分门别类的努力都以失败告终了。

[11] **the First Festival of Black Arts:** 1966年4月在塞内加尔举行的长达一个月的非洲文化与艺术盛事，由联合国教科文组织赞助。来自非洲本土与世界各地的非裔艺术家与表演者参加了本次盛会，涵盖领域包括诗歌、雕塑、绘画、音乐、舞蹈、电影、戏剧、时尚、建筑、以及设计等。

[12] **Second World Black and African Festival of Arts and Culture**：1977年1月至2月间，第二届世界黑人与非洲艺术和文化节在尼日利亚拉各斯（Lagos）盛大举行，它是有史以来规模最大的非洲盛会之一。这场长达一个月之久的庆祝活动向世人展示了灿烂悠久的非洲文化，包括音乐、舞蹈、文学、艺术、戏剧以及宗教等。来自世界各地的超过16,000名非裔艺术家与表演者参加了此次盛会。

[13] **Egungun:** 约鲁巴人的面具舞，约鲁巴人主要生活在西非尼日利亚与贝宁，跳这种舞蹈通常是为了纪念祖先。

[14] **Whereas royal rituals are generally associated with cosmological renewal, masquerades are usually oriented toward placating the dead,**

controlling witchcraft, and ostracizing malefactors in the community through ritually sanctioned accusations or parodic displays of antisocial behavior: 虽然皇家的宗教仪式通常和季节更替有关，但是面具舞的主要内容却是通过用仪式来批准指控或者模仿恶人反社会的行为，在社区里安抚亡灵、控制巫术、驱逐恶人。

［15］**Gelede**：格莱德是约鲁巴人的一种面具舞仪式，仪式上各种各样的面具舞表演起到了娱乐以及教化民众的作用，使得他们敬畏神灵。

［16］**Kola nut:** "可乐果"或"柯拉果"是西非可乐树的果实，味苦而涩，咀嚼后可以提神，是当地人民最喜爱的食物。尼日利亚伊博人非常推崇"柯拉果"，认为它们是解决所有问题的"金钥匙"，还有启发良心的神奇功效。每当遇到纠纷的时候，伊博人总要端出柯拉果，由德高望重的长者把它们切成小块分给当事人吃。一旦吃下这种果子，当事人的所有问题也就烟消云散。

［17］**Burying the dead in accordance with his or her faith plays a significant factor in the corpse's passage/transition into the ancestral world and the nature of the relationship he or she would establish with the living:** 根据逝者的信仰为他/她举行葬礼，尸体不但会顺利过渡到祖先世界，而且还能和生者建立和谐的关系。

［18］**Fufu:** "福福"是非洲许多国家和加勒比海地区的主食，通常由木薯粉、玉米粉等淀粉类材料制作而成，还可以加入山药和香蕉等成分，煮熟后拍打成面团状。吃福福的时候，人们用手指揪下一小块面团揉成小球形状，然后蘸汤汁或酱汁咽下去。

［19］**Tower of Babel:** "通天塔"取材自《圣经》旧约全书中的《创世纪》（Genesis）。在大洪水退去以后，诺亚（Noah）的后人向东迁移，在西纳（Shinar）定居下来。为了流芳百世，他们决定要建一个城市，以及一座通天高塔。上帝知道以后非常恼怒，于是就创造出不同的语言。由于语言障碍和沟通困难，大家无法齐心协力建塔，宏伟计划只能不了了之。这些人觉得没有必要继续在一起生活，于是就分道扬镳了。他们迁徙到世界的不同地区，分别成为七大洲的祖先。Babel一词在英语中也就被赋予了"嘈杂声"等含义。

Exercises

I. Read the following statements and decide whether they are true (T) or false (F):

_____ 1. Festivals have long been at the center of African cultural and social life.

_____ 2. Since colonial times, many Africans have celebrated certain Muslim festivals.

_____ 3. The sequences of ritual performance, procession, costume, and eating of meals during the festivals celebrated by the Swazi serve to reveal both the power of the king or chief, and the splendor and wealth of the state he represents.

_____ 4. In terms of festivals, Africans innovate substantially, modifying festivals to fit changing circumstances and even using festivals to promote social and political change.

_____ 5. New babies are not considered members of the family until all traditional rites are carried out.

_____ 6. Few African traditional cosmological myths present the Supreme Being as the Creator of all things in heaven and on earth.

_____ 7. Virtually all African cosmologies agree that there was originally a terrible relationship between the Supreme Being and human beings.

_____ 8. In the traditional view of Africans, nearly all the divinities or spirits are believed to be kind and benevolent.

_____ 9. African cosmological myths and world views present the Supreme Being as the Ultimate Reality, from and through whom all other beings derived their existence.

_____ 10. It is rare in Africa to hear persons introducing themselves in terms of their ethnicity, clan, lineage, age grade, caste, residential unit and ritual cult.

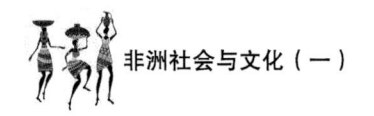

II. Fill in the following blanks with words that best complete the sentences.

1. At the core of African social experience and indigenous knowledge systems are _____ events designed to mark the critical moments of people's lives.
2. An essential and enduring feature of African festivals is _____, the content of which deals with libations, mythical themes, and creation narratives.
3. The dynamic nature and _____ of festivals that Africans celebrate across time and space defy previous attempts to classify them into fixed categories and genres.
4. Initiation rites are carried out for the purpose of admitting people into a new class, _____, or _____.
5. Africans believe that an individual exists in three different teleological realms: the world of the _____, that of the _____, and that of the generation unborn.
6. Adolescent initiation involves the passage from _____ to _____.
7. The rituals carried out for the dead are meant to initiate the dead into the world of the _____.
8. Africans generally have a strong belief in the existence of _____ or spirits.
9. The word "person" derives from the Latin persona, originally referring to a _____ in a drama, a mask, then applied to a human being.
10. Some individuals in Africa become persons at naming initiations, and other _____ _____, but proceed thereafter on a long multilinear journey toward fuller degrees of personhood.

Review and Reflect

- What do you think of the impact of colonialism on African festivals?
- What is the difference between the creation myth between Chinese culture and African culture?
- "Persona are not born persons, they become persons." How do you interpret this sentence?

Key to questions

Unit I

I. Read the following statements and decide whether they are true (T) or false (F).

F. F. T. T. F. T. F. T. T. F.

_____ 1. Sudan used to the largest before its separation into Sudan and South Sudan, covering an area of 2,505,813 square km. As they are now separate countries, the title of the largest country in Africa now falls to **Algeria**.

_____ 2. Africans speak **a vast number of** different languages.

_____ 3. Africa has five main kinds of ecosystems: forests and woodlands, savanna grasslands, deserts and semi-deserts, mountain environments, and coastal environments.

_____ 4. A savanna is a tropical **plain** with both **trees** and grass.

_____ 5. Africa may be divided into six general climatic regions.

_____ 6. Madagascar has a tropical rain forest climate, with heavy rain and high temperature throughout the year.

_____ 7. Though the diversity is huge between the countries, the cultural difference inside the countries is **even bigger**.

_____ 8. The most widely spoken languages in Africa are Arabic, Swahili and Hausa.

_____ 9. The European nations that colonized Africa hoped to exploit the continent's natural resources for their own benefit.

_____ 10. Because of colonial neglect, **few** countries had the infrastructure needed to support a modern economy.

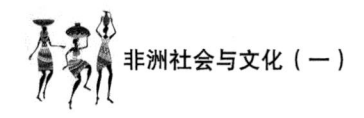

II. Fill in the following blanks with words that best complete the sentences.

1. **the birthplace**   2. **human activity**
3. **fine-leaved, broad-leaved**   4. **The Sahara Desert**
5. **the Nile, Tana rivers**   6. **Islam, Christianity**
7. **human history**   8. **rights, freedoms**
9. **international trade**   10. **strong central governments**

1. Africa was **the birthplace** of the human species between eight million and five million years ago.
2. The forests' boundaries are mainly established by water and **human activity**.
3. Africa has two main types of savannas, **fine-leaved** and **broad-leaved**.
4. **The Sahara Desert** in Northern Africa is the largest desert in the world
5. African mountain ranges are the headwaters of most of the large African rivers such as **the Nile** and **Tana rivers**.
6. **Islam** and **Christianity** are the most followed upon religions on the African continent.
7. Africa has the longest **human history** of any continent.
8. After World War II, the European powers moved to grant more **rights** and **freedoms** to Africans.
9. At the end of World War II, a rise in **international trade** spurred renewed exploitation of Africa's resources.
10. The most pressing issue for most African leaders was to build **strong central governments** in countries with deep racial and ethnic divisions.

Key to questions

Unit II

I. Read the following statements and decide whether they are true (T) or false (F).

F. F. F. F. T. F. T. T. F. F.

____ 1. Africa's climate became **cooler** and drier during the Middle Stone Age, producing environmental changes that challenged people to adapt to new conditions.

____ 2. In 1998, archaeologists discovered a boat more than 25 feet (7.6m) long near the Yobe River in northeastern **Nigeria**. Known as the Dufuna canoe, it dates from around 6500 B. C. and is thought to be Africa's oldest boat

____ 3. Evidence of domesticated wheat, grapes, and lentils has been found at other Ethiopian sites. Although grown in eastern Africa, all these food plants originated in the **Near East** and would have been introduced to the region.

____ 4. Archaeologists now believe that the Swahili coastal culture originated in Africa, but that colonists from southern **Arabia** influenced the culture.

____ 5. Archaeologists believe that Stone Age people had a strong sense of the spiritual world.

____ 6. European colonists, beginning with the **Portuguese** in the early 1500s, ventured into the interior.

____ 7. The great outer wall of the Elliptical Building of the Great Zimbabwe alone is said to be the largest single precolonial African structure in Sub-Saharan Africa.

____ 8. The Bantu-speaking people migrated from southern Cameroon through the Congo forest to several parts of central, eastern, and southern Africa and split into two major language families: the Eastern and the Western Bantu.

____ 9. **The learned men** in Timbuktu constituted its ruling elite, serving as imams and teachers, scribes, lawyers and judges.

____ 10. Arab, chinese and European writers of early documents about the East African coast had different interests and therefore their information was varied and diverse, though mainly related to commerce and religion.

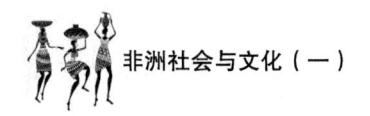

II. Fill in the following blanks with words that best complete the sentences.

1. **fossils, cradle**
2. **small game, carcasses**
3. **forts, castles, Europeans**
4. **tourist attractions, heritage**
5. **domesticated, camels**
6. **ivory, the Red Sea**
7. **nomadic, mountainous**
8. **grain farming, livestock raising**
9. **Axum, stelae**
10. **incompatible, subsistence agriculture**

1. Scientific evidence, which began with the study of **fossils**, shows that Africa was the **cradle** of human beings.
2. During the Early Stone Age in Africa from about 2. 6 million years ago, the early beings were believed to hunt **small game** and looked for **carcasses** that had been killed by large animals.
3. Archaeological sites along the coast of western Africa include **forts** and **castles** built by **Europeans** as they explored and traded in the area in the 1400s and later.
4. Eastern Africa has turned some archaeological sites into **tourist attractions** and has created local museums to educate schools and communities about their archaeological **heritage**.
5. The most common **domesticated** animals were cattle, sheep, and goats, though archaeologists have also uncovered bones of **camels** from sites in Ethiopia and northern Kenya.
6. Local African communities traded valuable raw materials, such as gold, skins, and **ivory** across **the Red Sea** to the Arabian Peninsula.
7. During the Late Stone Age, the peoples of central and southern Africa were largely **nomadic**, moving with the seasons between **mountainous** areas and low-lying lands.
8. In parts of central and southern Africa with fairly dependable summer rainfall,

people adopted a system of mixed agriculture, combining **grain farming** with **livestock raising**.

9. Even today, there are impressive remains at **Axum**, especially the royal tombs and their markers, the **stelae** or obelisks.

10. The elaborate and permanent nature of Zimbabwe's buildings was **incompatible** with the essentially **subsistence agriculture** on which the society was based, making its rulers heavily dependent upon tribute and external trade.

Unit III

I. Read the following statements and decide whether they are true (T) or false (F).

T. T. F. F. F. F. T. F. F. F.

____ 1. Africa's tapestry of hundreds of ethnic groups is woven of many strands formed in precolonial period, colonial period or modern times.

____ 2. Trade, war, and politics brought ethnic groups into contact and even some forms of unity in western Afica before the conquest by Europeans.

____ 3. The many ethnic conflicts that occur today in western Africa **do not represent** a return of ancient hostilities in the absence of colonialism.

____ 4. The political border that **the English** created between Kenya and Uganda cuts across ethnic groups linked by language, culture, and history.

____ 5. Swahili civilization, unlike that of neighboring African peoples, is urban, maritime, and based on **commerce**.

____ 6. In Maasai society, the **woman** is the one who builds the manyatta, sometimes with the help of **her co-wives**, but in most cases they do it alone.

____ 7. Kikongo is one of Congo/Zaire's four national languages.

____ 8. The Xhosa are one of **South Africa**'s black ethnic groups.

____ 9. The living conditions of Xhosa have improved after the apartheid regime ended in **1994**.

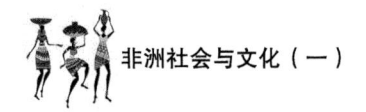

___ 10. It's claimed that Bushmen were not forced off the land for their own good, but rather because the land contains valuable **diamond** deposits.

II. Fill in the following blanks with words that best complete the sentences.

1. **kinship, geography**
2. **inspire, unite**
3. **colonialism**
4. **Swahili, national**
5. **stone-built, elegant, literary**
6. **cattle, medium, sacred**
7. **reinforce, favors**
8. **obedient, appointed, influenced**
9. **Zulu, European, autonomy**
10. **alcoholism, depression, AIDS**

1. Ethnic groups are populations that feel connected by a complex mix of **kinship**, culture, history, and **geography**.
2. Ethnic identity can **inspire** pride and hope and **unite** people in groups for effective political and social action.
3. The contemporary ethnic conflicts that plague western Africa are partly the result of **colonialism**.
4. Tanzanian government encourages the use of **Swahili**, the coastal language, as the **national** tongue, and people often identify themselves as belonging to several ethnic groups.
5. The Swahili are noted for their large, **stone-built** houses and towns, their **elegant** clothing and fool, and for a high level of **literary** achievement, especially in poetry.
6. Maasai economy revolves around livestock with **cattle** valued particularly high as a mobile form of wealth, **medium** of exchange, source of food, symbol of relationship and of **sacred** significance.
7. Even after independence, some central African politicians and intellectuals have continued to **reinforce** the colonial concept of tribes, which **favors** certain individuals and groups.
8. In South Africa, tribal identities kept people **obedient** to tribal leaders who were

either **appointed** or **influenced** by the colonial powers.

9. Besides losing their lands to both the **Zulu** and the **European** settlers, the Xhosa also faced restrictions on their political **autonomy** due to the various measures implemented by the British colonial authorities and subsequently by the South African government.

10. Critics argue that resettlement camps for the Bushmen are rife with **alcoholism**, **depression**, and a rising incidence of **AIDS**.

Unit IV

I. Read the following statements and decide whether they are true (T) or false (F).

F. T. F. T. T. T. T. F. F. T.

____ 1. In the modern era, Western European powers colonized nearly all parts of the continent, except **Liberia** and Ethiopia.

____ 2. The Berlin Conference of 1884 regulated European colonization and trade in Africa.

____ 3. The **Portuguese** had been the first Europeans to firmly establish settlements and trade posts along the coast of the African continent in the 15th century.

____ 4. As a result of colonialism and imperialism, Africa lost not only its sovereignty, but also control of its natural resources like gold, diamond and rubber, etc.

____ 5. Technological advancement facilitated European overseas expansionism. Industrialization brought about rapid advancement in transportation and communication, especially in the forms of steam navigation, railways, and telegraphs.

____ 6. Before the Scramble for Africa period, European powers' knowledge of the vast Africa hinterland was slight. Hitherto Europeans had known Africa more as a coastline than a continent.

____ 7. When marking out the boundaries of their new territories, European negotiators frequently resorted to drawing straight lines on the maps, taking little or no account of the myriad of traditional monarchies, chiefdoms and other African societies that existed on the ground.

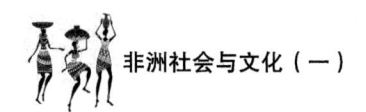

_____ 8. The **French** used the policy of assimilation, whereby through acculturation and education and the fulfillment of some formal conditions, some "natives" would become evolved and civilized French Africans.

_____ 9. In **Rwanda** in 1994 a Hutu-led government that provoked ethnic tensions leading to the genocide of nearly one million persons was overthrown by Tutsi-led forces.

_____ 10. Mindful of the Organization of African Unity's ineffectiveness in dealing with these issues and seeking an organization with greater powers to promote African economic, social, and political integration, African leaders established the African Union (AU), which superseded the OAU in 2002.

II. Fill in the following blanks with words that best complete the sentences.

1. **Partition, Conquest** 2. **10, 90**
3. **David Livingstone, H. M. Stanley** 4. **Italy, Ethiopia**
5. **population, settlers**
6. **settlement, sovereignty, indirect mechanisms** 7. **economic, political, social**
8. **centralized administrative** 9. **29, 1960**
10. **Nelson Mandela, the African National Congress/ANC**

1. "The Scramble for Africa" (also known as "the **Partition** of Africa" or "the **Conquest** of Africa"), was the invasion, occupation, colonization, and annexation of African territory by European powers during the period between 1881 and 1914.

2. In 1870, only **10** percent of Africa was under European control; by 1914, it was **90** percent.

3. In the middle decades of the 19th century, the most distinguished of the European explorers were **David Livingstone** and **H. M. Stanley**, both of whom mapped the

Key to questions

vast areas of southern Africa and central Africa.

4. In the 1880s, **Italy** failed to take Abyssinia (as **Ethiopia** was then known) as a colony.
5. The term colony comes from the Latin word "colonus", meaning "farmer". This root reminds us that the practice of colonialism usually involved the transfer of **population** to a new territory, where the arrivals lived as permanent **settlers** while maintaining political allegiance to their country of origin.
6. Imperialism, on the other hand, comes from the Latin term "imperium", meaning "to command". Thus, the term imperialism draws attention to the way that one country exercises power over another, whether through **settlement, sovereignty**, or **indirect mechanisms** of control.
7. The European imperialist push into Africa was motivated by three main factors: **economic, political**, and **social**.
8. While Britain organized its colonies at the central, provincial, and regional or district levels; the French, for their part, established a highly **centralized administrative** system.
9. Between 1956 and 1963, **29** African states gained their independence, and 17 of those countries became independent in the year **1960**.
10. South Africa's black majority participated in the country's first fully democratic election in 1994, which brought **Nelson Mandela** and **the African National Congress/ANC** to power.

Unit V

I. Read the following statements and decide whether they are true (T) or false (F).

T. T. F. F. T. T. T. F. F. F

_____ 1. Communication between the living and nonliving can occur through either human intermediaries or possession.

_____ 2. In different parts of Africa, both python and praying mantis play the role of creator.

_____ 3. **Cats** feature prominently in mythology as symbols of the seasons, of day and night, and of life and death.

_____ 4. The basic characteristic of African traditional religion is **holistic**.

_____ 5. The Christian Church and many of its missionaries played an important role in restricting and later abolishing slavery worldwide.

_____ 6. Johann Ludwig Kraph was convinced that the Oromo were the key to the evangelization of the African continent.

_____ 7. After David Livingstone died on first May 1873, his body was taken back to England and buried in Westminster Abbey.

_____ 8. **Unlike Christianity, Islam** tolerated traditional values, allowing a man to have more than one wife.

_____ 9. In Ethiopia, relatively the relationship between Christians and Muslims seemed to be **cooperative,** but nowadays this relationship becomes **competitive**.

_____ 10. The rich material and spiritual culture attained by medieval Ethiopia was almost completely destroyed in not more than a decade by the forces of **Ahmad ibn Ibrahim al-Ghazi/the "Gragn the left-handed"**.

II. Fill in the following blanks with words that best complete the sentences.

1. **supreme, particular**
2. **divination**
3. **Contact, communication**
4. **colonization, independence**
5. **crusade, colonizing**
6. **Christianity**
7. **Islamic, Christian**
8. **David Livingstone**
9. **denominations, Independent**
10. **conversion, marginalization, verbal**

1. While the God of Christians and Muslims is concerned about all humans, the **supreme** deity of African religions generally cares only for the people of a **particular** society.

2. Africans use **divination** to explain and combat forms of evil and to identify its source—either spirits or other humans.
3. **Contact** and **communication** between the living and the nonliving are at the heart of almost all African religions.
4. The social unrest caused by European **colonization** of Africa inspired many prophets who promoted political as well as religious change, including some who led their followers into battles for **independence**.
5. In the 19th century, increased Christian missions to Africa were driven by an antislavery **crusade** and the interest of Europeans in **colonizing** Africa.
6. With the dawn of the 21st century, **Christianity** is still the fastest growing religion in Africa.
7. Sudan, although it was declared an Islamic state in 1983, is still divided between an "**Islamic**" north (65% of the population) and a "**Christian**" south (23% of the population).
8. In 1855, **David Livingstone** discovered a spectacular waterfall which he named "Victoria Falls".
9. The modern Church in Africa comprises 15,000 different **denominations** and groups, of which 15% are Roman Catholic, 13% Protestant, 10% **Independent**, 6% Orthodox and 4% Anglican Christians.
10. In some places in Ethiopia, Christians have faced religious persecutions including forced **conversion** to Islam, **marginalization**, **verbal** violence and many other harsh modes of treatment.

Unit VI

I. Read the following statements and decide whether they are true (T) or false (F).

T. F. T. T. T. F. F. F. T. F.

_____ 1. Festivals have long been at the center of African cultural and social life.

_____ 2. Since **precolonial** times, many Africans have celebrated certain Muslim festivals.

_____ 3. The sequences of ritual performance, procession, costume, and eating of meals during the festivals celebrated by the Swazi serve to reveal both the power of the king or chief, and the splendor and wealth of the state he represents.

_____ 4. In terms of festivals, Africans innovate substantially, modifying festivals to fit changing circumstances and even using festivals to promote social and political change.

_____ 5. New babies are not considered members of the family until all traditional rites are carried out.

_____ 6. **Most** African traditional cosmological myths present the Supreme Being as the Creator of all things in heaven and on earth.

_____ 7. Virtually all African cosmologies agree that there was originally a **smooth** relationship between the Supreme Being and human beings.

_____ 8. In the traditional view of Africans, **a number of** the divinities or spirits are believed to be kind and benevolent.

_____ 9. African cosmological myths and world views present the Supreme Being as the Ultimate Reality, from and through whom all other beings derived their existence.

_____ 10. It is **common** in Africa to hear persons introducing themselves in terms of their ethnicity, clan, lineage, age-grade, caste, residential unit and ritual cult.

II. Fill in the following blanks with words that best complete the sentences.

1. **ceremonial**
2. **ritual practice**
3. **wide variety**
4. **organization, status**
5. **ancestors, living**
6. **childhood, adulthood**
7. **ancestors**
8. **divinities**
9. **character**
10. **critical junctures**

Key to questions

1. At the core of African social experience and indigenous knowledge systems are **ceremonial** events designed to mark the critical moments of people's lives.
2. An essential and enduring feature of African festivals is **ritual practice**, the content of which deals with libations, mythical themes, and creation narratives.
3. The dynamic nature and **wide variety** of festivals that Africans celebrate across time and space defy previous attempts to classify them into fixed categories and genres.
4. Initiation rites are carried out for the purpose of admitting people into a new class, **organization**, or **status**.
5. Africans believe that an individual exists in three different teleological realms: the world of the **ancestors**, that of the **living**, and that of the generation unborn.
6. Adolescent initiation involves the passage from **childhood** to **adulthood**.
7. The rituals carried out for the dead are meant to initiate the dead into the world of the **ancestors**.
8. Africans generally have a strong belief in the existence of **divinities** or spirits.
9. The word "person" derives from the Latin persona, originally referring to a **character** in a drama, a mask, then applied to a human being.
10. Some individuals in Africa become persons at naming initiations, and other **critical junctures**, but proceed thereafter on a long multilinear journey toward fuller degrees of personhood.

Reference

[1] Abiodun, R. Yoruba Art and Language: Seeking the African in African Art [M]. New York: Cambridge University Press, 2014.

[2] Adekunle, J. O. & Williams, H. V. (eds). Color Struck: Essays on Race and Ethnicity in Global Perspective [M]. Lanham: University Press of America, 2010.

[3] Adogame, A., Chitando, E. & Bateye, B (eds.). African Traditions in the Study of Religion in Africa: Emerging Trends, Indigenous Spirituality and the Interface with Other World Religions: Essays in Honour of Jacob Kehinde Olupuna [M]. Famham, Surrey, Burlinton, Vt.: Ashgate, 2012.

[4] African Development Bank. African Statistical Yearbook 2013 [R]. Herndon: African Development Bank, 2015.

[5] African Developmnet Bank. Africa in 50 Years' Time-The Road towards Inclusive Growth [R]. Tunis: African Development Bank, 2011.

[6] African Union Development Agency. Agriculture in Africa-Transformation and Outlook [R]. Johannesburg: African Union Development Agency, 2013.

[7] Akande, A. T & Taiwo, P. Contact Linguistics in Africa and Beyond [M]. New York: Nova Publishers, 2013.

[8] Appiah, K. A. & Gates, Jr. H. L (eds.). Encyclopedia of Africa, Vol. 1-4 [M]. Oxford: Oxford University Press, 2010.

[9] Bale, R. Netflix's 'The Ivory Game' Goes Undercover Into Poaching Crisis [J]. National Geographic, 2016.

[10] Bausi, A (ed.). Languages and Cultures of Eastern Christianity: Ethiopian [M]. Famham, Surrey, Burlinton, VT: Ashgate, 2012.

[11] Beegle, K., Christiaensen L., Dabalen A. & Isis Gaddis. Poverty in a Rising Africa [R]. Washington B.C.: World Bank Group, 2016.

[12] Boff, C. & C, J, Radcliff. Encyclopedia of African Literature [M]. Reference & User Services Quarterly, 2003.

[13] Bosman, M. History of Christianity in Africa [M]. Philadelphia Project.

[14] Brautigam, D. The Dragon's Gift: The Real Story of China in Africa [M]. Oxford: Oxford University Press, 2009.

[15] David Pilling. Chinese Investment in Africa: Beijing's Testing Ground [N]. Financial Times. 2017-6-13.

[16] Ekwe, H. A Required Reference for Understanding Contemporary Africa [J]. Journal of West African History, 2015.

[17] Entman, R. M. & Rojecki, A. The Black Image in the White Mind: Media and Race in America [M]. Chicago: University of Chicago Press, 2000.

[18] Erlich, H. Islam and Christianity in the Horn of Africa: Somalia, Ethiopia, Sudan [M]. Boulder, Colo.: Lynne Pienner Publishers, 2010.

[19] Fage, J. D. The Cambridge History of Africa, Volume 2: From c.500 B.C.to A.D. 1050 [M]. Cambridge: Cambridge University Press, 1979.

[20] Fetner, P. J. The African Safari: The Ultimate Wildlife and Photographic Adventure [M]. New York: St. Martin's Press, 1987.

[21] Gates, H. L. & Appiah K. A. (eds). Encyclopedia of Africa [M]. Oxford: Oxford University Press, 2010.

[22] Gulliver, P. H (ed.). Tradition and Transition in East Africa: Studies of the Tribal Element in the Modern Era [M]. London: Routledge, 2004.

[23] Harrison, D. Encyclopedia of African Literature [M]. New York: Routledge Press, 2003.

[24] Harry, N. U. African Youth, Innovation and the Changing Society [N]. The Huffington Post, 2013-11-9.

[25] Holmes, T. Journey to Livingstone: Exploration of an Imperial Myth [M]. Edinburgh: Canongate Press, 1993.

[26] Honey, M. Ecotourism and Sustainable Development: Who Owns Paradise? [M]. Washington, D.C.: Island Press, 1999.

[27] Horton, R. Patterns of Thought in Africa and the West [M]. Cambridge:

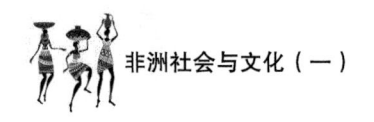

Cambridge University Press, 1993.

［28］ Hudson, G (ed.). Essays on Gurage Language and Culture: Dedicated to Wolf Leslau on the Occasion of his 90th Birthday ［M］. Wiesbade: Harrassowitz, 1996.

［29］ Imperato, P. J. & Imperato, G. H. Historical Dictionary of Mali ［M］. Lanham: Scarecrow Press, 2008.

［30］ Irele, A. The African Experience in Literature and Ideology ［M］. Bloomington: Indiana University Press, 1990.

［31］ Irele, A. The Cambridge History of African and Caribbean Literature ［M］. Cambridge: Cambridge University Press, 2004..

［32］ Irele, F. Abiola (eds.). The Oxford Encyclopedia of African Thought, Vol. 1 & 2 ［M］. Oxford: Oxford University Press, 2010.

［33］ Iverem, E. We Gotta Have it: Twenty Years of Seeing Black at the Movies, 1986—2006 ［M］. New York: Thunder's Mouth Press, 2007.

［34］ Johnson K. & Jacobs S. (eds.). Encyclopedia of South Africa ［M］. Boulder, Colorado: Lynne Rienner Publishers, 2011.

［35］ July, Robert. A History of the African People ［M］. Longrove: Waveland Press, 1998.

［36］ Kalu, W. J., Wariboko, N. & Falola, T (eds.). Religions in Africa: Conflicts, Politics, and Social Ethics ［M］. Trenton, New Jersey: Africa World Press, 2010.

［37］ Kasomo, D. W. African Traditional Culture and Religion is Alive and Dynamic ［M］. Saarbrucken: LAP Lambert Academic Publishing AG & Co KG, 2010.

［38］ Kasomo, D. W. African Traditional Religion: Meaning, Significance and Relevance［M］. Saabrucken, LAP Lambert Academic Publishing, 2010.

［39］ Kerr, D. African Popular Theatre: From Pre-colonial Times to the Present Day ［M］. London: Heinemann Educational Publishers, 1995.

［40］ Klaus K, Frieder, L, & Marian, D (eds.). History of Christianity in Asia, Africa, and Latin America, 1450—1990［M］. Grand Rapids: Wm. B.

Eerdmans Publishing Company, 2007.

[41] Kretzmann, Paul E. John Ludwig Krapf: The Explorer-Missionary of Northeastern Africa. [M]. London: Forgotten Books, 2012.

[42] Kuo F. What China Knows about Africa That the West Doesn't [N]. The National Interest, 2016-5-22.

[43] Lewis, P. M. Growing Apart: Oil, Politics, and Economic Change in Indonesia and Nigeria [J] African Studies Review, 2009.Vol. 52.

[44] Li, Anshan. 2011. Chinese Medical Cooperation in Africa, with Special Emphasis on the Medical Teams and Anti-Malaria Campaign [M]. Uppsala: Nordic Africa Institute.

[45] Li,Anshan. 2014. Understanding Modern China Sino-African Relations: a Lifetime from Historical Cooperation to Today's Co-dependence. Retrieved August, 11, 2017 from https://uosm2018.wordpress.com/2014/03/27/sino-african-relations-a-timeline-from-historical-cooperation-to-todays-co-dependence/.

[46] Martelli, G. 1970. Livingstone's River: A History of the Zambezi Expedition, 1858—1864 [M]. London: Chatto & Windus.

[47] Mazonde, Issac Ncube. Culture and Education in the Development of Africa [P// C]. Paper Presented at the International Conference on the Cultural Approach to Development in Africa. Dakar: Senegal, 2001.

[48] Mbiti, J. S. Christian Spirituality in Africa: Biblical, Historical, and Cultural Perspectives from Kenya [M]. Eugene, Oregon: Pickwick Publications, 2013.

[49] McGrail, S. Boats of the World [M]. Oxfordshire: Oxford University Press, 2004.

[50] Meredith, Martin. The State of Africa, A History of Fifty Years of Independence [M]. London: The Free Press, 2006.

[51] Middleton, J. Africa: an Encyclopedia for Students, vol. 1-4 [M]. Detroit: Gale, 2001.

[52] Middleton, J. & Miller, J. C (eds.). New Encyclopedia of Africa, vol.1-4

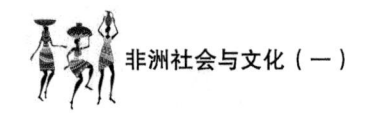

[M]. Detroit: Thomson/Gale, 2008.

［53］ Middleton, John (eds.). Africa, an Encyclopedia for Students, Vol. 2 [M]. New York: The Gale Group, 2002.

［54］ Middleton, John (eds.). Encyclopedia of Africa: South of the Sahara, Vol. 2, Vol. 3 [M]. New York: C. Scribners Sons, 1997.

［55］ Mitchell, P. & Lane, P. (eds). The Oxford Handbook of African Archaeology [M]. Oxford: Oxford University Press, 2013.

［56］ Mokhtar, G. Ancient Africa [M]. California: University of California Press, 1990.

［57］ Moran, S. Representing Bushmen: South Africa and the Origin of Language [M]. Rochester, New York: University of Rochester Press, 2009.

［58］ Morrill, L. & Haines M. Livingstone, Trail Blazer for God [M]. Mountain View: Pacific Press Publication Association, 1959.

［59］ Muthwii, M. J. & Kioko, A. N. New Language Bearings in Africa: a Fresh Quest [M]. Buffalo, New York: Multilingual Matters, 2004.

［60］ Nelson, F (ed.). Community Rights, Conservation and Contested Land: the Politics of Natural Resource Governance in Africa [M]. London: Earthscan, 2010.

［61］ NourbeSe, P. M. Looking for Liviparingstone: An Odyssey of Silence [M]. Stratford: The Mercury Press, 1991.

［62］ Oliver, R & A. Atmore. Africa since 1800 [M]. Cambridge: Cambridge University Press, 1994.

［63］ Olney, J. Tell Me Africa: An Approach to African Literature [M]. Princeton: Princeton University Press, 1973.

［64］ Owusu-Ansah, D. Historical Dictionary of Ghana [M]. Lanham: Littlefield Publishers, 2014.

［65］ Page, Willie F. (eds.). Encyclopedia of African History and Culture: from conquest to colonization (1500—1850) [M]. New York: Learning Source Books, 2001.

［66］ Paris, P. J (ed.). Religion and Poverty: Pan-African Perspectives [M].

Durham: Duke University Press, 2009.

[67] Rodney, W. How Europe Underdeveloped Africa [M]. London and Dar Es Salaam: Bogle-L'Ouverture Publications, 1973.

[68] Ross, A. C. David Livingstone: Mission and Empire [M]. London and New York: Hambledon and London, 2002.

[69] Saul, M. & Austen, R. A (eds.). Viewing African Cinema in the Twenty-first Century: Art Films and the Hollywood Video Revolution [M]. Athens: Ohio University Press, 2010.

[70] Seaver, G. David Livingston: His Life and Letters [M]. London: Lutterworth Press, 1957.

[71] Shavit, J. & Yaacov. History in Black: African-Americans in Search of an Ancient Past [M]. Abingdon: Taylor & Francis, 2001.

[72] Shinn, D. H. & Ofcansky, T. P. Historical Dictionary of Ethiopia [M]. Lanham, Maryland: Scarecrow Press, 2013.

[73] Soares, B. F (ed.). Muslim-Christian Encounters in Africa [M]. Leiden, Boston: Brill, 2006.

[74] Stewart, J. N. Migrating to the Movies: Cinema and Black Urban Modernity [M]. Berkeley: University of California Press, 2005.

[75] Suberu, R. T. Federalism and Ethnic Conflict in Nigeria [M]. Washington: US Institute of Peace Press, 2001.

[76] Taye, B. A. Islamic Fundamentalism in East Africa: Ethiopia in Focus [M]. Saarbrucken: Scholar's Press, 2013.

[77] Toyin, F & Ann, G. Historical Dictionary of Nigeria [M] Lanham: Scarecrow Press, 2009.

Trimingham, J. S. Islam in Ethiopia [M]. London, New York: Routledge, 2008.

[78] Tudge, C. The Variety of Life [M]. Oxfordshire: Oxford University Press, 2002.

[79] UNDP. If Africa builds nests, will the birds come? Comparative Study on Special Economic Zones in Africa and China [R]. Beijing: International

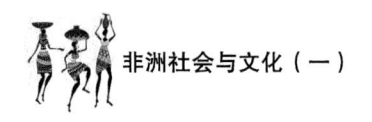

Poverty Reduction Center in China & UNDP China, July 2015.

[80] UNESCO. EFA Global Monitoring Report, 2015-Education for All 2000—2015 Achievements and Challenges [R]. Paris: UNESCO, 2015.

[81] UNESCO. Global Education Monitoring Report 2016-Education for People and Planet: Creating Sustainable Futures for all [R]. Paris: UNESCO, 2016.

[82] United Nations Economic Commission for Africa. Economic Report on Africa: Industrializing Through Trade [R]. Addis Ababa: United Nations Economic Commission for Africa, 2015.

[83] Wei Jianguo. Africa: A Lifetime of Memories [R]. Beijing: Foreign Languages Press, 2012.

[84] Williams, D. L. & Challis, S. Deciphering Ancient Minds: The Mystery of San Bushman Rock Art [M]. New York: Thames & Hudson, 2011.

[85] Winkler, A. M. Uncertain Safari: Kenyan Encounters and African Dreams [M]. Dallas: Hamilton Books, 2004.

[86] World Bank. Africa Can Help Feed Africa-Removing Barriers to Regional Trade in Food Staples [R]. Washington D.C.: World Bank, 2012.

[87] World Economic Forum. The Travel & Tourism Competitiveness Report 2017 [R]. Geneva: World Economic Forum, 2017.

[88] 艾周昌, 舒运国. 非洲黑人文明 [M]. 福州: 福建教育出版社, 2008.

[89] 李安山. 非洲古代王国 [M]. 北京: 北京大学出版社, 2011.

[90] 贺文萍. 中国在非洲的软实力建设: 问题与出路 [C]. 北京: 社会科学文献出版社, 2015.

[91] 孙丽华, 穆育枫, 韩红, 蒋春生. 非洲部族文化纵览（第二辑）[M]. 北京: 知识产权出版社, 2016.

[92] 孙丽华, 穆育枫, 蒋春生, 韩红. 非洲部族文化纵览（第一辑）[M]. 北京: 知识产权出版社, 2015.

[93] 王飞鸿. 非洲简史 [M]. 长春: 吉林大学出版社, 2010.

[94] http://africanhistory.about.com. Retrieved on July, 7, 2016.

[95] http://africanhistory.about.com/library/timelines/blIndependenceTime.htm. Retrieved on Sept. 5, 2016.

[96] http://exhibitions.nypl.org/africanaage/essay-colonization-of-africa.html. Retrieved on August, 5, 2016.

[97] http://muse.jhu.edu/article/543062. Retrieved on August, 5, 2016.

[98] http://plato.stanford.edu/entries/colonialism/ Stanford Encyclopedia of Philosophy. Retrieved on August, 5, 2016.

[99] http://www.ascleiden.nl/content/webdossiers/african-cinema. Retrieved on August, 25, 2016.

[100] http://www.focusfeatures.com/article/hooray_for_nollywood_/print. Retrieved on August, 17, 2016.

[101] http://www.imdb.com/title/tt0416991/. Retrieved on August, 9, 2016.

[102] http://www.jrmartinmedia.com/documentary/virunga/. Retrieved on August, 2, 2016.

[103] http://www.modernghana.com/movie/211/3/the-birth-of-nigerian-films-and-movies.html. Retrieved on August, 19, 2016.

[104] https://africa.si.edu/exhibits/kente/strips. htm.

[105] https://nationalinterest.org/feature/what-china-knows-about-africa-the-west-doesnt-16295?page=0%2C1, Retrieved on August, 14, 2017.

[106] https://www.enca.com/africa/nigerias-nollywood-seeks-worldwide-audience. Retrieved on August, 11, 2016.

[107] https://www.ft.com/content/0f534aa4-4549-11e7-8519-9f94ee97d996, Retrieved on August, 14, 2017.

Vocabulary List

A

aardvark *n.* 土豚

Aba Women's Riots 阿巴妇女反殖民斗争

abduct *v.* 劫持

abet *v.* 煽动

abode *n.* 黏土

Abyssinia（埃塞俄比亚旧称）阿比西尼亚

Abyssinia（埃塞俄比亚旧称）阿比西尼亚

acacia *n.* 金合欢树

accelerate *v.* 加速

accord *v.* 给予

accountable *adj.* 负有责任的

acculturation *n.* 文化交流

acephalous *adj.* 没有首领的

acquisition *n.* 获取

Acropolis 雅典卫城

Addis Ababa（埃塞俄比亚首都）亚的斯亚贝巴

adherent *n.* 追随者

adjacent *adj.* 邻近的

adjudicate *v.* 裁决

administration *n.* 政府

adolescent *n./adj.* 青少年（的）

adornment *n.* 装饰物

adorn *v.* 装饰

Adulis（古城）阿杜利斯

advent *n.* 到来

advocate *n.* 拥护者

affirmation *n.* 确认

afflict *v.* 使……痛苦

affluent *adj.* 富裕的

Afikpo（伊博族的一支）阿菲克波族

Africanity 非洲文化特性

Afrikaner 阿非利卡人

Afro-Caribbean 非裔加勒比人

agentive *adj.* 表示动作主体的

age set/grade 年龄组

age-set *n.*（男性的）年龄组

agitate *v.* 激烈争辩

agriculturalist *n.* 农业专家

Ahanta（阿坎族的一支）阿涵塔族

Ahmad ibn Ibrahim al Ghazi 阿达尔苏丹国教长、将军艾哈迈德·伊本·伊布拉欣

Akan 阿坎族

Aksumite Kingdom 阿克苏姆王国

Akure in Ondo State（尼日利亚）翁多州阿库雷

Albanian 阿尔巴尼亚

alcoholism *n.* 酗酒

Alexandria（埃及）亚历山大港

algae *n.* 海藻

alien *adj.* 外国的

allegiance *n.* 忠诚，效忠

alliance *n.* 联盟

alternative *adj.* 可供替代的

altitude *n.* 海拔

amalgamate *v.* 合并

Amhara 阿姆哈拉人

Amharic 阿姆哈拉语

Amr ibn al-Asi 阿莫尔·伊本·阿尔-阿斯将军

ancestor *n.* 祖先

ancestral *adj.* 祖先的

ancestral *adj.* 祖先的

ancestry *n.* 血统

ANC （南非）非洲人国民大会/非国大

annexation *n.* 兼并

annex *v.* 吞并

antagonistic *adj.* 敌对的

antelope *n.* 羚羊

anthropological *adj.* 人类学的

anthropologist *n.* 人类学家

antisocial *adj.* 危害社会的

apartheid *n.* (948—1994年间南非的）种族隔离政策

appointee *n.* 被委任者

apprehend *v.* 理解

appropriate *v.* 非法占用

Arabian Peninsula 阿拉伯半岛

Arabia 阿拉伯半岛

archaeological *adj.* 考古学的

archaeological *adj.* 考古的

archaeology *n.* 考古学

arc *n.* 弧形

arduous *adj.* 艰苦的

aridity *n.* 干旱

arm-twisting *adj.* 施加压力的

arrowhead *n.* 箭头

artifact *n.* 人工制品

artificial *adj.* 人造的

Asante/Akuapem （阿坎族的两支）阿散蒂族/阿夸佩姆族

Asante 阿散蒂王国

assembly *n.* 会议

assimilation *n.* 同化

astride *prep.* 跨在……上

astute *adj.* 精明的

asymmetry *n.* 不对称性

atop *prep.* 在……顶上

attribute *n.* 属性

attune *v.* 使……一致

australopithecine *n.* 南方古猿

Australopithecus afarensis 南方古猿阿法种

authoritarian *adj.* 独裁的

authoritatively *adv.* 权威性地

autocratic *adj.* 专制的

autonomy *n.* 独立自主，自治权

awe *n.* 敬畏

Axumite Kingdom 阿克苏姆王国

Axum 阿克苏姆古城

B

backwardness *n.* 落后状况

Bakongo 巴刚果人

Bakongo 巴刚果族

Bamana 巴马纳族

Bambuti 班布蒂族

Bandawe Missionary Station 班德伟传教站

bandit *n.* 匪徒

Bantu-speaking *adj.* 说班图语的

Bantustan 班图家园

Bantu 班图人，班图族，班图语支

baptize *v.* 施洗礼

bargain *v.* 讨价还价

bark *n.* 树皮

barley *n.* 大麦

barnacle *n.* 藤壶

Basuto 巴苏托族

Battle of Magdala 马格达拉战役

Bavarian *adj.* 巴伐利亚的

bead *n.* （有孔的）珠子

Bechuanaland （博茨瓦纳旧称）贝专纳兰

Bemba 本巴族，本巴语

benevolent *adj.* 仁慈的

benighted *adj.* 愚昧无知的

bequeath *v.* 把……传给

Berlin Act 《柏林公约》

bewilder *v.* 使迷惑

biblical *adj.* 《圣经》中的

biblical *adj.* 圣经中的

Bight of Benin 贝宁湾

Bight of Biafra 比夫拉湾

biodiversity *n.* 生物多样性

bipartite *adj.* 由两部分组成的

bipedal *adj.* 双足行走的

Bishop Gobot （英国圣公会）戈巴主教

bishop *n.* 主教

blade *n.* 刀片

blur *v.* （使）难以区分

Boer （阿非利堪人的旧称）南非布尔人

bolster *v.* 加强

Boma 刚果民主共和国博马港

bona fide 真实的

bond *v.* 使牢固结合

Borgu （贝宁）博尔古省

bori （豪萨人的）灵魂附体

Borno （尼日利亚）博尔诺州

boundary *n.* 边界

bound *v.* 形成……边界

bracelet *n.* 手链

brass *n.* 黄铜

bribery *n.* 贿赂

British West Africa 英属西非

Briton 英国人

broad-leaved *adj.* 阔叶植物的

bronze *n.* 青铜

Brussels 布鲁塞尔

BSAC 英国南非公司

Buddhism 佛教

buffalo *n.* 非洲野牛

Buganda 布干达王国

Buganda 布干达王国

bulk *n*. 大部分

Bunyoro 巴尼奥洛王国

bureaucratic *adj*. 官僚的

burial chamber 墓室

Bushmen 布须曼人

Byzantine Empire 拜占庭帝国

C

cadre *n*. 骨干队伍

calendric *adj*. 历法的

callousness *n*. 麻木不仁

caloric *adj*. 热量的

cannibal *n*. 食人族

canoe *n*. 独木舟

Cape Agulhas 厄加勒斯角

Cape Blanc 布朗角

Cape Colony 开普殖民地

Cape of Good Hope 好望角

Cape Verde 佛得角

captive *n*. 俘虏

carcass *n*. 动物尸体

caretaker *n*. 管理员

caricature *n*. 人物漫画

carpenter *n*. 木匠

cassava *n*. 木薯

caste *n*. 等级

cataclysm *n*. 大灾难

catalog *v*. 编目录

caterpillar *n*. 毛毛虫

cater to 迎合

cement *v*. 加强

centralist *adj*. 中央集权的

centralization *n*. 中央集权

Central Kalahari Game Reserve 卡拉哈里野生动物保护区

ceramics *n*. 陶器

Ceylon（斯里兰卡旧称）锡兰

Chaga 查加族

chancellery *n*. 办事处

chancellor *n*. （德国或奥地利）总理

chaplain *n*. 牧师

chart *v*. 绘制地图

chessboard *n*. 国际象棋棋盘

chevron *n*. V形线条

chickpea *n*. 鹰嘴豆

chiefdom *n*. 酋邦社会

chiefly *adj*. 领袖的

chief *n*. 酋长

chieftaincy *n*. 氏族部落国家

Christian *adj*. 基督教的

Christianity 基督教

Christian 基督徒（的），基督教的

chronicle *n*. 记录

chronicler *n*. 编年史家

circular *adj*. 圆形的

circumcise *v*. 举行割礼

circumcision *n*. 割礼

circumference *n*. 圆周长

city-state 城邦

civic *adj.* 公民的

civilization *n.* 文明

civilize *v.* 使……文明

civil servant 公务员

claim *n.* 要求合法权利

clan *n.* 氏族

clause *n.*（法律）条款

cleanse *v.* 净化

clothed *adj.* 穿着……衣服

cluster *n.* 群

CMS 英国海外传道会

cocoa *n.* 可可豆

cognitive *adj.* 感知的

coinage *n.* 金属货币

coincide *v.* 与……相符

colonialism *n.* 殖民主义

colonist *n.* 殖民者

commentator *n.* 时事评论员

commerce *n.* 商业

commissioner *n.* 专员

commission *v.* 正式委托……完成

commonwealth *n.* 共和国

communal *adj.* 公共的，（居住在一起的人）共用的

commune *v.* 交谈

communion *n.*（思想感情的）交流

complementarity *n.* 互补关系

complementary *adj.* 互补的

complement *v.* 补充

complex *n.* 建筑群

comprise *v.* 包括

concomitant *adj.* 伴随而来的

confrontation *n.* 冲突，对抗

Congo-Brazzaville 刚果–布拉柴维尔

conical *adj.* 圆锥形的

consensus *n.* 共识

consent *n.* 同意

Constantine （罗马皇帝）君士坦丁

constitution *n.* 宪法

constitutive *adj.* 组成部分的

consultation *n.* 咨询，问卦

contamination *n.* 污染

contemporary *adj.* 当代的

contestation *n.* 争论

contiguous *adj.* 相接的

continental shelf 大陆架

contract *v.* 收缩

controversy *n.* 争论

convene *v.* 召集

convergent *adj.* 汇聚的

conversion *n.* 皈依

convert *vt.* 使转变；转换…；使改变信仰

convert *vi.* 转变，变换；皈依；改变信仰

convert *n.* 皈依者；改变宗教信仰者

convert *v.* 改变宗教信仰

convert *v.* 皈依

copper *n.* 铜

coral *n.* 珊瑚

coral reef 珊瑚礁

cordial *adj.* 热情友好的

coronation *n.* 加冕典礼

corpse *n.* 尸体

correspondence *n.* 来往信件

cosmogony *n.* 宇宙进化论

cosmological *adj.* 宇宙观的

cosmology *n.* 宇宙观

cotton mill 棉纺厂

council *n.* 委员会

counterbalance *v.* 平衡

counter *v.* 抵制

coup *n.* 政变

courtier *n.* 朝臣

court *n.* 宫廷

cowrie *n.* 贝壳

crack *n.* 裂缝

cradle *n.* 发源地

craft *n.* 手艺

critic *n.* 批评家

crossroads *n.* 交叉路口

crown *n.* 树冠，花冠；王冠

crucible *n.* 熔炉

crumble *v.* 瓦解，破碎

crusade *n.* 坚持不懈的斗争

cuisine *n.* 烹饪

culminate *v.* 达到顶点

cult *n.* 异教团体

cult *n.* （有极端宗教信仰的）异教团体

curriculum *n.* 课程设置

Cushitic 库希特语族的

customary *adj.* 独特的

customs duty 关税

cynically *adv.* 悲观地

D

Dagaaba 达嘎巴族

daga *n.* 砖头

Dahomey（贝宁旧称）达荷美

dairy *n.* 乳制品

Daniel arap Moi 丹尼尔·阿拉普·莫伊

Darfur 达尔富尔

date-tree 椰枣树

David Livingstone 大卫·利文斯顿

David Randall-MacIver 美国考古学家、人类学家大卫·兰德尔–麦克艾维

dazzle *v.* 令人眼花缭乱

deceased *adj.* 亡故的

decentralize *v.* 分散行政权

decolonization *n.* 去殖民化

degenerate *adj.* 退化的

deity *n.* 神

delineate *v.* （详细地）描述

delta *n.* 三角洲

demographic *adj.* 人口的，人口统计的

denomination *n.* 宗派

dependency *n.* 附属国

deplete *v.* 使枯竭

depot *n.* 仓库

depravity *n.* 堕落

depression *n.* 抑郁

dereliction *n.* 荒废

derogatory *adj.* 贬义的

descendant *n.* 后代

descend *v.* 降落

descent *n.* 血统

desiccate *v.* 使……变干

designate *v.* 指定

destabilize *v.* 破坏稳定

devotee *n.* 信徒

diachronic *adj.* 历时的

diaspora *n.* 侨民

diaspora *n.* 海外侨民

diasporic *adj.* 流散的

dictatorial *adj.* 独裁的

differentiation *n.* 区分

Dinka 丁卡族

Diogo Cão 葡萄牙航海家迪奥戈·康

diplomatic *adj.* 外交的

diplomat *n.* 外交官

directive *n.* 指令

discern *v.* 辨别

discrimination *n.* 歧视

disembodied *adj.* 脱离肉体的

disintegrate *v.* 解体

dismantle *v.* 分解，废除；拆除

disperse *v.* 散开

dispersion *n.* 散布

displacement *n.* 被迫离开家园

disregard *v.* 忽视，漠视

disruption *n.* 瓦解

dissenter *n.* 持不同意见者

distinction *n.* 区分，区别

distort *v.* 扭曲

distribution *n.* 分配

disturbance *n.* 动乱

ditch *n.* 沟渠

divergence *n.* 偏离，分歧

diverge *v.* 偏离

diversity *n.* 多样性

divert *v.* 使……绕道

divination *n.* 占卜

divine *adj.* 神的

diviner *n.* 占卜者

divinity *n.* 神

Djenné-Djenno 杰内-杰诺

doctorate *n.* 博士学位

doctrine *n.* （政府的）正式声明

dogma *n.* 教条

domesticate *v.* 驯化

domesticity *n.* 家庭生活

domination *n.* 控制

Donald Johanson 美国古人类学家唐纳德·约翰逊

donor *n.* 捐赠者

doomed *adj.* 注定失败的

DRC 刚果民主共和国

dressed *adj.* 磨光的

drought *n.* 旱灾

Duarte Barbosa 葡萄牙作家杜阿尔特·巴博萨

due *adv.* 正对着

duel *n.* 决斗

duly *adv.* 适时地

dung *n.* 畜粪

Dutch Reform Church 荷兰改革宗教会

dwarf *n..* 矮生植物

dwarf *v.* 使……相形见绌

dwelling *n.* 住所

dynamics *n.* 动态

E

Early Stone Age 旧石器时代

earthen *adj.* 土质的

earthly *adj.* 人间的，俗世的

Eastern Nilotic 东尼罗语支的

ecstatic *adj.* 欣喜若狂的

edifice *n.* 宏伟建筑

Edo State （尼日利亚）埃多州

Efik 埃菲克族

elaborate *v.* 详细说明

elevation *n.* 海拔

ELF 厄立特里亚解放阵线

elite *n.* 精英

Elizabethan 和伊丽莎白一世同时代的人

ellipse *n.* 椭圆

elliptical *adj.* 椭圆形的

elusive *adj.* 难以解释的

embroidery *n.* 刺绣

emergence *n.* 出现

emigrate *v.* 迁出

emirate *n.* 酋长国

emir *n.*（穆斯林国家的首脑）埃米尔

Empire Day （英联邦日的前身）大英帝国日

emporium/emporia *n.* 商业中心

enclave *n.*（某国或某地隶属外国或外地的）领土

enclose *v.* 把……围起来

enclosure *n.* 围场

encroachment *n.* 侵占

entity *n.* 实体

entrepreneur *n.* 创业者

entrust *v.* 委托

Enugu 尼日利亚埃努古州

equatorial *adj.* 赤道附近的

Eritrea 厄立特里亚

erosion *n.* 侵蚀

erratic *adj.* 不稳定的

escarpment *n.* 悬崖

esoteric *adj.* 秘不外传的

esteem *n.* 尊重，尊敬

eternally *adv.* 永恒地

Ethiopia Orthodox Christian 埃塞俄比亚东正教基督徒

ethnicity *n.* 族群性

ethnicity *n.* 民族

ethnographic *adj.* 人种学的

ethnography *n.* 民族志

ethno-linguistic 民族语言的

etymology *n.* 词源学

evangelical *adj.* 基督教福音派的

evangelism *n.* 传播福音

evangelist *n.* 福音作者

evangelize *v.* 使……皈依基督教

evict *v.* 驱逐

evildoer *n.* 坏人

excavate *v.* 挖掘

excavation *n.* （对古建筑或文物的）发掘

excavator *n.* 发掘者，开凿者

exclusive *adj.* 独有的

exclusively *adv.* 仅仅

excretory *adj.* 排泄的

executive *adj.* 行政的

exfoliation *n.* 剥落

exigency *n.* 迫切需要

exotic *adj.* 奇异的

exotic *adj.* 有异国情调的

expedition *n.* 探险

explicit *adj.* 清楚的

exploitation *n.* 剥削

exploratory *adj.* 探险的

exposition *n.* 产品博览会

exterminate *v.* 消灭

extract *n.* 节录

extract *v.* 获得

extremity *n.* 尽头

Ezana（埃塞国王）埃扎纳

F

fanciful *adj.* 富于想象力的

fantasy *n.* 幻想

far-flung *adj.* 广泛的

favored *adj.* 受优待的

fealty *n.* （对君主的）效忠宣誓

fecundity *n.* 肥沃

federation *n.* 联邦

fester *v.* 恶化

fidelity *n.* 忠实

figurine *n.* 小雕像

fine-leaved *adj.* 窄叶植物的

flake *n.* 薄片

flare *v.* 突然加剧

flea *n.* 跳蚤

fluidity *n.* 多变性

folklore *n.* 民间传说

forage *v.* （尤指用手）搜寻（东西）

forcibly *adv.* 强行地

foretell *v.* 预言

forge *v.* （坚定地）前进

fortification *n.* 防御工事

fort *n.* 要塞

fossilize *v.* 使……成化石

fossil *n.* 化石

Francisco Álvares 葡萄牙探险家弗朗西斯科·阿尔瓦雷斯

frankincense *n.* 乳香

Frederick Lugard 弗雷德里克·卢押爵士

free-born *adj.* 生来自由的

freestanding *adj.* （建筑物等）独立的

Freetown（塞拉利昂首都）弗里敦

frenzied *adj.* 疯狂的

freshwater *adj.* 淡水的

frieze *n.* 饰带

fringe *n.* 边缘

frontier *n.* 边疆地区

Fulani 富拉尼族

fury *n.* 狂怒

fusion *n.* 融合

F. W. de Klerk （南非前总统）德克勒克（1986—1994）

G

Ganda 干达族

Gaza 加沙地带

Ga 加族

Ge'ez 吉兹语

gender specific 与性别有关的

genocidal *adj.* 种族灭绝的

genocide *n.* 种族屠杀，种族灭绝

genre *n.* 流派

gentile *n.* 非犹太人

geometric *adj.* 几何的

Gertrude Caton-Thompson 英国考古学家格特鲁德·卡顿–汤普森

Glasgow （苏格兰）格拉斯哥

glean *v.* 四处收集

God Save the King/Queen （英国国歌）《天佑吾王》

Gondar （埃塞俄比亚古都）贡德尔

Gospels of John and Matthew 《约翰福音》和《马太福音》

Gospel 福音

governor-general 大总督

governor *n.* 总督

governorship *n.* 省长职位

Gragn 艾哈迈德·伊本·伊布拉欣·阿尔-加齐

Gragn （阿姆哈拉语）征服者

Grain Coast （西非利比里亚梅苏拉多角和帕尔马斯角之间的）谷物海岸

granite *n.* 花岗岩

grasshopper *n.* 蚱蜢

grave *n.* 坟墓

graveyard *n.* 墓地

graze *v.* 吃草

Great Lakes Region 东非湖区

Great Zimbabwe 大津巴布韦

grove *n.* 小树林

gruesome *adj.* 令人毛骨悚然的

guerrilla *n.* 游击队

Guinea·Bissau 几内亚比绍

Guinea 几内亚

Gulf of Guinea 几内亚湾

Gusii 盖斯族

H

habitat *n.* 栖息地

haggle *v.* 讨价还价

Haile Selassie （埃塞俄比亚皇帝）海尔·塞拉西一世

hamper *v.* 阻碍

handle *n.* 把手

hangover *n.* 残留

Harar 哈勒尔

harden *v.* 固化

harness *v.* 利用

harpoon *n.* 鱼叉

Hausa （西非）豪萨族

Haya 哈亚族

headwater *n.* 上游源头

heathen *adj.* 异教徒的

hectare *n.* 公顷

Heligoland 赫里戈尔岛

hemisphere *n.* （地球的）半球

Henry Stanley 亨利·斯坦利

herald *v.* 宣称……是好的或重要的

herder *n.* 牧民

heritage *n.* 传承，遗产

heritage tourist 参观文化遗产的游客

hewer *n.* 砍伐者

hierarchical *adj.* 按等级划分的

hierarchy *n.* 等级制度

highlight *v.* 突出

hinterland *n.* 内陆地区

hippopotamus *n.* 河马

historiographic *adj.* 编史的

historiography *n.* 历史编撰学

hitherto *adv.* 到那时为止

hitherto *adv.* 直到那时

holding *n.* 私有财产

holistic *adj.* 整体的

Holy Cross Cathedral 圣十字主教座堂

homage *n.* 表示敬意的举动

hominid *adj.* 人科的

hominid *n.* 人科动物

Homo sapien 智人

honorary *adj.* 荣誉的

hostility *n.* 战争行为

hot spring 温泉

hub *n.* （某地或活动的）中心

humanitarian *n.* 人道主义者

human sacrifice 人祭

Hutu 胡图族

hydroelectricity *n.* 水电

hyperventilation *n.* 换气过度

I

Ian Smith（南罗德西亚白人总理）伊恩·史密斯

identical *adj.* 与……完全相同的，同一的

ideological *adj.* 思想体系的

ideology *n.* 思想意识

idolatry *n.* 神像崇拜

Igbo/Ibo 伊博族

Igboland 伊博家园

Ile-Ife 伊莱–伊费

illustrious *adj.* 著名的

imam *n.* 伊斯兰教教长

Imam （伊斯兰教领袖）伊玛目

immaterial *adj.* 无关紧要的

immemorial *adj.* 远古的

immortal *adj.* 长生不老的

impassioned *adj.* 热情洋溢的

impede *v.* 妨碍

imperative *adj./n.* 非常必要的（事情）

imperative *n.* 必要条件

imperial *adj.* 帝国的

imperialism *n.* 帝国主义

imperviousness *n.* 防渗透性

impetus *n.* 动力

implore *v.* 恳求

impose *v.* 把……强加于

imposition *n.*（新税的）征收

impoverished *adj.* 赤贫的

improvise *v.* 临时拼凑

in alliance with 联合

incompatible *adj.* 矛盾的

incorporate *v.* 将……包括在内

incremental *adj.* 渐进性的

indigénat *n.*（法语）在殖民地实行的土著管理制度

indigenous *adj.* 土生土长的

indigenous *adj.* 本土的

infidel *n.* 异教徒

inflict *v.* 造成

infrastructure *n.* 基础设施

infringement *n.* 侵犯

infuriate *v.* 激怒

inhabitant *n.* 居民

inhabit *vt.* 在……居住

inhabit *v.* 占据

initiate *v.* 开始

initiation *n.*（常指通过特殊仪式）入会

insatiable *adj.* 贪得无厌的

insignia *n.* 徽章

inspire *v.* 激发

instantiation *n.* 实例化

instigate *v.* 使……发生

institute *v.* 实行

insurgent *n.* 叛乱分子

intact *adj.* 完好无损的

integral *adj.* 不可或缺的

intellectual *n.* 知识分子

interior *n.* 内陆

interlacustrine *adj.* 湖间的

interlock *v.* 紧密连接

intermarriage *n.* 异族通婚

intermarry *v.* 不同种族（或国家、教派）的人结婚

intermediary *n.* 中间人

intermediate *adj.* 中间的

interplay *n.* 相互作用

interpretation *n.* 解释

inter-regional *adj.* 区域之间的

interventionist *adj.* 主张进行干涉的

intrusion *n.* 入侵

inundation *n.* 泛滥

invalid *v.* 令……（因伤病）退役

inversely *adv.* 相反地

isiXhosa 科萨语

Islam 伊斯兰教

issue *v.* 发布

Iteso 特索族

ivory *n.* 象牙

J

James Grant 苏格兰探险家詹姆斯·格兰特

Jamie Uys 南非导演加美·尤伊斯

jaw *n.* 下颌

Jerusalem 耶路撒冷

jihad *n.*（伊斯兰教徒的）圣战

Jimma 季马

Joãode Barros 葡萄牙历史学家若昂·德·巴罗斯

Johannes Rebmann 约翰·雷布曼

Johann Ludwig Krapf 约翰·路德维希·克拉普夫

John Speke 英国探险家约翰·斯皮克

Joseph Jenkins Roberts 约瑟夫·詹吉斯·罗伯茨

Joseph Kasavubu 约瑟夫·卡萨武布

Judaism 犹太教

judicial *adj.* 司法的

juncture *n.* 特定时刻

jural *adj.* 法律上的

justify *v.* 证明……有理

K

Kalahari Desert 卡拉哈里沙漠

Kalenjin 卡伦金族

Karl Mauch 德国地理学家卡尔·莫赫

Kemise 凯米斯

Khami National Monument 卡米国家遗址纪念地

Khedive 埃及总督

Khoikhoi 科伊科伊族

Khoisan 科伊桑人，科伊桑语

Kikamba 康巴语

Kikongo 刚果语

Kilwa 基尔瓦

King George V 英王乔治五世（1910—1936在位）

kingship *n.* 王权

Kinshasa （刚果民主共和国首都）金沙萨

kinship *n.* 血缘关系

Kiswahili 斯瓦希里语

Klasies River Mouth 克莱西斯河口

know-how *n.* 技术诀窍

kola nut 柯拉果

Kongo/Congolese 刚果族

kopje *n.* 丘陵

Kuranko 库兰科族

Kuruman （南非）库鲁曼

Kush 库施王国

KwaZulu （南非）夸祖鲁地区

Kwa 克瓦语

L

laborious *adj.* 耗时费力的

labor union 工会

labyrinth *n.* 迷宫

lagoon *n.* 环礁湖

lag *v.* 滞后

Lake Malawi 马拉维湖

Lake Nakuru 纳库鲁湖

Lake Tanganyika 坦噶尼喀湖

Lake Turkana 图尔卡纳湖

Lake Victoria 维多利亚湖

Lake Zway 兹怀湖

Lalibela Cave 拉利贝拉岩洞

Lamu（肯尼亚）拉穆岛

latent *adj.* 潜在的

Late Stone Age 新石器时代

latitude *n.* 纬度

latitude *n.* 纬度地区

legacy *n.* 后遗症

legislative *adj.* 立法的

legitimacy *n.* 合法性

legitimate *adj.* 合法的

legitimize *v.* 使……合法

lentil *n.* 扁豆

Leo Africanus 欧洲旅行家利奥·阿非利加努斯

Leopoldville（金沙萨旧称）利奥波德维尔

Lesotho 莱索托

libation *n.*（旧时供奉神的）祭酒

Liberia 利比里亚

Lij Iyasu 伊亚苏五世

limestone *n.* 石灰岩

Limpopo River 林波波河

lineage *n.* 宗系

linguistic *adj.* 语言的

linguist *n.* 语言学家

linteled *adj.* 有门楣的

Lisbon（葡萄牙首都）里斯本

literary *adj.* 文学的

literature *n.* 文献

littoral *n.* 沿海地区

livestock *n.* 家畜

LMS 伦敦传道会

Lobi 露比族

locust *n.* 蝗虫

longitude *n.* 经度

lore *n.*（某一群体的）传说

Lovedu 勒夫杜族

loyalty *n.* 效忠于……的强烈感情

Loziland 洛兹家园

Luba 卢巴族

Lugbara 卢格巴拉族

Luo 卢奥族

lurk *v.* 潜伏

Lutheran 路德教（派）的

Luvale 卢瓦勒族

M

Maasai 马赛族，马赛语

machination *n.* 阴谋诡计

Madagascar 马达加斯加

Maghreb 马格里布

Mahdist 苏丹马赫迪派

Mahdi（伊斯兰教）救世主马赫迪

maintenance *n.* 保养

malaria *n.* 疟疾

malefactor *n.* 作恶者

Mali Empire 马里帝国

Mali 马里

malnutrition *n.* 营养不良

maneuver *v.* 操纵

mangrove *n.* 红树林

manifold *adj.* 由许多部分组成的

mansion *n.* 豪宅

manuscript *n.* 手抄本

manyatta *n.*（外面有栅栏的）传统非洲茅草村庄

Mapungabwe（南非）马蓬古布韦

marginalization *n.* 边缘化

marine *adj.* 海洋的

mariner *n.* 水手

maritime *adj.* 海上的

Marjorie Shostak 美国人类学家马乔里·肖斯塔克

market-oriented *adj.* 以市场为导向的

Mark（福音使者）马可

Marxist *adj.* 马克思主义的

Mashonaland（津巴布韦）马绍纳兰

masquerade *n.* 面具舞会

massacre *n.* 屠杀

v. 屠杀

Matadi 刚果民主共和国马塔迪港

matrilineal *adj.* 母系的

Mau Mau Uprising 茅茅起义（1952—1960）

Mauritania 毛里塔尼亚

Mauritius 毛里求斯

mediate *v.* 调解

medieval *adj.* 中世纪的

Mediterranean 地中海

medium *n.* 灵媒

mega *adj.* 巨大的

Mende 曼德族

Menelik 孟尼利克二世

mercantile *adj.* 商人的

mercenary *n.* 雇佣兵/军

merge *v.* 合并，融合

meritoriously *adv.* 非常好

Meroë（古城）麦罗埃

Meru 梅鲁族

messenger *n.* 信使

Middle Stone Age 中石器时代

migrant *adj.* 迁移的

migrant *n.* 移民

migration *n.* 迁移

milestone *n.* 里程碑

milieu *n.* 环境

millennium *n.* 一千年

millet *n.* 小米

mimetic *adj.* 模仿的

minority *n.* 少数族群

minor *n.* 未成年人

mint *v.* 铸造（硬币）

mischievous *adj.* 招惹是非的

misfortune *n.* 不幸

missionary *adj.* 传教士的

missionary *n./adj.* 传教士（的）

missionary *n.* 传教士

Missionary Travels and Researches in South Africa 《南非传教旅行考察记》

mission *n.* （基督教海外）传教

mist-wrapped *adj.* 迷雾笼罩的

mobilize *v.* 调动

mock *adj.* 模拟的

mockery *n.* 嘲笑

modality *n.* 形态

moderate *v.* 缓和

Mohammed 先知穆罕默德

Mombasa 蒙巴萨

momentum *n.* 动力

monarch *n.* 统治者

monarchy *n.* 君主国

monograph *n.* 专著

monolith *n.* 单块巨石

Monomotapa Empire 莫纳莫塔帕王国

Monomotapa 莫诺莫塔帕王国

monopoly *n.* 垄断　独占

monotheistic *adj.* 一神论的

Moors 摩尔人

moral *n.* 品行

moratorium *n.* 暂停

Moroccan 摩洛哥人

morphology *n.* 形态学

mortal *n.* 凡人

mosaic *n.* 马赛克

Moshoeshoe 莫修修一世

mound *n.* 土墩

mountainous *adj.* 多山的

Mount Kilimanjaro 乞力马扎罗山

mount *v.* 跨上马

mount *v.* 逐步增加

multilinear *adj.* 多线性的

multiparty *adj.* 多党的

multiple *adj.* 多重的

multistory *adj.* 多层的

Mussolini 墨索里尼

mutinous *adj.* 参与叛乱的

myriad *n.* 极大数量

mystical *adj.* 神秘的

mythical *adj.* 神话的

N

Nama 那马族

Namib Desert 纳米布沙漠

naming ceremony 命名仪式

Nandi 南迪族

narrative *n.* 叙述，描述

nationalism *n.* 民族主义

nationalist *n.* 民族主义者

navigable *adj.* 可通航的

navigation *n.* 航海

Nazi（德国）纳粹

Ndebele 恩德贝勒族

nefarious *adj.* 罪恶的

neocolonialism *n.* 新殖民主义

neotraditional *adj.* 新传统的

Newfoundland 纽芬兰岛

Ngala 恩加拉族

Ngewo 恩盖欧

Ngulu 奴卢族

Nguni 恩古尼族

niche *n.* 小环境

Niger-Benue confluence 尼日尔河–贝努埃河交汇处

Niger-Congo family 尼日尔–刚果语系

Niger-Congo 尼日尔—刚果语系

Niger Delta 尼日尔三角洲

Niger River 尼日尔河

Niger 尼日尔

Nilo-Saharan 尼罗–撒哈拉语系的

Nilotic 尼罗族系的

Nilotic 尼罗语的

Nisa《尼萨》

nomadic *adj.* 游牧的

nomadic *adj.* 游牧的

normative *adj.* 规范的

Northern Rhodesia（赞比亚旧称）北罗德西亚

notable *adj.* 值得注意的

notion *n.* 观念

notoriously *adv.* 众所周知地

Nuer 努尔族

Nyame 尼阿美

Nyonmo 尼欧莫

O

oasis *n.* 绿洲

OAU 非洲统一组织

Obatala （约鲁巴神话中的造物主）欧巴塔拉

obelisk *n.* 方尖碑

objectification *n.* 人格物化

obligation *n.* 职责

oblong *adj.* 长方形的

observance *n.* 庆祝

obsidian *n.* 黑曜石

occupant *n.* 居住者

Oduduwa 奥杜杜瓦

Ogun （约鲁巴人神话中的战神）欧贡

Ohaneze Ndigbo 伊博人的奥哈奈兹大会

oil spill 原油泄漏

Olorun 奥罗伦

Omani 阿曼人

Oman 阿曼

ontological *adj.* 存在论的

opposition *n.* 对抗

oppressor *n.* 压迫者

opt *v.* 选择

oracle *n.* 神谕

oracular *adj.* 谜一样的

oral tradition 口述传统

ordain *v.* 授予圣职

oriental *adj.* 东方的

Oromo 奥罗莫族，奥罗莫语

Vocabulary List

ostracize *v.* 放逐

Osun（尼日利亚）奥孙州

Ottomans 奥斯曼土耳其人

Ottoman 奥斯曼帝国

outcrop *v.* 出露地表

outgrowth *n.* 副作用

outlet *n.* 出路

outpost *n.* 前哨

overgrow *v.*（杂草等）在……上蔓生

overlord *n.*（旧时的）领主

oversimplify *v.* 过度简化

overthrow *n.* 推翻

overture *n.* 友好姿态

Oyo Empire 奥约帝国

oyster *n.* 牡蛎

P

pageantry *n.* 盛典

paleoanthropologist *n.* 古人类学家

paleoarchaeological *adj.* 古考古学的

paleoarchaeology *n.* 古考古学

paleontologist *n.* 古生物学家

pan-African *adj.* 泛非的

pantheon *n.* 万神殿，众神

parallel *adj.* 同时发生的

parallel *n.* 平行的

paramount *adj.* 首要的

par excellence 最优秀的

paring *n.* 削下来的皮

parodic *adj.* 模仿的

parsimonious *adj.* 抠门的

partial *adj.* 不完整的

partition *n.* 划分

passage *n.* 走廊

Pass Laws（种族隔离时代南非政府限制有色人种的）通行证法

pastoral *adj.* 畜牧的

pastoralism *n.* 游牧业

pastoralist *n.* 牧民

pastor *n.* 牧师

Pate（肯尼亚）帕泰岛

patriarchy *n.* 父权制度

patrilineal *adj.* 父系的

Pemba（坦桑尼亚）彭巴岛

penetrate *v.* 进入

peninsula *n.* 半岛

people *v.* 住满居民

per annum 每年

perennially *adv.* 常年

perforate *v.* 穿孔，打眼

periodize *v.* 划分时期

periphery *n.* 周围

perishable *adj.* 易腐烂的

permeate *v.* 渗透

persecution *n.* 迫害

Persian 波斯人

Persia 波斯

perturb *v.* 使……混乱

pervasive *adj.* 普遍的

perverse *adj.* 不通情理的

pestle *n.* 杵

pest *n.* 害虫

phenomenal *adj.* 惊人的

Pietist 虔敬派

pillage *v.* 劫掠

placate *v.* 安抚

plague *v.* 使……受煎熬

plague *v.* 困扰

plantation *n.* 种植园

plaster *v.* 往……上涂抹

plateau *n.* 高原

plunder *v.* 抢劫

Pokot 波科特族

poleward *adv.* 向两极

polity *n.* 国家组织

polity *n.* 政治形态

ponder *v.* 仔细思考

Pope *n.* 教皇

populate *v.* 居住在……

port of call 停泊港

Portuguese 葡萄牙人

possession *n.* 鬼魂附身

post-colonial *adj.* 后殖民时期的

posture *n.* 姿态

pottery *n.* 陶器

power plant 发电站

practitioner *n.* 实践者

pragmatic *adj.* 务实的

praying mantis 螳螂

preach *v.* 传道

precipitation *n.* 降水

precolonial *adj.* 沦为殖民地以前的

predate *v.* 先于……产生

predictable *adj.* 可预见的

predominantly *adv.* 主要地

preeminence *n.* 卓越

prefect *n.* 长官

preoccupation *n.* 当务之急

prerogative *n.* 特权

press for 迫切要求

prestige *n.* 威望

prey *v.* 捕食

priest *n.* 牧师

primate *n.* 灵长类动物

primordial *adj.* 原始的

Prince Henry the Navigator 葡萄牙"航海家"亨利亲王

procession *n.* 列队行进

processual *adj.* 过程性的

proclaim *v.* 宣告

productivity *n.* 生产率

progenitor *n.* 祖先

pro-independence *adj.* 支持独立的

proliferate *v.* 猛增

proliferation *n.* 数量激增

prominence *n.* 重要性

pronounced *adj.* 显著的

propagate *v.* 传播

prophecy *n.* 预言

prophet *n.* 先知，预言家

protectorate *n.*（一国对另一国的）保护关系/受保护国

Protestant *adj.* 新教徒的

prototype *n.* 典型

provincial *adj.* 省级的

provision *n.* 条款

proximity *n.* 接近

pseudoscientific *adj.* 伪科学的

Ptolemy/Claudius Ptolemaeus 古希腊天文学家、地理学家、数学家克劳狄斯·托勒密

puberty *n.* 青春期

publicize *v.* 宣传

Puerto Rico 波多黎各

pupil *n.* 瞳孔

puppet *n.* 木偶

purification *n.* 净化

purportedly *adv.* 据称

python *n.* 蟒蛇

Q

Qadi（伊斯兰教法官）卡迪

quinine *n.* 奎宁

R

radical *adj.* 激进的

raid *n.* 突击检查

rally *v.* 召集

rank and file 普通士兵

rapid *n.* 湍流

ration *v.* 配给

reaches *n.* 边远地带

realm *n.* 领域

reconcile *v.* 调解

recreational *adj.* 休闲的，娱乐的

refinement *n.* 经过改进的东西

reformation *n.* 宗教改革

refugee *n.* 难民

refuge *n.* 庇护

regeneration *n.* 更新

regime *n.* 政权

reign *v.* 统治

reinforce *v.* 强化

relic *n.* 遗物，遗迹

relocate *v.* 重新安置

remains *n.* 遗迹

remedy *n.* 处理方法

removed *adj.* 无关的

renounce *v.* 声明放弃

repository *n.* 储存库

repression *n.* 镇压

reputed *adj.* 有名气的

requisite *n.* 必需的事物

resemble *v.* 与……相似

resentment *n.* 愤恨

reservoir *n.* 水库

residence *n.* 住所

reside *v.* 居住在……

resolve *v.* 决心

resonate *v.*（使）回响

retinue *n.* 随从

revenue *n.* 税收，财政收入

reverence *n.* 尊崇

reverend *n.* 牧师

reversal *n.* 逆转

reversible *adj.* 可逆的

revert *v.* 恢复原来的信仰

revival *n.* 复兴

revive *v.* 使……复活

revolutionary *n.* 革命者

revolve *v.* 以……为中心

Richard Burton 英国探险家理查德·波顿

Richard Nicklin Hall 理查德·尼克林·霍尔

ridge *n.* 山脊

rife *adj.* 充斥

rigid *adj.* 严格的　僵化的

rite *n.* 仪式

rite of passage 成年礼；（标志人生重要阶段的）仪式重大事件

ritualize *v.* 使……仪式化

ritual *n.* （宗教）仪式

rivalry *n.* 敌对状态

riverine *n.* 河流附近的

roam *v.* 在……漫步

Robert Napier 英国陆军元帅罗伯特·皮内

Roger Summers 津巴布韦考古学家罗杰·萨默斯

Roman Empire 罗马帝国

royalty *n.* 皇族

ruin *n.* 废墟

ruthlessly *adv.* 冷酷无情地

Rwanda 卢旺达

S

sack *v.*（旧时军队的）破坏

sack *v.* 洗劫

sacred *adj.* 神圣的

sacrifice *n.* 祭品

Sahel 萨赫勒地带

Saint Mary 圣母玛利亚

Sallah Festival 宰牲节

salt marsh 盐沼

salvation *n.* 救赎

sanctify *v.* 使……正当化

sanction *n.* 制裁

v. 制裁

Sande 桑德社

sandstone *n.* 砂岩

San 桑人

São Tomé and Príncipe 圣多美和普林西比

savage *n.* 不懂礼仪的人

savanna *n.* 热带稀树草原

scavenge *v.* 吃（动物尸体）

scholarship *n.* 学问

scourge *n.* 灾害

scraper *n.* 刮刀

scribe *n.* 抄写员

Scripture *n.*《圣经》

sculpture *n.* 雕塑

seafarer *n.* 海员

seafaring *adj.* 航海的

Vocabulary List

secession *n.* 分裂

seclusion *n.* 与世隔绝

secretariat *n.* 秘书处

secular *adj.* 世俗的

sedimentary *adj.* 沉积物的

seesaw *adj.* 拉锯性的

segment *v.* 分割

segregate *v.* 隔离并区别对待

segregation *n.* 种族隔离

segregation *n.* 种族隔离

self-contained *adj.* 独立的

self-containment *n.* 自我封闭

self-deployment *n.* 自配置

selfhood *n.* 人格

self-sufficient *adj.* 自给自足的

semiarid *adj.* 半干旱的

seminal *adj.* 开创性的

Semitic 闪米特语族的

Senegal 塞内加尔

Senufo 塞努福族

sequence *n.* 顺序

service *v.* 保养

Seth 赛斯

settlement *n.* 定居点

Seychelles 塞舌尔群岛

Shango "雷电之神"商加

shatter *v.* 使……破碎

shellfish *n.* 水生贝类动物

Shirazi 设拉子王朝

Shona 绍纳族

shot *n.* 镜头

shrine *n.* 圣地

sight *v.* 看到

Sinai Peninsula 西奈半岛

Sir James Frazer（英国人类学家）詹姆士·弗雷泽爵士

skeleton *n.* 骨架

slaughter *v.* 宰杀

small game 小型猎物

smelt *v.* 冶炼

sociability *n.* 社交性

Sofala 索法拉港

solar radiation 日照

Somaliland 索马里兰

Somerset East（南非东开普省）东索美塞特

Songhai 桑海族

sorcerer *n.* 巫师

sorcery *n.* 巫术

southerly *adj.* 来自南方的

Southern Rhodesia（津巴布韦旧称）南罗德西亚

sovereign *n.* 君主

sovereignty *n.* 国家主权

spectacle *n.* 壮观的场面

speculation *n.* 猜测

speculator *n.* 投机商

SPG 福音传播协会

sphere *n.* 领域

spin *v.* 纺纱

spiritual world 灵界

splendor *n.* 灿烂

sponsor *v.* 主办

spur *v.* 刺激

stairway *n.* 楼梯

stake *n.* 重大利害关系

stateless *adj.* 没有国籍的

static *adj.* 静止不变的

statue *n.* 雕像

status quo 现状

steadfast *adj.* 坚定不移的

stelae *n.* 石柱

steppe *n.* 温带草原

stereotype *n.* 成见

stereotype *n.* 模式化的形象

straddle *v.* 横跨

strand *n.* 一股绳、线

strangulation *n.* 勒死

stratigraphical *adj.* 地层学的

stride *n.* 进展

strife *n.* 冲突

striking *adj.* 显著的

stringent *adj.* 苛刻的

strive *v.* 努力奋斗

stronghold *n.* 根据地

subject *n.* 臣民

subjugate *v.* 征服

subjugation *n.* 屈服

Sub-Saharan Africa 撒哈拉以南非洲

subservient *adj.* 恭顺的

subsistence agriculture 温饱型农业

succession *n.* 继承

successor *n.* 继任者

superiority *n.* 优越感

superpower *n.* 超级大国

supersede *v.* 代替

suppression *n.* 镇压

Supreme Being 至高神

sustain *v.* 维持

Swahili 斯瓦希里语

swamp *n.* 湿地

Swaziland 斯威士兰

Swazi 斯威士族

symbiotic *adj.* 共生的

symmetrical *adj.* 对称的

synonym *n.* 同义词

T

taboo *n.* 戒律

Tabwa 塔布瓦人

Taita 泰塔族

Tallensi 塔伦西族

Tana River 塔纳河

Tanganyika 坦噶尼喀

Tangier 丹吉尔

Tangier（摩洛哥）丹吉尔

tapestry *n.* 织锦画

tariff *n.* 关税

Tarzan 泰山（指健壮的男子）

telegraph *n.* 电报

teleological *adj.* 目的论的

Vocabulary List

temperate *adj.* 温带的

tension *n.* 紧张状况

terminology *n.* （某学科的）术语

terracotta *n.* 赤陶土

terra incognita 未知领域

terrain *n.* 地形

terrain *n.* 地形

territory *n.* 领土

testament *n.* 证据

testimony *n.* 证明

thatch *n.* 茅草屋顶

the Algerian War of Independence 阿尔及利亚独立战争（1954—1962）

the Anglican Church 英国圣公会

the Battle of Metema 梅特马战役

the Berlin Conference《柏林会议》

the Black Death 黑死病

The Christian Topography of Cosmas Indicopleutes 希腊人科斯马斯·印第科普莱特斯的《世界基督风土志》

The Chronicle of Kilwa《基尔瓦编年史》

The Church of Scotland 苏格兰长老会

the Comoro Islands 科摩罗群岛

the Congo Basin 刚果盆地

the Congo River 刚果河

the Coptic Church 科普特教会

the Democratic Republic of the Congo 刚果民主共和国

The Descent of Man, and Selection in Relationship to Sex《人类的由来与性选择》

the Eastern Arc Mountains 东弧山

The Geography《地理学》

The Gods Must Be Crazy 电影《上帝也疯狂》

the Great Depression 经济大萧条（1929—1939）

the Kalahari Desert 卡拉哈里沙漠

the League of Nations （联合国前身）国际联盟

the Mediterranean Sea 地中海

the Niger Bend 尼日尔河大拐弯

the Niger Delta 尼日尔三角洲

the Niger River and Delta 尼日尔河及尼日尔三角洲

the Nile 尼罗河

the Nok 诺克文化

theologian *n.* 宗教研究家

theological *adj.* 神学的

theology *n.* 神学

the Pantaleon Monastery 庞塔莱昂修道院

The Periplus of the Erythraean Sea《厄立特里亚海航行记》

The Persian Gulf 波斯湾

the Philippines 菲律宾

the queen of Sheba 示巴女王

thereafter *adv.* 从那以后

the Roman Catholic Church 罗马天主教会

the Sahara 撒哈拉沙漠

the Sahel region 萨赫勒地区

the Soweto Uprising 索韦托（学生）起义

the Suez Canal 苏伊士运河

the United Methodist Church（美国）联合卫理公会

throne *n.* 帝位，王位

throng *n.* 聚集的人群

Tigray Region （埃塞俄比亚）提格雷州

Tigrinya 提格雷尼亚语

timber *n.* 木料，木材

Timbuktu 廷巴克图

Tiv 蒂夫族

tonal *adj.* 音调的

torment *v.* 烦扰

totemic *adj.* 图腾的

tragedy *n.* 悲剧

trance *n.* 催眠状态

transaction *n.* 业务

transition *n.* 过渡

transsaharan 跨撒哈拉的

treachery *n.* 背叛

treasury *n.* 财政部

trekker *n.* 远足的人

triangular *adj.* 三角形的

tribalism *n.* 部族意识

tributary *adj.* 附庸的

tribute *n.* 贡品

Tripolitania （利比亚西北部）的黎波里塔尼亚

trove *n.* 收藏的东西

tsetse fly 采采蝇

Tsonga 聪加族

Tswana 茨瓦纳族

Tuareg Uprising 图阿雷格族反政府武装叛乱

Tuareg 图阿雷格族

Tübingen University（德国）图宾根大学

turbulent *adj.* 动荡的

Turkana 图尔卡纳族

Turkish *n.* 土耳其人

adj. 土耳其的

turret *n.* 角楼

Tutsi 图西族

typology *n.* 分类法

tyrant *n.* 暴君

U

Ubangi-Shari （中非共和国旧称）乌班吉沙里

umbilical cord 脐带

uncaused *adj.* 非创造的

unconstitutional *adj.* 违背宪法的

uncoursed *adj.* 不分层的

uncover *v.* 发现

underclass *n.* 社会底层

underfunded *adj.* 缺乏资金的

underlie *v.* 构成……的基础

undermine *v.* 逐渐削弱

underpinning *n.* 基础

understaffed *adj.* 人手不足的

undulate *v.* 波动起伏

unearth *v.* 挖掘

uneven *adj.* 不平衡的

unilaterally *adv.* 单方面地

unilinear *adj.* 单线性的

unmortared *adj.* 未用灰浆涂抹的

unoccupied *adj.* 没人居住的

unpopulated *adj.* 无人居住的

unprecedented *adj.* 前所未有的

unrest *n.* 动乱，动荡

upheaval *n.* 动乱，动荡，激变

Upper Volta （布基纳法索旧称）上沃尔特

usher in ……引进

U.S.S.R 前苏联

V

variation *n.* 变体

vassal *adj.* 附庸的

vassalize *v.* 使……成为附庸

vegetation *n.* 植物

venture *v.* 敢去（危险的地方）

verbal *adj.* 口头的

vessel *n.* 器皿

veteran *n.* 退伍军人

viable *adj.* 切实可行的

vice versa 反之亦然

vicinity *n.* 周围地区

vicissitude *n.* 变迁

victimize *v.* 使……受苦

Victorial Falls 维多利亚瀑布

vilify *v.* 诋毁

Virginia （美国）弗吉尼亚州

visual art 视觉艺术

vocal *adj.* 直言不讳的

volcanic *adj.* 火山的

vowel *n.* 元音

W

wane *v.* 衰落

warehouse *n.* 仓库

warrant *n.* 授权令

warrior *n.* 勇士

water hyacinth 水葫芦

waterlogged *adj.* 被水淹的

weave *v.* 编织

well-being *n.* 福祉

Westminster Abbey （英国伦敦）威斯敏斯特大教堂

wickedness *n.* 恶行

wield *v.* 运用

windward *adj.* 迎风的

witchcraft *n.* 巫术

witch *n.* 女巫

WMMS 循道宗传教会

wooded *adj.* 树木覆盖的

X

Xhosa 科萨族

Y

yam *n.* 薯类

Yemeni 也门人的

Yoruba 约鲁巴人，约鲁巴族

Z

Zaïre（刚果民主共和国旧称）扎伊尔

Zambezi River 赞比西河

Zanzibar（坦桑尼亚）桑给巴尔岛

zar cult（东北非的）灵魂附体

zenith *n.* 鼎盛时期

Zion Church 锡安教会

Zulu 祖鲁族